W9-APZ-525

WITHDRAWN

SOCIOLOGY
a multiple paradigm science

George Ritzer

University of Maryland

Allyn and Bacon, Inc.
Boston

With Love To Sue,
Who Makes It All Worthwhile

Extracts on pp. 198, 199, 216 from *Social Behavior: Its Elementary Forms* by George C. Homans, © 1961 by Harcourt Brace Jovanovich, Inc. and reprinted with their permission.

Library of Congress Cataloging in Publication Data
Ritzer, George.
    Sociology: a multiple paradigm science.
    1. Sociology.   I. Title.
HM24.R494   301   74-10739

Contents

Preface

This book constitutes an effort to analyze the current status of sociology using concepts developed by Thomas Kuhn in *The Structure of Scientific Revolutions*. Particularly useful is Kuhn's concept of a *paradigm*. By carefully redefining the concept and rigorously applying it to sociology, I conclude that there are *at the present time* three sociological paradigms: The Social Facts, Social Definition, and Social Behavior Paradigms. This tripartite differentiation explains the sources of many differences in contemporary sociology. Although no one of the paradigms is in itself adequate to explain any single social phenomenon, adherents of each of the paradigms claim that their perspective explains most, if not all, social phenomena. These exaggerated claims emanating from each of the paradigms makes for considerable political conflict in sociology. Adherents of each paradigm not only make exaggerated claims for their perspective, they also seek to destroy the competing paradigms through vicious political attacks on their validity and utility. The application of the paradigm concept to sociology allows us to see clearly the nature of political conflict in contemporary sociology. In my view, this conflict has far more destructive than constructive effects on the state of sociology.

The paradigmatic analysis of sociology also allows us to see that theory and method, often thought to be unrelated, are interrelated under a broader paradigm. Structural-functionalism and conflict theory are subsumed by the social facts paradigm and they are linked to the preferred method of the social factist, the interview/questionnaire. Within the social definition paradigm we find three theories—action theory, symbolic interactionism, and phenomenology—and they are tied to the observation technique most often employed by the social definitionist. Finally, the social behavior paradigm includes two theories: behavioral sociology and exchange theory and the experimental method. This book makes explicit something that has been generally unrecognized in sociology—the linkage between theory and method. This linkage has important implications for the way sociology is currently practiced.

Another important theme in this book is the high degree of irrationality in contemporary sociology. Adherents of each paradigm claim more for their perspective than it can possibly deliver. They seek to destroy other paradigms without attempting to extract at least the useful perspectives contained in the other paradigms. Methods are used that are ill-suited to answer questions raised by the paradigm. Specific works are viewed as exemplars for a given paradigm even though they do not fit well into the paradigm. The list is practically endless and the unmistakable conclusion is that contemporary sociology is a highly irrational enterprise.

There are a number of additional insights into the current status of sociology throughout this book. For one, behaviorism is, in my view, a major and growing sociological paradigm. Despite its significance, most sociologists have been oblivious to the growing importance of behaviorism. For another, the tripartite paradigmatic split makes it clear that despite what most sociologists believe, the debate between structural-functionalism and conflict theory is *not the* basic difference, or major source of conflict, in sociology. In fact, in my view, structural-functionalism and conflict theory have a number of commonalities as theories sharing the social facts paradigm.

In sum, the application of the paradigm concept to sociology is designed to shed new light on the current status of sociology. It is hoped that these new insights can lead to changes in a number of the negative aspects of the way sociology is currently practiced.

There are innumerable people to thank for their help in the development of this manuscript. Foremost, is Professor Norman R. Yetman who contributed numerous insights to this book as well as transforming many incomprehensible sentences into acceptable English. He refused to allow me to be satisfied with anything but the best I could do. Professor Robert Antonio wrote the section in Chapter 3 on phenomenology and many of his other ideas are found throughout the pages of the book. Professor Charles K. Warriner, whose work is seen as the exemplar for the social facts paradigm, was a great personal source of help, support, and ideas. Professor Hernan Vera-Godoy spent many hours discussing his ideas with me and they too will be found throughout this manuscript. Professors Kenneth Kammeyer, Shirley Harkess, and Leonard Reissman also offered some very useful suggestions. Finally, the students in my graduate theory classes contributed a great deal to this manuscript. In particular, I would like to thank Gary Long, Richard Bell, and Jill Quadango for numerous ideas.

In the end, the greatest help of all came from my children, David and Jeremy, and my wife, Sue. They helped me succeed in finishing this manuscript by being the most wonderful people in the world.

George Ritzer

1

The Paradigmatic Status of Sociology

In 1962 Thomas Kuhn published *The Structure of Scientific Revolutions,* a part of the *International Encyclopedia of Unified Science.* It appeared fated to marginal status within sociology because it seemed of interest to only a relatively few sociologists concerned with the philosophy and sociology of science. Kuhn's work has come to occupy an increasingly central place in sociology over the years because of the realization that it offered sociologists a useful way of looking at their own discipline. The importance of Kuhn's work to sociology was underscored by the publication of Robert Friedrichs' *A Sociology of Sociology,* in 1970, which involved an application of Kuhn's ideas to sociology. With the publication of this influential and controversial book, Kuhn's central concept of a *paradigm* became an important addition to sociological terminology. Friedrichs' work was followed by further analyses of the paradigmatic status of sociology by Lodahl and Gordon (1972), Phillips (1973), Effrat (1972), and Friedrichs himself (1972a; 1972b).

This list promises to grow within the next few years. Sociological interest in paradigms was further kindled in 1970 by the publication of the second, enlarged edition of Kuhn's book, plus critical analyses of his work (Lakatos and Musgrave, 1970). Despite all of this attention, it is my contention that the concept of a paradigm has yet to be applied adequately to sociology. It is the goal of this book to reanalyze the status of contemporary sociology using Kuhn's ideas, particularly his concept of a paradigm. Let me begin by summarizing some of Kuhn's basic ideas in order to better understand this concept.

One of Kuhn's goals in *The Structure of Scientific Revolutions* is to challenge commonly-held assumptions about the way in which science changes. In the view of most laymen, science advances in a cumulative manner with each advance building inexorably on all of those that precede it. Science has achieved its present state through slow and steady increments of knowledge. It will advance to even greater heights in the future. Kuhn regards this conception of the development of science as a myth and seeks to debunk it. He lays much of the blame for this misconception on science textbooks, which systematically disguise "the existence and significance of scientific revolutions." (Kuhn, 1970:135)

Why do the sciences, through their textbooks, engage in this form of deception? I think two reasons exist, only one of which involves deception. First, a science need only convey to beginning students its current state of knowledge. It need not expose the student to the blind alleys, dead ends, discoveries, and revolutions that led to its present state. These occur, *being important in their time,* but are of little more than historical interest to the modern student in the field. The authors are not engaging in deception when they ignore their past failures and successes, but are simply making a decision on what information is essential to the student. Second, authors of science textbooks often engage in an effort to consciously deceive the student. While this occurs in all sciences, I think it occurs more frequently in the social sciences. Such authors seek to hide the errors, confusion, blind alleys, and revolutions from their students, thinking they reflect badly on the field. A falsely coherent picture of both the past and present is drawn so the student thinks more highly of the field in question. Introductory textbooks systematically seek to sweep past confusion and present confusion under a rug of coherence.

Despite the differences between fields, the authors of science textbooks convey an image of accumulation of knowledge rather than changes in scientific knowledge through revolution. This falsely coherent picture, repeated in textbook after textbook gives the impression that science develops cumulatively. To Kuhn, it is not cumulation that marks the important changes in science, but revolution. Kuhn argues that while accumulation plays a role in the advance of science, the truly major changes come about as a result of revolutions. Kuhn's model of scientific changes may be represented as follows:

PARADIGM I → NORMAL SCIENCE → ANOMALIES →

CRISIS → REVOLUTION → PARADIGM II

I will explore this model in some detail, but a brief description is in order at this point. Kuhn sees a science at any given point in time as dominated by a specific *paradigm* (defined for the moment as a fundamental image of the science's subject matter.) *Normal science* is a period of accumulation of knowledge in which scientists work and expand the reigning paradigm. Such work inevitably spawns *anomalies,* or things that cannot be explained by the existing paradigm. A *crisis stage* occurs if these anomalies mount, which ultimately may end in a *revolution.* The reigning paradigm is overthrown and a new one takes its place at the center of the science. A new reigning *paradigm* is born. The stage is set for the cycle to repeat itself. It is during the period of revolution that great changes in science take place. This view clearly places Kuhn at odds with the lay conception of scientific development.

The key term in Kuhn's model, the one that is the backbone of this book as well, is his concept of a paradigm. The concept of a paradigm itself is elusive since, according to Masterman (1970), Kuhn uses it in at least twenty-one different ways. Understanding of the concept can be facilitated by referring to a definition originally used by Friedrichs (1970:55) in his effort to analyze the state of sociology from a paradigmatic perspective: "A fundamental image a discipline has of its subject matter." This definition, simple and manageable, is of such a general nature that it would prove useless were we to try to apply it in any depth. We must therefore look for a more precise definition of this pivotal concept.

Masterman (1970) has performed a very useful function by reducing Kuhn's twenty-one different uses of the paradigm concept to three broad types. I will use Masterman's threefold typology as a lever to develop a more coherent definition of paradigm.

The first type is labelled, *metaphysical* paradigm (or metaparadigm), a total world view, gestalt, or *Weltanschauung* within a given science. Kuhn seems to be describing this type of paradigm at several points in his book. At one point he discusses a paradigm as a new way of "seeing"; at another as a general organizing principle governing perception; and at still another point as a "map" that describes which entities exist (and, conversely, which do not) and how they behave. Such a map, or Weltanschauung, allows the scientist to explore the vast and complex world otherwise inpenetrable were he to explore randomly. The metaphysical paradigm performs several functions:

4

1. It defines what entities are (and are not) the concern of a particular scientific community.
2. It tells the scientist where to look (and where not to look) in order to find the entities of concern to him.
3. It tells the scientist what he can expect to discover when he finds and examines the entities of concern to his field.

The metaphysical paradigm is the broadest unit of consensus within a given science. It serves to define the broad parameters of the field, or subareas within a field, giving the scientist a broad orientation from which to operate.

Although I believe the thrust of Kuhn's original work was to define a paradigm as what Masterman calls the metaphysical paradigm, Kuhn tends to retreat from that definition in the postscript to the 1970 edition of his book. Kuhn (1970:175) recognizes his original use of the term paradigm as "the entire constellation of beliefs, values, techniques, and so on shared by the members of a given community," but then goes on to say that the use of the term paradigm in this sense is "inappropriate." Kuhn prefers to define this phenomenon as a "disciplinary matrix."

Kuhn argues that the term paradigm can only be applied to, what he calls, an "exemplar." The exemplar is defined by Kuhn (1970:175) as "one sort of element in that constellation [the metaphysical paradigm]; the concrete puzzle solutions which when employed as models or examples, can replace explicit rules as a basis for the solution of the remaining puzzles of normal science." To Kuhn, an exemplar is a far "deeper" concept than the metaphysical paradigm, or disciplinary matrix. An exemplar is much more concrete and specific. It is these characteristics that lead Kuhn to reserve the term paradigm for it. In making this substantial shift, Kuhn is obviously responding to those who criticized his original work viewing science in terms of its "irrationality." (Kuhn, 1970:191)

An exemplar is only a part of the broader metaphysical paradigm. The emphasis on irrationality in science is a positive asset as far as sociologists are concerned. Most analysts of science have tended to view it as a highly rational enterprise. The sociologist is debunking some of the myths that abound about the nature of science in emphasizing the irrationality of science. Thus, in my opinion, the concept of a metaphysical paradigm is far more useful in analyzing the status of any science than the concept of an exemplar. An exemplar is an important part of metaphysical paradigm, but it is still only a portion of that more inclusive phenomenon.*

It is interesting to note in Masterman's work that the second type of paradigm in her scheme, the *sociological* paradigm, is very similar to Kuhn's exemplar. Kuhn, in the first edition of his book, discusses a variety of phenomena that could be included under this heading such as a concrete set of habits, an accepted judicial decision, a concrete scientific achievement, or a universally recognized scientific achievement. It is this last meaning that comes closest to the later idea of an exemplar. Watson and Crick's (1968) discovery of the DNA double helix is a clear example of a universally recognized scientific achievement that has acquired the status of an exemplar.

Finally, there is what Masterman calls the *construct* paradigm. This is the narrowest of the three types in that specific *tools* or *instruments* are viewed as paradigms. For example, the development of the nuclear reactor performed a paradigmatic function for nuclear scientists. My problem with this third type of paradigm is identical to my difficulty with the concept of an exemplar. They are both far too narrow to qualify for the paradigm label which I reserve for the broader notion of a science's Weltanschauung. I think that the idea of a construct paradigm, like that of an exemplar, can and should be subsumed under the heading of a metaphysical paradigm.

I have not gone through all three of the types of paradigms discussed because I believe that the threefold typology is particularly useful. I have reviewed Masterman's work because I think it demonstrates that the term paradigm is best reserved for the broadest possible notion—what she calls the metaphysical paradigm, or the science's Weltanschauung. A paradigm is all three of the types discussed by Masterman. Masterman's metaphysical paradigm subsumes exemplars as well as tools and instruments.

A paradigm, in my view, serves to differentiate one scientific community (or subcommunity) from another. A given scientific community has a different Weltanschauung than another scientific community, *even when both communities exist within the same science*. A paradigm not only differentiates between sciences, but also

---

* Friedrichs (1972:448) comes to a similar conclusion about the relative importance of exemplars and metaphysical paradigms.

between subcommunities within any given science. I disagree with the position taken by Kuhn (1970:176) in the 1970 postscript in which he argues, "Scientific communities can and should be isolated without prior recourse to paradigms . . ." *In my opinion, the shared paradigm is the major dimension setting one scientific community or subcommunity off from another.*

We have now arrived at the point where I am finally prepared to offer a definition of the knotty concept of a paradigm. The definition that follows is a synthesis of the threefold typology presented by Masterman.

> A paradigm is a fundamental image of the subject matter within a science. It serves to define what should be studied, what questions should be asked, how they should be asked, and what rules should be followed in interpreting the answers obtained. The paradigm is the broadest unit of consensus within a science and serves to differentiate one scientific community (*or subcommunity*) from another. It subsumes, defines, and interrelates the exemplars, theories, and methods and instruments* that exist within it.

This definition is the basis of this entire book, but before we begin to apply it to sociology, let us return to Kuhn's schema and outline the other stages in the revolutionary development of science. Before I do, however, I would like to emphasize one point. A paradigm can apply to an entire scientific community *as well as* to specific subcommunities within a broad scientific community. As you will see, this is very different from the approach taken by most other people who have dealt with the paradigm concept. They have generally restricted a paradigm to an entire scientific community. The importance of this point will be seen when we examine the paradigmatic status of sociology.

The period of normal science is entered when a specific paradigm has gained hegemony within a science. To Kuhn normal science is basically a "mopping up operation." The paradigm has already gained ascendency and it is during this period that normal science seeks to solidify and expand the position of the paradigm. The paradigm is expanded in three different ways:

---

* Although I include instruments as a part of the definition of a paradigm, I will not use them in my analysis of sociology. Sociology is a field notably lacking in instrumentation.

1. "Extending the knowledge of those facts that the paradigm displays as particularly revealing."
2. "Increasing the extent of the match between those facts and the paradigm's predictions."
3. "Further articulation of the paradigm itself."   (Kuhn, 1970:24)

Kuhn argues that these activities can be subsumed under what he calls "puzzle solving," a trademark of normal science.   Extending factual knowledge, increasing the congruity between knowledge and predictions, and articulating the paradigm itself are not innovative activities.   "Perhaps the most striking feature of the normal research problems . . . is how little they aim to produce major novelties, conceptual or phenomenal."   (Kuhn, 1970:35)   Most of the life of a science is spent in periods of normal science.   Most scientists are better described as puzzle-solvers than as innovators and creators using predefined methods to explore the problems defined by the paradigm.

It is these periods of normal science that receive the attention of textbook authors.   These periods do adhere to the textbook author's image of cumulative development of science, but textbooks only cover the period from the end of the last paradigmatic revolution.   They ignore many past revolutions, in addition to the likelihood that the future will bring still further scientific revolutions.

Scientists are generally engaged in puzzle-solving, or paradigmatic articulation, raising the question, "How do the crucial revolutions in the history of science occur?"   "No part of the aim of normal science is to call forth new sorts of phenomena; indeed those that will not fit the box are often not seen at all."   (Kuhn, 1970:24) How can those busy solving puzzles possibly make great innovations? Kuhn offers two different answers to this question, only one of which is truly satisfactory.   Kuhn argues on the unsatisfactory side that novelties are produced "inadvertently."   In the course of conducting normal science, scientists accidentally stumble on a fact or an observation that casts doubt on the dominant paradigm.   Accidents are never very appealing explanations of social regularities; Kuhn offers us a more attractive answer.   He argues that the existence of a dominant paradigm allows the scientist to accept basic assumptions of his field unquestioningly freeing him to focus on minute issues in almost unimaginable detail and depth.   The scientist can operate in the protected milieu of an unquestioned paradigm, unencumbered by the need to defend his basic assumptions.   A few scientists are likely to uncover findings that are at variance with the dominant paradigm. These findings, which Kuhn labels *anomalies,* play a key role in the advent of scientific revolutions.   At first, efforts are made to explain anomalies in terms of the dominant paradigm.   The crisis phase of Kuhn's model is entered as the number of anomalies increase, and it becomes more and more difficult to accommodate these anomalies within the existing paradigm.   As these efforts fail, and more and more holes appear in the paradigm, we are on the way toward a scientific *revolution.*   As the anomalies grow, they become the object of study of some scientists rather than normal science.   If the dominant paradigm is unable to accommodate or explain these anomalies, a new paradigm will ultimately emerge.   It will be seen as being able to explain these anomalies as well as things covered by the preceding paradigm.

A new paradigm, in order to emerge, must have a number of other characteristics in addition to its *perceived* ability to explain anomalies.   The new paradigm must be "sufficiently unprecedented to attract an enduring group of adherents away from competing modes of scientific inquiry."   (Kuhn, 1970:10)   This means that the new paradigm must be different from its predecessor in the sense that it *seems* to explain demonstrably more than the one before it. The new paradigm must not, paradoxically, seem to offer all of the answers.   It must not be fully closed, and it must leave open a series of problems for solution by the new group of scientists who will become its adherents during the coming period of normal science.   The new paradigm must include within it the exemplars, theories, methods, and instruments that will aid in the scientific research to come.

Even if the new paradigm has these characteristics, scientific revolutions do not come easily.   They are always preceded and accompanied by lengthy periods of *crisis.*   A number of competing schools of thought arise, each seeking preeminence as the dominant paradigm begins its decline under a mounting number of anomalies. Each school of thought questions the basic assumptions of its competitors as they seek to dominate the field.   Most of the scientists continue to subscribe to the old paradigm and defend it from attack. They have, after all, been trained under the threatened paradigm and are highly committed to it, especially since its demise would also represent their demise in the sense that they would not fit into the new era of the science dominated by an unfamiliar paradigm. Some do try to convert in the face of growing anomalies. Those who do not convert will ultimately die or retire. The crisis ends when all who remain are converts or younger scientists trained under the new paradigm. The stage is now set for a new period of normal science, but the spectre of a new crisis and a new paradigm lurks in the misty future.

One of the key points in Kuhn's analysis, one on which he is most ambivalent, is the reason one paradigm wins out over another paradigm. The thrust of Kuhn's original work is in the direction of arguing that this is a political phenomenon. The paradigm that emerges victorious is the one that is able to win the most converts. It need not necessarily have greater explanatory power in order to emerge victorious. Irrational and subjective factors may affect, even determine, the emergence of a new paradigm. Such a view is in stark contrast to the lay conception of scientific advance and one which is highly attractive to the sociologist. Kuhn has retreated from this position in the face of criticisms that he overemphasized irrational factors. (Kuhn, 1970b)   He argues that one paradigm wins out over another for "good" reasons. These good reasons include "accuracy, scope, simplicity, fruitfulness, and the like." (Kuhn, 1970b: 261)   Kuhn seems to be retreating to a more "scientific" conception of scientific revolutions. "Good" reasons have replaced irrationality. This equivocation, like others in his later work, has worked to the detriment of Kuhn's perspective, in my opinion. He has disowned many of the original ideas that made his book most attractive to one interested in the sociology of science.

Phillips (1973:19) argues that Kuhn's later work has left open the question that Kuhn began with: "Are there good objective reasons for scientists proceeding as they do, or do we merely term them good because they are endorsed by members of a certain scientific community?" The weight of the evidence points in the direction of the latter interpretation in Phillips' view, and mine. Notions, such as "accuracy, scope, simplicity, and fruitfulness would be regarded as paradigm dependent." (Phillips, 1973:18)   Put another way, paradigms rise and fall as a result of subjective, not objective, factors.

Basic to Kuhn's model is the idea that science makes its great changes during periods of revolution, not during the more lengthy periods of normal science. This idea clearly stands in direct opposition to the commonsense notion that science develops cumulatively. Although the new paradigm that emerges after a revolution contains elements of its predecessor, it is radically different and *it is the difference that is crucial,* not the similarities. New entities have been defined, and new questions have been raised. The methods, exemplars, instruments, and theories have shifted. This is not cumulative development, it is revolution—scientific revolution—and it is the way great changes in science occur.

It is Kuhn's concept of a paradigm that is most crucial to an understanding of science in general, and more specifically sociology. Masterman contends that the paradigm concept can be used to differentiate between sciences. In her view there are four types of science in terms of their paradigmatic status: *paradigmatic, nonparadigmatic, dual paradigmatic,* and *multiple paradigmatic.* Let us critically examine her fourfold classification.

A science can be labelled *paradigmatic,* in Masterman's view, when it possesses a discipline-wide paradigm over which there is broad consensus. There are a *few* examples of a science achieving the paradigmatic state, but even in these few cases, the paradigmatic state has *not* been a permanent situation. Take the case of physics. The Newtonian paradigm dominated physics from the latter part of the 1600s until the birth of the Einsteinian paradigm in the early 1900s. There were certainly those who doubted the Newtonian paradigm. The number of anomalies mounted over the years, but the physics of the period between Newton and Einstein is as close as one can come to the paradigmatic state. In the early 1900s, in the face of increasing anomalies, Einstein developed his paradigm which coped with the problems handled by Newton as well as at least some of the anomalies that Newton's paradigm could not deal with. The Einsteinian paradigm dominated physics in the early 1900s, but new anomalies arose rather quickly. In particular, the Einsteinian paradigm was not able to cope with the atomic and subatomic level. Other paradigms, such as the one developed by Heisenberg, seemed to be better able to explain atomic and subatomic behavior. (Clark, 1971) While the paradigmatic state is a viable possibility, few sciences ever achieve it. Even those that do only manage to maintain it for a relatively short period of time.

The second paradigmatic state discussed by Masterman is the

nonparadigmatic science.   This is a situation in which there are no paradigms, hence the scientist cannot differentiate the basic subject matter of his field from that of other disciplines.   One might question whether such a discipline can be labelled a science.

Dual paradigmatic science exists immediately before a scientific revolution, when two paradigms are vying for hegemony, a dominance that one of them will ultimately achieve.   An example of a dual paradigmatic science is the historical point when Einsteinian physics was dueling with Newtonian physics for preeminence.

This raises an important point; all sciences at a given point in their history may fall into each of the types of paradigmatic states. We have already seen how physics could be categorized as a paradigmatic science at one point in its history and as a dual paradigmatic science at another point.   In its early stage of development it presumably lacked any paradigm and therefore was, at that time, a nonparadigmatic science.

Finally, there is the *multiple paradigm* science.   This is the situation in which there are several paradigms vying for hegemony within the field as a whole.   One of the defining characteristics of a multiple paradigm science is that supporters of one paradigm are constantly questioning the basic assumptions of those who accept other paradigms.   Thus, scientists have a difficult time conducting "normal science" because they are constantly defending their flanks against attacks from those who support other paradigms.   *It is in the category of a multiple paradigm science that I would place sociology, as well as the other social sciences.*

The problem with Masterman's analysis is she conceives of paradigms applying only to an *entire discipline.*   A paradigm either gains hegemony within an entire science or tries to achieve that dominance. *Paradigms need not, as Masterman argues, apply to the discipline as a whole.   Paradigms can, in a sense, co-exist within a given science.* It is my thesis that multiple paradigms co-exist within contemporary sociology, but they do not co-exist peacefully.   They are engaged in political efforts to gain hegemony within the discipline as a whole as well as within virtually every sub-area in sociology.

We are now approaching the point where we must apply Kuhn's ideas to sociology. Those ideas were developed by Kuhn for the natural sciences, not the social sciences.   A useful intermediary step would be to demonstrate the applicability of Kuhn's ideas to a field that stands somewhere between physics and sociology, namely, linguistics.

Linguistics was regarded as a classificatory science prior to 1957. The goal of the linguist was to classify the elements of the human languages. John Searle (1971:16) offered the following description of the subject matter of linguistics prior to 1957:

> Suppose, for example, that such a linguist [a pre-1957 linguist] is given a description of a language, whether an exotic language like Cherokee or a familiar one like English. He proceeds by first collecting his data, he gathers a large number of utterances of the language, which he records on his tape recorder or in phonetic script. This "corpus" of the language constitutes the subject matter. He then classifies the elements of the corpus at their different linguistic levels. . . . The aim of linguistic theory was to provide the linguist with a set of rigorous methods, a set of discovery procedures which he could use. . . .

In addition to defining classification as its main mission, pre-1957 linguists defined certain topics as outside their domain:

> Meanings, scientifically constructed, were thought to be patterns of behavior determined by stimulus and response; they were properly speaking the subject matter of psychologists. Alternatively they might be some mysterious mental entities altogether outside the scope of a sober science or, worse yet, they might involve the speaker's whole knowledge of the world around him and thus fall beyond the scope of a study restricted only to linguistic facts. (Searle, 1972:16)

Pre-1957 linguistics was labelled *structural linguistics* or structuralism. It defined as its subject matter the objective utterances of a given population. It sought to use objective and precise methods in order to investigate these phenomena. Conversely, it refused to get into any metaphysical issues such as the meanings of sentences, mental entities, or unobservable facts. Pre-1957 linguistics truly sought to be a behavioral science focusing only on observable behavior patterns and not on the mental processes that may have preceded those behaviors.

The 1957 revolution in linguistics was ushered in by the publication of Noam Chomsky's *Syntactic Structures*. Chomsky was trained in the structuralist tradition outlined above, but he found as early as his graduate school days that there were things (anomalies) with which the structuralists could not cope.   The structuralist could not account for the infinite number of sentences within a language, the internal relationships within sentences, the relationships between sentences, and the existence of ambiguous sentences.   These anomalies led to the crisis stage in the revolution in linguistics.   Chomsky's new paradigm sought to account for the infinite number of sentences of a natural language.   It attempted to show which strings of words were sentences and which were not, in addition to providing a description of the grammatical structure of each sentence.   This paradigm was labelled *generative grammar* "because of its aim of constructing a device that would generate all and only the sentences of a language."   (Searle, 1972:17)   The new paradigm, true to Kuhn's predictions, led to wide-scale changes within linguistics.

Chomsky was not content with the traditional subject matter of linguistics.   He felt, for example, that any body of published sentences, even all those to be found in the Library of Congress, was trivially small.   It was not the sentence that was the proper subject of study, "the proper object of study was the speaker's underlying knowledge of the language, his 'linguistic competence' that enables him to produce and understand sentences he has never heard before."   (Searle, 1972:17)   This shift from a body of sentences as the subject matter of linguistics to the speaker's linguistic competence was obviously revolutionary.   It sought to include subjects consciously excluded by the structuralists.   It also carried with it enormous changes in the methods employed by the linguist in his research.   The objective methods used to collect data on sentences were markedly different from those needed to collect information about the linguistic competence of the speaker.

Publication of Chomsky's revolutionary statement was met with a predictable reaction from structuralists—they rejected it.   Trained in the old school, structuralists found it difficult to accept generative grammar.   But Chomsky's position did not fall on totally deaf ears. Graduate students of the structuralists were young enough not to be sold on the structuralist position. They were able to see the merits of a new, albeit revolutionary, position.   Under the noses of their structuralist mentors, graduate students flocked to the banner of generative grammar. In a very few years generative grammar became an established paradigm in linguistics in spite of the resistance of the old Turks. A brief period of normal science had returned, at least for the young linguist attempting to articulate the new paradigm. It is interesting to note that a new revolution seems to be inundating linguistics. Many of Chomsky's disciples and even some of his best students are challenging generative grammar with a new paradigm that Searle labels "generative semantics." Scientific revolutions seem to be occurring in linguistics at a breakneck pace.

One of the ironies of the Chomsky revolution is that, in the short period of time since it began, Chomsky has been relegated to a minority status within linguistics. Most of the young people active in the field have come to regard many of Chomsky's ideas as obsolete. The older structuralists are delighted by the struggle between Chomsky and those who have followed up on his work. One structuralist said: "Those . . . people are in deep trouble." (Searle, 1972:20) Yet Searle (1972:20) is quite right in noting that the "conflict is being carried on entirely within a conceptual system that Chomsky created." Thus, in the end, structuralism will not emerge as the winner; it will not reemerge as the dominant paradigm in linguistics. That honor will go either to one of the paradigms currently competing for center stage or to one that is as yet unborn.

I have clearly not done justice to the situation in linguistics in these few paragraphs, but my goal was not to give you a complete picture of the situation in linguistics. Rather, I wanted to use the case of linguistics as a transition to a discussion of the applicability of Kuhn's ideas to sociology. If Kuhn's ideas apply to linguistics, as they seem to, we are on firmer ground in trying to apply them to sociology.

There are important lessons to be learned from the example of linguistics. It demonstrates the clearly political character of the struggle between paradigms for preeminence within a field. This underscores the importance of irrationality in the development of the sciences. Paradigms do not simply gain hegemony because they are better than their predecessors. Paradigms gain the center stage because they are able to attract adherents and ward off attacks from those who support other positions. Irrational factors enter into the emergence of any paradigm. The victory of the Chomsky paradigm was a political victory and the attacks by Chomsky's disciples were similarly motivated, at least in part. The glee of the structuralists over the conflict between Chomsky and his disciples was also motivated by political factors.

One of the major contributions of Kuhn's work is to point out the irrational and the political factors that affect the development of any science. We have seen how this applies to linguistics and we will see throughout this book how it also applies to sociology.

A second reason for the inclusion of the discussion of linguistics is the similarity between it and sociology. At the present time both linguistics and sociology lack a dominant, discipline-wide paradigm. The multiple paradigms within linguistics, like those in sociology, are competing and conflicting within the field as a whole as well as within virtually every sub-area in the discipline. Because of this fact, it is almost impossible to get down to normal science within linguistics or sociology. Normal science is not currently open to the linguist or the sociologist since any work he undertakes is likely to be criticized in terms of its basic assumptions by those who accept alternate paradigms.

We have finally arrived at the point where we can directly consider the paradigmatic state of sociology. A critical analysis of previous work on this issue will be useful as a starting point for the analysis that will be developed in the remainder of this book. We will begin with an empirical study of the paradigmatic development of a variety of sciences conducted by Lodahl and Gordon (1972).

Lodahl and Gordon (1972:58) designed their research to determine if they could "operationalize the paradigm concept in a manner that will be viable in terms of research, and then, in testing key hypotheses based on the paradigm concept, which, if supported, could provide the framework for increased investigation of differences between scientific fields." They tested two sets of hypotheses derived from Kuhn's work. First, Lodahl and Gordon (1972:58) tested Kuhn's idea that "paradigms are more *highly developed* in the physical than in the social sciences." (italics mine)   Second, they tested the hypothesis that "the great consensus of fields with *high paradigm development* would facilitate teaching and research activities as compared to fields with *low paradigm development*." (italics mine) (Lodahl and Gordon, 1972:8)   Lodahl and Gordon gathered data from 1,161 people in the fields of sociology, political science, chemistry, and physics. These four disciplines were chosen because they represented a range of high and low paradigm development with physics and chemistry representing the former and sociology and political science representing the latter. What is it that differentiates a high paradigm field from a low paradigm field? Lodahl and Gordon simply arbitrarily labelled chemistry and physics high paradigm fields and sociology and political science low paradigm fields. However, they did seek to evaluate the validity of their categorization by asking their respondents to evaluate seven fields (biology, chemistry, economics, physics, political science, psychology, and sociology) in terms of "the degree to which . . . there is consensus over paradigms (law, theory, and methodology) within the field." (Lodahl and Gordon, 1972:59)   Table 1–1 summarizes the results.

TABLE 1–1. *Rankings of Selected Scientific Fields on Paradigm Development*

	Respondent Fields			
Fields Ranked	Physics	Chemistry	Sociology	Political Science
Biology	3	3	3	3
Chemistry	2	2	2	2
Economics	4	4	4	4
Physics	1	1	1	1
Political Science	6	6	7	7
Psychology	5	5	5	5
Sociology	7	7	6	6

Adapted from: Janice Lodahl and Gerald Gordon, "The Structure of Scientific Fields, and the Functioning of University Graduate Departments," *American Sociological Review*, Feb. 1972, p. 60.

Some interesting conclusions emerge from Table 1–1. Of greatest significance is the fact that there is high agreement among those in the fields studied on the relative ranking of the seven disciplines in terms of paradigmatic development. Since sociology is ranked at, or near, the bottom in terms of paradigmatic development, those active in various fields agree with the position taken in this chapter on the paradigmatic status of sociology.   Sociology is a low paradigm science, or in my terms, a science in which a paradigm has not been able to achieve preeminence within a given area or within the field as a whole. It is interesting to note that the only disagreements on the list are over the two least developed fields paradigmatically, sociology and political science.   Those in the two most developed fields (physics and chemistry) view sociology as least developed paradigmatically; those in the two least developed fields (sociology and political science) believe that political science is less developed than sociology.

The key to whether a field is a high paradigm science is the amount of agreement within it.   This agreement should manifest itself in several areas, including the basic survey course.   Where there is high paradigmatic agreement, one would hypothesize that there would be less variation in the content of the survey course than there would be in fields where there is low paradigmatic agreement.   Respondents in each field were asked "how much basic or survey undergraduate courses varied in content from their department to others of a comparable quality."   (Lodahl and Gordon, 1972:60)   The responses could vary from 1 (very little difference between departments) to 10 (great differences between departments).   Differences between the fields in terms of mean responses were as follows:

Physics—3.61
Chemistry—4.67
Sociology—4.90
Political Science—5.82

The differences were statistically significant, indicating that the social sciences had less paradigmatic development than the natural sciences.

Lodahl and Gordon also hypothesized that the same sort of relationship would hold in terms of graduate education with paradigmatically developed fields exhibiting more agreement over such things as course content and degree requirements than paradigmatically undeveloped fields.   This time they asked about agreements on these issues within the respondent's department rather than between departments.   The results tend to confirm this hypothesis.   The most important finding, from our point of view, is that sociologists exhibit significantly less agreement in these areas of graduate studies than the natural scientists studied.   Similar findings on a number of other variables tend to support the idea that sociology exhibits low paradigmatic development, or lacks a single dominant paradigm or one that has been able to gain preeminence within any subarea within the discipline.

More generally, Lodahl and Gordon have provided some empirical support for the entire base upon which this book is built. They have tended to confirm Kuhn's idea that there is variation among fields in terms of paradigmatic development. More specifically, they have shown that the social sciences are less developed paradigmatically than the natural sciences. Sociology is at, or near, the bottom of paradigmatic development in terms of those fields studied by Lodahl and Gordon. It is my thesis that this lowly status is attributable to the fact that paradigms within sociology have not been able to maintain preeminence within specified areas, let alone the field as a whole. Each paradigm is contested by those who accept the other paradigms. In my opinion, the finding that sociology is a low paradigm science results from this fact.

We have an image of Kuhn's schema, a definition of a paradigm, and some idea of the paradigmatic status of sociology. I would like to turn to Robert Friedrichs' (1970) effort to analyze sociology using the paradigm concept. I think that Friedrichs' work has certain inherent weaknesses and I would like to examine those weaknesses in the next few pages. In baring the weaknesses of Friedrichs' analysis, and later Effrat's, I hope to set the stage for my own effort to pinpoint the basic paradigms within sociology.

The real problem with Friedrichs' *A Sociology of Sociology* is it operates within the confines of Kuhn's first, admittedly vague, notion of a paradigm. Friedrichs' analysis of the paradigmatic status of sociology fails because it lacks a usable definition of a paradigm. Friedrichs makes no real effort to redefine the term. He is generally satisfied to operate with Kuhn's diverse definitions. If he uses any single definition to orient his work, it is the idea that a paradigm is a discipline's "fundamental image" of its subject matter. The problem with this definition is that it is extremely vague and hardly useful in trying to determine the paradigmatic status of sociology or any other field. Operating with diverse and vague definitions of a paradigm, it is hardly surprising that Friedrichs' analysis of the paradigmatic status of sociology is highly limited. In fact, Friedrichs was forced to conclude that Kuhn's ideas did not fit sociology very well and that in sociology, unlike the natural sciences, there were two types of paradigms, first-order and second-order paradigms.

He begins with a direct application of Kuhn's idea of a paradigm to the subject matter of sociology. He proceeds to label almost every *theory* in sociology a paradigm, or at least a would-be paradigm. System and conflict theories emerge as the dominant "paradigms" in sociology. Marxism, dialectics, action theory, exchange theory, and phenomenology are defined as pretenders to that lofty status. However, as our definition has made clear, theories are *not* paradigms, but only one aspect of a far broader unit that is a paradigm. Friedrichs labels theories as paradigms because he lacks a good definition of a paradigm.

Working with a weak definition of the paradigm concept, Friedrichs argues that sociology did, at one time, have a dominant paradigm. Friedrichs is working with the same misconception that has plagued many of the authors discussed in this chapter. That is, Friedrichs mistakenly assumes that a paradigm must apply to a discipline as a whole. This further weakens Friedrichs' case. He argues that in the fifteen years following the Second World War sociology was dominated by what he calls the *system paradigm*. Although it is broader in some respects, the system paradigm seems to be very close to structural-functional theory. The end of the Second World War marked a turning point, according to Friedrichs (1970:20), that led to the emergence of the system paradigm: "Sociology's preparadigmatic period of adolescence was drawing to an end. A core vocabulary and a common theoretical posture was beginning to emerge. With them sociology seemed finally on the point of moving from the ordering of its own house to cumulative research." Even though Friedrichs argues that the system paradigm gained hegemony within the discipline as a whole, directly following the Second World War, he recognizes its shaky status:

> Although the consolidation about the system paradigm in the decade and a half following World War II was far from total, the field of force that the image exerted was remarkable in light of the eclectic state of the discipline before the war. Furthermore, the *actually* operative images may be less crucial for our analysis than the image that was *thought* at the time to be dominant. Thus, although any

sociologist active during the period could easily recall many a limited battle that continued to rage, the fact that stands out in retrospect is that system and its antecedent notion, functionalism, was deemed by the well-informed professional to represent sociological orthodoxy in the "fifties."   (Friedrichs, 1970:19)

Friedrichs clearly weakens his case by admitting that the system model was not actually dominant, but only *thought* to be dominant. He nevertheless clings to his idea that there was a paradigm and it was best described by the term *system*.

Friedrichs goes on to argue that by the 1960s the system paradigm was breaking down because of a series of anomalies, the most important of which was its inability to deal with conflict and change. A series of "paradigms" (really theories) came to the fore in the wake of the demise of the system "paradigm."   "But as intriguing as this assortment of candidates for paradigmatic status may have appeared, there could be no doubt whatsoever that the most popular pretender to the throne was *conflict*."   (Friedrichs, 1970:45)   Friedrichs is as wrong here as he was regarding the system paradigm.   As the system model was not a paradigm but a theory, conflict is nothing more than another theoretical alternative.

Thus, Friedrichs' inadequate definition of a paradigm led him to accord paradigmatic status to system and conflict theory.   He also accorded the possibility of that status to a variety of other theoretical perspectives that have arisen in light of the decline of system theory. Marxism, dialectics, action theory, exchange theory, and phenomenology were defined as possible inheritors of paradigmatic status.

His usage of the paradigm concept leaves Friedrichs with a bewildering array of paradigms and would-be paradigms.   It is perhaps because he recognizes that his perspective is overly splintered, that Friedrichs decides to differentiate between first-order and second-order paradigms.   He recognizes that the theories he has been calling paradigms may not be the "most controlling" fundamental images in sociology.   He relegates his theories to second-order paradigms.   The first-order, or most controlling, paradigms in sociology relate to the image the sociologist has of "himself as a scientific agent," rather than his basic image of the subject matter.   There are only two such self-images, the *priestly* and the *prophetic*.   They are the most controlling.   This idea of first-order paradigms allows Friedrichs to come to

a much more parsimonious analysis of the paradigmatic status of sociology. This perspective allows Friedrichs to conclude that there are
only two first-order paradigms, instead of many different paradigms in
sociology.

   To support his notion of the existence of two orders of paradigms in sociology, Friedrichs argues that sociologists have a very
different relationship with their subject matter than biological or
physical scientists. He argues, somewhat seductively, that social scientists are more "intimate" with their subject matter than natural
scientists. Intimacy is obviously hard to deal with in any science, so
Friedrichs (1970:56) extends his argument: "And whereas atoms and
cells are *not in any consequential* way influenced by the image the
physicist and the biologist hold of themselves as scientists, social phenomena may be immediately and profoundly conditioned by the
image the social scientist has internalized regarding the nature of his
activity." (italics mine)   Friedrichs argues that images of the subject
matter of sociology may be a function of a more fundamental paradigm—the images sociologists have of themselves. Thus, the self-
image becomes the first-order paradigm. This determines the nature
of the second order paradigms—the fundamental images of the subject
matter. Sociology, in Friedrichs' view, was dominated by the prophetic paradigm prior to World War II. Although sociology did not
have a dominant paradigm in terms of its subject matter at this time,
it did achieve a dominant paradigm in terms of the image sociologists
had of themselves. The prophetic sociologist conceives of himself as
a social critic oriented toward debunking our social myths. The
prophet is far more committed to social change than to the development of scientific sociology. The major sociological prophet was, of
course, C. Wright Mills (1959). Friedrichs links the preeminence of
the prophetic mode prior to World War II with the lack of a dominant substantive paradigm during that period. The prophets are far
more inclined toward the destruction of social myths than they are
to the construction of sociological thought. In any case, by the mid-
1950s all of the major sociological prophets, except for Mills, were
either dead or retired.

   In the decade and a half following the Second World War the
early prophetic leaders of the field passed from the scene. They were
replaced by a new breed of sociologist, well trained in empirical

methods and opposed to the prophetic orientation of their mentors. They urged a more scientific sociology, a value-free sociology. These were the sociologists who fit what Friedrichs calls the *priestly paradigm*. These sociologists were oriented toward the development of scientific sociology instead of social change. These sociologists tended to withdraw from the problems of the real world and turned their attention toward personal success within the discipline of sociology. This swing to the priestly mode was not without its opponents. Friedrichs notes evidence within the discipline of a "return to prophecy." We are at the stage where we have two such first-order paradigms vying for preeminence within the discipline.

Although I have no quarrel with the differentiation between priestly and prophetic sociology, I do not accept the necessity of resorting to this different level of analysis. Friedrichs was forced to look for paradigms based on self-images of sociologists because he was working with an inadequate definition of a paradigm relating to the subject matter of sociology. This inadequate definition led him to mistake theories for paradigms and to label almost every sociological theory a paradigm, or a would-be paradigm. This, in turn, led to the unesthetic conclusion that there are innumerable paradigms in sociology. Uncomfortable with this, Friedrichs turned to the self-images of sociologists in order to come up with a more parsimonious paradigm system. My point is that Friedrichs would not have had to go to this level if he had a better definition of a paradigm. Furthermore, the different images of the *subject matter* are the key paradigmatic splits in sociology, as they are in all other sciences. The definition offered in this chapter will allow us to parsimoniously identify the major paradigms in sociology in terms of the different images of the subject matter of the discipline.

Parsimony is also the problem facing Effrat (1972) in his effort to analyze the paradigmatic status of sociology. Effrat has an adequate definition of a paradigm. In fact, his definition is very close to the one employed in this book. He fully recognizes the irrational and political character of paradigmatic revolutions and, in fact, criticizes Kuhn for underestimating these dimensions. Although he starts out well, Effrat becomes careless and begins to use the term "theories" interchangeably with the paradigm concept. This leads him to the same problem that stalked Friedrichs. In calling theories paradigms, Effrat ends up with a cumbersome list of paradigms. Among the theoretical orientations which Effrat labels paradigms are the following: Marxist, Freudian, Durkheimian, Weberian, Parsonian, phenomenological, ethnomethodological, symbolic interaction, and exchange theory. He lists a number of other theoretical perspectives that he is willing to call paradigms and furthermore implies that there are still other paradigms that he has not had time to discuss. If there really were this many paradigms in sociology, the concept would be a useless tool in analyzing the status of the discipline. In fact, the paradigm concept *is* a useful tool for analyzing sociology. Now that I have covered the work of some of my predecessors, I will demonstrate that the paradigm concept is truly a useful tool for analyzing sociology.

A rigorous application of the paradigm concept to sociology leads me to the conclusion that there are at this time only *three basic paradigms in sociology*. The discussion at this point will be brief since the ensuing chapters will deal with each paradigm in great detail. In my view the three basic paradigms within sociology are as follows:

1. The Social Facts Paradigm
2. The Social Definition Paradigm
3. The Social Behavior Paradigm

These three paradigms, unlike Friedrichs' first-order paradigms, relate to the sociologist's fundamental image of his subject matter. These paradigms are the broadest units of consensus within sociology, although no individual paradigm is accepted by a majority of sociologists. The brief initial descriptions of the three paradigms that follow, simply outline the major components of each paradigm—their exemplars, images of the subject matter, theories, and methods.*

---

* Some theorists, such as Phillips (1973) , include values as part of a paradigm. I have chosen not to include values as part of a discipline's paradigm, although I recognize the strength of Phillips' argument. I will simply mention the different value systems that could have been included within each paradigm.

The *social factist* tends to be committed to professional goals. He is interested in the development of grand, abstract theory. If he is a researcher, he is interested in using sophisticated and elaborate statistics. The social factist fits Friedrichs' "priestly" mode.

The *social definitionist* tends to reject grand theory and elaborate statistics. He is more oriented to the idea that he possesses peculiar skills. These skills are a result of

THE SOCIAL FACTS PARADIGM

EXEMPLAR

The exemplar for the social factist is the work of Emile Durkheim, in particular, *The Rules of Sociological Method* (1964) and *Suicide* (1951).

IMAGE OF THE SUBJECT MATTER

In *The Rules of Sociological Method* Durkheim argued that the basic subject matter of sociology is the social fact. He demonstrated that contention empirically in *Suicide*. As Blau (1960) has pointed out, there are two types of social facts—social structures and social institutions. Sociologists who define either, or both, of these types as the basic subject matter of sociology are social factists. They accept, following Durkheim, that these social facts should be treated as "real" things. Some even go further arguing that they *are* real things. (Warriner, 1956)   A social fact can be a "real" structure (such as a group or a bureaucracy) or a "real" institution (such as the family or religion). The social factist focuses on the nature of these structures and institutions and their interrelationships. He is usually not

---

his training and allow him to see things that would escape the layman. (This is Mills' "sociological imagination" and Weber's Verstehen.) The social definitionist tends to be what Friedrichs called the "prophet." The social definitionist is particularly interested in debunking myths about society and changing various things that he regards as detrimental.

The *social behaviorist* tends to stand somewhere between the social factist and the social definitionist. He accepts the need to develop theory and use sophisticated methods and statistics. He also accepts a prophetic role within society. He tends to use his theories and methods to debunk myths, as well as lay the groundwork for improving society.

content to remain at this level and frequently encroaches on the subject matter of the other two paradigms. He also endeavors to explain social definitions and behavior. Conversely, those who accept the other two paradigms are far from reluctant, as we will see, to try to explain social structures and social institutions. In fact, *the adherents of each paradigm attempt to deny the validity of the other paradigms.* The social factist sees behavior and social definitions more or less determined by social structures and institutions.

THEORIES

The social facts paradigm encompasses a number of theoretical perspectives. Structural-functional theory tends to see social facts as rather neatly interrelated. Conflict theory tends to emphasize disorder among social facts, or the fact that order is maintained by coercive forces within society. Structural-functional and conflict theory are the two dominant theories within the social facts paradigm. Systems theory is another, but much of systems theory can be included under the heading of modern structural-functionalism. It is important to emphasize the point that structural-functionalism and conflict theory are *theories, not paradigms* as both Friedrichs and Effrat would have us believe. They both can be included under the heading of the social facts paradigm since they both accept the centrality of the study of social facts. I believe this approach is far more parsimonious and realistic than the ones presented by Friedrichs or Effrat.

METHODS

The preferred method of the social factist engaged in empirical research is the questionnaire and/or interview. This preference is an anomaly since questionnaires and interviews are designed to gather information from individuals. How can one study social facts by asking individuals questions? I will argue later that one cannot really study social facts in this way. Instead, the comparative and historical method should be used by those who seek to study social facts.

THE SOCIAL DEFINITION PARADIGM

EXEMPLAR

To the social definitionist, the unifying exemplar is Max Weber's (Gerth and Mills, 1958) work on social action.

IMAGE OF THE SUBJECT MATTER

Weber's work led to an interest in the way individuals define their social situations and the effect of this definition on ensuing action. This is the basic subject matter of the social definition paradigm. The subject matter is not social facts, but the way in which people define those social facts. The basic premise here is W. I. Thomas' dictum: if people define things as real, they will be real in their consequences. The crucial object of study is intrasubjectivity and intersubjectivity and the action that results. This also entails a rejection of the behaviorist position. Behavior is not seen as a simple stimulus–response phenomenon, but rather as a result of an evaluative process undertaken by the individual. The acceptance of the social definition paradigm entails a simultaneous rejection of the validity of the other two sociological paradigms.

THEORIES

There are three major theories that can be subsumed under the social definitionist paradigm. The first is action theory, stemming directly from Weber and later in the work of Parsons (1937) and MacIver (1942). The second theory is symbolic interactionism, which also owes a debt to Weber, but developed primarily at the University of Chicago in the 1920s and 1930s in the work of Mead (1956), Cooley (1902), Thomas (1951), and later, Blumer (1969) and others. Finally, there is phenomenological sociology. This theoretical orientation was also influenced by Weber, as well as Schutz (1971), Husserl (1965), and Garfinkel (1967).

METHODS

The social definitionist tends to use some form of observation if he is oriented toward research. Although other methods are used by some in this paradigm and others shun empirical methodology altogether, observation is the preferred method of the social definitionist. As with the questionnaire/interview methods of the social factist, I will later question whether the observation method really allows the social definitionist to study the subject matter of concern to him—intrasubjectivity and intersubjectivity and the resulting action.

THE SOCIAL BEHAVIOR PARADIGM

EXEMPLAR

The major exemplar for the sociologist who accepts the social behavior paradigm* is the work of the psychologist, B. F. Skinner (1971).

IMAGE OF THE
SUBJECT MATTER

The behaviorist downgrades the importance of social definitions and social facts. To the behaviorist, these are metaphysical concepts which get in the way of the real subject matter of sociology—human behavior. The behaviorist seeks to understand, predict, and even determine the behavior of man. Of particular interest are the rewards that elicit desirable behaviors and the punishments that inhibit undesirable behavior.

THEORIES

There are two theoretical approaches in sociology that can be included under the heading of social behaviorism. The first is behavioral sociology, which is very close to pure psychological behaviorism

---

* The meaning of the phrase social behavior should not be confused with Mead's use of the same phrase. Mead used the phrase to differentiate his brand of social definitionism from behaviorism, while I use it for the sociological variant of behaviorism. I am indebted to Marston McCluggage for this point.

applied to sociological questions. The work of Burgess and Bushell (1969) is of this genre. The second is exchange theory, which is most often associated with George Homans (1961).* Homans integrates pure behaviorism with some elements native to sociology.

METHODS

Owing a heavy debt to psychology, it is not surprising to find that the behaviorist tends to use experimental methods when conducting research. This may take the form of laboratory experiments or experiments conducted in real-life situations. I will argue that the method of the behaviorist comes closest to tapping the subject matter of concern to his paradigm.

Although trichotomizing sociology in this way is original in this work, some support for its efficacy can be found in a study by Brown and Gilmartin (1969). The type of variable analyzed is one of the things in which they were interested, in their comparative study of articles published in the *American Journal of Sociology* in the periods 1940–1941 and 1965–1966. They divided the variables into three categories that roughly parallel the three types of sociological paradigms discussed above. The first variable analyzed by Brown and Gilmartin is the "individual," the primary focus of those who accept the behavioral sociology paradigm. The second is the "individual-group." Those who subscribe to the social definition paradigm would be most likely to concentrate on it. Finally, there is the "group" variable. It is primarily the concern of those who accept the social facts paradigm.

Brown and Gilmartin's findings on the percentage of articles focusing on each of these three variables tends to confirm my idea that sociologists are divided among the three paradigms. Their findings also indicate that the relative strength of the three paradigms has remained relatively constant over time. The following data derived from the study by Brown and Gilmartin support these contentions:

* A new edition of Homans' book appeared as this manuscript was going to press.

TABLE 1–2. *Comparison of Articles Published in the* American Journal of Sociology *(1940–1941 and 1965–1966) by Type of Variable Analyzed*

	Year	
Type of Variable Analyzed	1940–1941	1965–1966
Individual (Social Behavior Paradigm)	30.9%	36.5%
Individual-Group (Social Definition Paradigm)	33.2%	32.3%
Group (Social Facts Paradigm)	35.9%	31.2%

Adapted from: Julia S. Brown and Brian G. Gilmartin, "Sociology Today: Lacunae, Emphases and Surfeits," *American Sociologist,* 4:283–90, 1969.

The variable scheme employed by Brown and Gilmartin does not exactly parallel my three paradigms. Most questionable is the linkage between the individual variable and the social behavior paradigm. It is clear that many sociologists who have studied the individual never accepted the behaviorist paradigm. Nevertheless, the Brown and Gilmartin research lends at least *some* empirical validity to the position outlined here.

Conclusion

The basic thesis of this book is that sociology is characterized by three competing paradigms. On the one hand, each is striving to achieve hegemony within the discipline as a whole. However, as of this writing, and in the foreseeable future, none of the paradigms is likely to gain discipline-wide dominance. On the other hand, each paradigm has also been unable to win unquestioned supremacy within a specific area within sociology. Each paradigm competes with the others within every area in sociology. Sociology is characterized by an extraordinary amount of political conflict because of this competition. Adherents of one paradigm are constantly attacking those who support the other two. One of my goals in the remainder of this book will be to detail the political nature of conflict within sociology. We will see that sociologists are often more interested in winning a victory for their paradigm than expanding sociological knowledge. This reflects a more general theme in this book, the irrationality of the sociological enterprise. We will see this manifested not only in the political conflicts, but also in such areas as the choice of exemplar and methodology.

Although the analysis of political conflict and irrationality in sociology are major concerns in this book, I am also interested in describing the nature of each of the three major paradigms in sociology. It is my belief that most sociologists do not really grasp the basic differences within the field. It is my hope that this book will rectify this failing. I believe that sociologists must gain a better understanding of their real differences before they can even begin to tackle the problems of political conflict and irrationality.

It is important at this early point to caution the reader not to reify the paradigms discussed in these pages. They are *not* social facts that are external to sociologists and coercive on them. In my view, the paradigms are nothing more than descriptions of the way sociologists currently practice their craft. As such, they can be changed by those sociologists who desire to alter the way in which sociology is currently practiced. However, change is not possible until sociologists understand the real nature of their differences.

Finally, I would like to point out that this book focuses on *differences within sociology*. I have deliberately ignored the common core of agreement that exists within the discipline. Nevertheless, such a common core exists and I underscore that point here so the reader is not misled into believing there is nothing in sociology but differences.

Although the tripartite paradigmatic split is an original contribution of this book, the idea that sociology is radically split into a number of competing perspectives is not. Alfred Schutz (1967:10), the eminent phenomenologist, articulates a position that can be seen as the basic or underlying principle of this book:

> What is happening at the present time in sociology is that different schools are each choosing . . . levels of interpretation as a starting point. Each school then develops a methodology suitable to that level and initiates a whole new line of research. The level of structure of meaning which was the starting point soon gets defined as the exclusive, or at least the essential, subject matter of sociology.

BIBLIOGRAPHY

Berger, Peter. *Invitation to Sociology.* New York: Doubleday, 1963.

Blau, Peter. "Structural Effects." *American Sociological Review* 19 (1960) :178–93.

Blumer, Herbert. *Symbolic Interactionism: Perspective and Method.* Englewood Cliffs, New Jersey: Prentice-Hall, Inc., 1969.

Brown, Julia S., and Gilmartin, Brian G. "Sociology Today: Lacunae, Emphases and Surfeits." *American Sociologist* 4 (1969) :283–90.

Burgess, Robert, and Bushell, Donald, Jr. *Behavioral Sociology.* New York: Columbia University Press, 1969.

Chomsky, Noam. *Syntactic Structures.* New York: Humanities Press, 1957.

Clark, Ronald. *Einstein: The Life and Times.* New York: Avon Books, 1971.

Cooley, Charles H. *Human Nature and the Social Order.* New York: Scribner, 1902.

Durkheim, Emile. *Suicide.* New York: The Free Press, 1951.

———. *The Rules of Sociological Method.* New York: The Free Press, 1964.

Effrat, Andrew. "Power to the Paradigms: An Editorial Introduction." *Sociological Inquiry* 42 (1972) :3–33.

Friedrichs, Robert. *A Sociology of Sociology.* New York: The Free Press, 1970.

———. "Dialectical Sociology: Toward a Resolution of the Current 'Crises' in Western Sociology." *British Journal of Sociology* 13 (1972) :263–74.

———. "Dialectical Sociology: An Exemplar for the 1970's." *Social Forces* 50 (1972) :447–55.

Garfinkel, Harold. *Studies in Ethnomethodology.* Englewood Cliffs, New Jersey: Prentice-Hall, Inc., 1967.

Gerth, Hans, and Mills, C. Wright. *From Max Weber: Essays in Sociology.* New York: Oxford University Press, 1958.

Homans, George. *Social Behavior: Its Elementary Forms.* New York: Harcourt, Brace and World, 1961.

Husserl, Edmund. *Phenomenology and the Crisis of Western Philosophy.* New York: Harper and Row, 1965.

Kuhn, Thomas. *The Structure of Scientific Revolutions.* Chicago: University of Chicago Press, 1962.

———. *The Structure of Scientific Revolutions.* 2d ed. Chicago: University of Chicago Press, 1970.

———. "Reflections on My Critics." *Criticism and the Growth of Knowledge.* Edited by Imre Lakatos and Alan Musgrave. Cambridge: Cambridge University Press, 1970.

Lakatos, Imre, and Musgrave, Alan, eds. *Criticism and the Growth of Knowledge.* Cambridge: Cambridge University Press, 1970.

Lodahl, Janice Beyer, and Gordon, Gerald. "The Structure of Scientific Fields and the Functioning of University Graduate Departments." *American Sociological Review* 37 (1972) :57–72.

MacIver, Robert. *Social Causation.* New York: Harper and Row, 1942.

Marx, Karl. *The Essential Writings.* Edited by Frederick Bender. New York: Harper and Row, 1970.

Masterman, Margaret. "The Nature of a Paradigm." *Criticism and the Growth of Knowledge.* Edited by Imre Lakatos and Alan Musgrave. Cambridge: Cambridge University Press (1970):59–89.

Mead, George Herbert. *On Social Psychology.* Chicago: University of Chicago Press, 1956.

Mills, C. Wright. *The Sociological Imagination.* New York: Oxford University Press, 1959.

Parsons, Talcott. *The Structure of Social Action.* New York: The Free Press, 1937.

Phillips, Derek. "Paradigms, Falsifications and Sociology." *Acta Sociologica* 16 (1973) :13–31.

Schutz, Alfred J. Collected Papers, Vol. I. The Hague: Martinus Nijhoff, 1971.

Searle, John. "Chomsky's Revolution in Linguistics." *New York Review of Books* 18 (June 29, 1972):16–24.

Skinner, B. F. *Beyond Freedom and Dignity.* New York: Knopf, 1971.

Thomas, W. I. "The Persistence of Primary Group-Norms in Present-Day Society." *Social Behavior and Personality.* Edited by E. H. Volkart. New York: SSRC (1951) : 35–38.

Warriner, Charles K. "Groups Are Real." *American Sociological Review* 21 (October, 1956) :549–54.

Watson, James D. *The Double Helix.* New York: New American Library, 1968.

2

*The
Social
Facts
Paradigm*

I will follow the schema laid out in Chapter 1 in this chapter and the following two chapters. I will deal in sequence with each paradigm's exemplars, images of the subject matter, theories, and methods beginning with the social facts paradigm. One who works within this paradigm is labelled a social factist.

EXEMPLARS

Emile Durkheim in *The Rules of Sociological Method* (1895) and *Suicide* (1897) * laid the groundwork for what I label the Social Facts Paradigm. Writing in the late 1890s, Durkheim saw the infant sociology he was trying to nurture surrounded by hostile disciplines having a vested interest in preventing it from gaining independent status. On one side stood philosophy, on the other, psychology.

Durkheim felt philosophy was threatening to destroy sociology from within. The two dominant sociologists of the day, August Comte and Herbert Spencer, were viewed as being far more philosophical than sociological. By this, Durkheim meant they preferred armchair theorizing to actually testing their ideas against real data. In Durkheim's opinion, empirical research distinguished sociology from philosophy. He felt if the field was to continue in the direction laid down by Comte and Spencer, it would end as nothing more than a branch of philosophy. Thus, Durkheim found it necessary to attack both Comte and Spencer.

---

* These are the original publication dates. The bibliography found at the end of this chapter indicates the most recent publication.

Comte and Spencer were interested in the process of evolution, but instead of studying that process empirically, they imposed their preconceived theories on it. Durkheim (1964:19) said of Comte:

> He too, takes ideas for the subject matter of study. It is the course of human progress that forms the chief subject of his sociology. He begins with the *idea* that there is a continuous evolution of the human species, consisting in an ever more complete perfection of human nature; and his problem is to discover the order of this evolution. Now, the existence of this assumed evolution can be established only by an already completed science; it cannot, then, constitute the immediate subject of research, except as a conception of the mind and not as a thing. And indeed, this "representation" is so *completely subjective* that, as a matter of fact, this progress of humanity cannot be said to exist at all.* (italics mine)

Comte substituted his philosophy of evolution for what actually transpired in the real world. There was, in Durkheim's view, a place for this kind of thinking, but it was in philosophy not sociology.

Durkheim (1964:20) offered a similar criticism of Herbert Spencer's brand of sociology:

> With him societies, and not humanity, become the subject matter of science. However, in the definition he gives of society at the outset, the thing itself disappears, giving way to the preconception he has of it. He postulates as a self-evident proposition that "a society is formed only when, in addition to juxtaposition, there is cooperation"—that only by this combination does the union of individuals become a society in the strict sense of the word . . . mere inspection does not reveal that cooperation is the core of social life . . . So here again a certain conception of social reality is substituted for reality itself. What is thus defined is clearly not society but Spencer's idea of it.

Spencer, like Comte, imposed his idea of social order on society rather than empirically investigating it. In Durkheim's view, both Spencer and Comte were guilty of turning sociology into a branch of philosophy rather than into an empirical science.

To move sociology away from philosophy and to help it chart

---

* Emile Durkheim, *The Rules of Sociological Method* (New York: The Free Press, 1964). Reprinted by permission of Macmillan Publishing Co., Inc.

out its own distinctive area, Durkheim developed the concept of a *social fact*. A social fact was to be *treated* as a *thing:*

> A thing differs from an idea in the same way as that which we know from without differs from that which we know from within. Things include all objects of knowledge that cannot be conceived by purely mental activity, those that require for their conception data from outside the mind, those which are built up from the more external and immediately accessible characteristics to the less visible and more profound. (Durkheim, 1964:xliii)

The import of this statement lay in its effort to clarify that social facts could not be studied by introspection. They must be researched in the real, empirical world just as we investigate other "things." This position, of course, further served to set sociology, as Durkheim saw it, apart from the brand of sociology developed by people like Comte and Spencer.

Although he is not always clear on this point, social facts seem to take two basic forms for Durkheim. First, social facts may be real material entities. In *Suicide,* Durkheim (1951:313) says: "The social fact is sometimes materialized as to become an element of the external world." He discusses architecture and law as examples of material social facts. Second, most of Durkheim's work emphasizes a kind of social fact that lacks a material existence.

> Of course it is true that not all social consciousness achieves such externalization and materialization. Not all aesthetic spirit of a nation is embodied in the works it inspires; not all of morality is formulated in clear precepts. The greater part is diffused. There is a large collective life which is at liberty; all sorts of currents come, go, circulate everywhere, cross and mingle in a thousand different ways, and just because they are constantly mobile are never crystalized in an objective form. Today a breath of sadness and discouragement descends on society; tomorrow, one of joyous confidence will uplift all hearts. (Durkheim, 1951:315)

These social currents do not have material existence; they can only exist within and between consciousness. In *Suicide,* Durkheim concentrates on examples of this kind of social fact. He relates differences in suicide rates to differences in social currents. Thus, for example, where there are strong currents of anomie, we will find high rates of anomic suicide. Social currents, such as anomie, egoism, and altruism, clearly do not have a material existence, although they may have a material effect by causing differences in suicide rates. Rather, they are intersubjective phenomena that can only exist in the consciousness of man.

It is important to emphasize at this point, that Durkheim did not say that social facts were things, only that *they should be treated as things.* Some social facts, such as law and architecture, are material things, while others, such as currents of opinion, are only to be treated as things. Remember that Durkheim makes this argument so that sociology can move away from armchair theorizing and in the direction of empirical research. He demonstrates how this might be accomplished in his study of suicide.

To Durkheim, both types of social facts are external to the individual and coercive on him. We have no problem with the material social fact on this score. Laws are clearly external to man and coercive on him. Similarly, the architectural design of a man's office is external to him and may also coerce him into behaving differently than he otherwise might. But how could the nonmaterial type of social fact be external to the individual and coercive on him? I think the terms *external* and *coercive* have a different meaning when Durkheim is talking about nonmaterial social facts.

In order to understand how nonmaterial social facts can be external and coercive, we must be aware of Durkheim's battle with psychology. As was the case with philosophy, Durkheim considered psychology as a threat to the existence of sociology. Psychology was already well established when sociology began to come to the fore. Since both fields seemed to deal with the same subject matter, a struggle for supremacy was in progress. It was a struggle that psychology was destined to win *unless* the subject matter of sociology could be distinguished from the subject matter of psychology. This is another of the tasks Durkheim set for himself in *The Rules of Sociological Method.*

In order to set sociology apart from psychology Durkheim differentiated between social facts and psychological facts. Psychological facts, according to Durkheim, were inherited phenomena. Although such a definition would no longer fit psychology, it was appropriate at the time Durkheim was writing. Durkheim relegated the task of studying psychological facts to psychology. That left social facts as the subject matter of sociology. One social fact could only be explained by another social fact. Conversely, a psychological fact could not explain a social fact. Thus, psychologists were warned that they were wasting their time if they tried to deal with the social phenomena of concern to sociologists. As Durkheim (1964:110) put it, "The determining cause of a social fact should be sought among the social facts preceding it."

This brings us back to the external and coercive character of nonmaterial social facts. Unlike material social facts, they are *not* external to, and coercive on, the individual. Instead, nonmaterial social facts are best seen as being external to, and coercive on, psychological facts. *Both* psychological and nonmaterial social facts exist within and between consciousness. Durkheim makes this clear in a number of places. At one point he says of social facts: "Individual minds, forming groups by mingling and fusing, give birth to a being, *psychological if you will,* but constituting of a psychic individuality of a new sort." (Durkheim, 1964:103)   At another point Durkheim (1964:xlix) says: "This does not mean that they are not also mental after a fashion, since they all consist of ways of thinking or behaving." Thus, nonmaterial social facts are external to, and coercive on, psychological facts, not individual consciousness. Nonmaterial social facts, like psychological facts, can only exist within and between consciousness.

It is interesting to note that most social factists have ignored the fine points in Durkheim's argument. They have lumped all social facts together and have gone far beyond Durkheim's idea of simply *treating* social facts as things. They have come to believe, and argue, that all social facts *are* things, real material entities. When the modern-day social factist is examining the relationship between the political, religious, and familial institutions, he is not simply treating them as real things, he believes that they are real things. When he discusses the relationship between these institutions, he is discussing them as if they are real things apart from the men who perceive and construct them.

It is important to note that a social fact need not necessarily be granted the ontological status of a material entity. It can be treated as an intrasubjective and intersubjective phenomenon (in much the same way that Durkheim used it most of the time), that is *experienced* as a coercive externality, but is not reified. Had those who followed Durkheim stayed with this type of analysis, they would have taken a position close to that of the social definitionist. That is, social facts are experienced as material entities and it is the task of sociology to understand the process by which such an experience takes place. However, many of those who thought they were following Durkheim ignored this theme in his work and tended to adopt a position that granted a creation of man (social facts) the status of a separate material entity that is beyond the control of man. This is what upsets the radical sociologists. They argue that treating social facts in this way forces the social factists into a static conception of social reality where social facts are seen to be beyond man's control despite the fact that it is man who created them.

In the remainder of this chapter I will use the term *social fact* in its post-Durkheim, reified sense. It is interesting to note that the social facts paradigm, which got its impetus from Durkheim, would probably be unacceptable to him in its present form because of its belief that all social facts *are* real entities that exist external to the individual and are coercive on him. Although Durkheim accorded some social facts the ontological status of material entities, the body of his work indicates that he saw most social facts as intrasubjective and intersubjective phenomena.

Durkheim's work constitutes the exemplar for the social facts paradigm, but it has a serious weakness. Although many have overlooked it, Durkheim argued that social facts be *treated* as things, not that social facts are real things. This is a serious problem since most of those who accept the social facts paradigm believe that social facts are real. There is, however, another exemplar which argues that social facts are real things. It is Charles K. Warriner's (1956) well-known paper "Groups Are Real: A Reaffirmation." Although Warriner focuses on only one social fact—the group—the same case could be made for any other social fact. Warriner chose to focus on the group because it is one of the most important, if not the most important, social facts. Some have gone as far as to define the field of sociology as the study of groups. Note this definition of the field used in the best selling introductory text in the field. (Broom and Selznick,

1963:7) "Sociology is complementary to the other social sciences. It explores the varieties of *group* structure and the ways they affect political, psychological, and economic relationships." (italics mine) A definition of sociology in another influential textbook not only defines the field in terms of the study of groups, but rules out the study of our other two paradigms: "Sociology, in contrast, has no primary interest in the individual, nor his personality, nor in his behavior, but concerns itself rather with the nature of the *groups* to which individuals belong and the nature of societies in which they live." (Bierstedt, 1970:9) (italics mine)

The title of Warriner's article is extremely intriguing given our focus. For one thing, the title makes it clear that Warriner is arguing that the group is a "real" social fact, although not in the physical sense that a chair is real. It is also clear that the idea that groups are real is under attack by behaviorists and social definitionists and Warriner is being goaded into reaffirming his notion of the Durkheimian argument. Let us examine Warriner's argument in some detail because it is one of the clearest examples of the social facts paradigm as it applies to the concept of a group.

Warriner sees four major ways in which the issue of the "reality" of the group is viewed. The first he labels the *nominalist* position. This maintains "that the group is not a real entity, but is merely a term used to refer to 'an assemblage of individuals.'" (Warriner, 1956:549, citing Malinowski)   The group, in this view, is nothing more than the sum of the individuals in it. Thus the task of sociology is to explain individual behavior, either singly or collectively. Sociology, much to the chagrin of the Durkheimian, is reduced by this perspective to a branch of psychology.

The second position, according to Warriner, is *interactionism.* The interactionists reject the individual-group dichotomy and treat the two as indivisible phenomena. Warriner cites Wirth as an exponent of this position: "Rather than settling the issue as to whether the individual or the group is the ultimate unit in terms of which social life must be analyzed, the mainstream of sociological and social-psychological thought has forgotten this issue and proceeded to analyze social phenomena as complexes of the meaningfully oriented actions of persons reciprocally related to one another." (Warriner, 1939: 966)   Warriner sees the interactionist as taking the position that *neither the individual nor the group is real* except in terms of the other.   We do not have individuals without groups.   Conversely, we do not have groups without individuals.   This seems to be the position accepted by those who are identified with the social definition paradigm.

The third position in this debate is labelled by Warriner as *neo-nominalism*.   The neo-nominalist "accepts the proposition that the term 'group' refers to an objective reality, but claims that the group is less real than persons, for it is, after all, made up of persons and of processes which have their locus and immediate origin in the person." (Warriner, 1956:550)   It is certainly strange to argue that the group is real, but *less real* than individuals.   This raises the philosophical question of whether there is such a thing as degrees of reality.   Can one thing be more real than another?   Aren't things either real or unreal?

The final position in this debate, according to Warriner (1956: 550–551), is *realism:* "This doctrine holds that (1) the group is just as real as the person, but that (2) both are abstract, analytical units, and that (3) the group is understandable and explicable solely in terms of distinctly social processes and factors, not by reference to individual psychology."   It is this position that best expresses the social facts paradigm being discussed in this chapter.   It is the position that Warriner (1956:551) defends: "The purpose here is calling attention to and defending the legitimacy and validity of the realist position, and to propose that this is the most valid and potentially fruitful sociological approach to the study of group and society." Warriner is therefore waging a battle similar to the one waged by Durkheim, although he is more definite in his defense of the realist position than was Durkheim   (1964:551).   Warriner (1956:551) cites the following quotation as the kind of reductionism that led to his defense of the realist position: "We have . . . to establish a branch of psychology concerned with the 'personality' of groups . . . in spite of much talk about 'culture patterns,' methods and concepts simply do not exist.   The sociologists, recognizing that a group cannot be defined in merely political or economic terms have turned to the psychologist for a science of the living group entity."   Like Durkheim before him, Warriner is seeking to differentiate sociology from psychology, a field that still seems eager to swallow it up.

Critics of the "groups are real" position offer, according to Warriner, four propositions to support their position:

1. We can see persons, but we cannot see groups except by observing persons.
2. Groups are composed of persons.
3. Social phenomena have their reality only in persons, this is the only possible location of such phenomena.
4. The purpose for studying groups is to facilitate explanations and predictions of individual behavior." (Warriner, 1956:552)

Warriner's critiques of each of these propositions provide a concise statement of the social facts paradigm. I will summarize his replies point by point.

Warriner replies to the argument that we can only see persons (not groups) in two ways. First, he argues that it is only partially true that we can see a person. We can see the entire biological structure, but we can only see *part* of the person through his actions and behaviors:

> The only thing which we as humans can observe are events within a relatively limited time and space location. Any unity that is microscopic, that extends beyond the scope of our perceptual equipment in space, or whose structural processes are too fast for our perception must be inferred from partial observations made via instruments or through time series. The fact that we cannot directly perceive their unity does not detract from their essential empirical reality: it merely reflects the human reality. This appears to be no less true of social phenomena than of physical ones. (Warriner, 1956:552)

Thus, Warriner is arguing that we cannot see *either individuals or groups*. They are both realities that extend beyond the capacity of human perception, and we are forced to construct a reality out of the bits and pieces of both that we do see. Warriner also indicates that the assumption that "the only realities are physical realities" has been undermined by contemporary physics which notes the "interchangeability of matter and motion."

Warriner interprets the second argument, that groups are composed of persons, as leading to the conclusion that groups are more abstract, less real than persons, and that groups are explained by their component individuals. He believes this position loses strength if we accept his first argument that persons are no more concrete than groups. He also feels that the position is worthy of independent examination. First, Warriner observes that many studies of group interaction recognize the emergence of new phenomena that are not explicable in terms of the nature of the individuals involved nor of what they bring with them to the interaction. Second, the fact that an entity is composed of parts tells us nothing about the entity itself. It is true a chair is composed of atoms, but that tells us little about the chair. Similarly, "the proposition that groups are composed of persons tells us nothing about the groups as such, but merely says that persons are characteristic of human life." (Warriner, 1956:553)

The assumption that social phenomena exist only in individuals is based, according to Warriner, on the fallacious idea that for something to be real it must be internalized by the individual. He differentiates between knowing something and internalization. The fact that one can know something *without internalizing* it gives social phenomena an existence independent of the individual.

Regarding the final proposition (the purpose of studying groups is to facilitate the understanding of individual behavior), Warriner takes the position that it is a value statement and therefore not amenable to argumentation. He, and most other sociologists, believe that the purpose of studying groups is to facilitate explanations and predictions of *group behavior*.

Warriner's summary of his position is a good statement of the social facts paradigm as it applies to groups:

> I propose that if we treat groups as real units or systems, if we cease to identify group phenomena with a particular personnel and with personality, if we cease to look for group phenomena in persons, and if we study groups for the sake of learning more about groups, only then will we begin to make real strides in a uniquely sociological problem. (Warriner, 1956:554)

IMAGE OF THE SUBJECT MATTER

The basic subject matter of sociology to those who adopt this paradigm is the social fact. There are a large number of phenomena that could be labelled social facts: groups, societies, social systems, positions, roles, norms, values, the family, the polity, etc. Peter Blau

(1960) has performed a useful service by differentiating between two basic types of social facts. There are "the common values and norms embodied in a culture or subculture." (Blau, 1960:178)   Such normative and value patterns are often labelled *institutions* by sociologists. There are also "the networks of social relations in which processes of social interaction become organized and through which social positions of individuals and subgroups become differentiated." (Blau, 1960:178)   Such networks are frequently labelled *social structures* by sociologists. Institutions and structures are the two basic types of social facts. They constitute the subject matter for the social factist. Let us examine each of these types of social facts.

In his later work Emile Durkheim equated social facts with institutions. This was not made clear in the first edition (1895) of *The Rules of Sociological Method.* A few years later, however, in the preface to the second edition of that book, Durkheim made the link between social facts and institutions. Discussing social facts, he said:

> It has been pointed out that the word "institution" well expresses this special mode of reality, provided that the ordinary significance of it can be slightly extended. One can, indeed, without distorting the meaning of the expression, designate as "institutions" all the beliefs and all the modes of conduct instituted by the collectivity. Sociology can then be defined as the science of institutions, of their genesis and of their functioning.   (Durkheim, 1964:lvi)

By the second edition of *The Rules of Sociological Method,* the concepts of a social fact and an institution had become interchangeable. Furthermore, social facts or institutions constituted *the subject matter of sociology.*

The transition from social facts to institutions cannot be credited to Durkheim, but to his nephew Marcel Mauss in collaboration with Paul Fauconnet (1901).* They used the term *institution* to include "ways of acting and thinking that the individual finds pre-established, . . . already made, . . . imposed more or less on him . . . and that will survive him." (Vera-Godoy, 1971:52)   All of these meanings of the term *institution* were derived from Durkheim's definition of a social fact. However, an important transition had taken place.

* I would like to thank Hernan Vera-Godoy for pointing this out to me.

Social facts were no longer to be *treated* simply as external to the individual; they *were external* to the individual. All social facts had acquired the ontological status of material entities with an existence separate from the individual. It is this step that gave shape to modern social fact analysis.

In modern sociology, institutions tend to be viewed as interrelated sets of norms and values that surround a particular human activity or bothersome problem. There are clearly numerous institutions, but some of the more important are the family, the polity, the economy, education, religion, and science. Institutions can also take more specific forms such as the nuclear family, parenthood, and childhood. All institutions clearly have a structural existence. The polity has laws, offices, and organizations; the same is true of all other institutions. But the analyst of institutions often accords the nonmaterial aspects of institutions the status of material things. When the student of institutions examines the relationship between family and political norms, he often assumes that these norms have an existence outside of man's consciousness. In making this assumption, the modern-day social factist is going far beyond Durkheim's position that nonmaterial social facts exist within and between consciousness. In terms of Warriner's realist position, an institution is as real as a person or a group.

This brings us to the other major type of social fact—social structures. As pointed out above, some sociologists view institutions as structures rather than conglomerations of norms and values. Parsons (1951:39) is of this genre: "An *institution* will be said to be a complex of institutionalized role integrates which is of strategic significance in the social system in question. The institution should be considered to be a higher order unit of social structure . . ." However, other social units are more often accorded the status of social structures. Among them are roles, positions, organizations, groups, collectivities, social systems, and even societies. Whether they work with social structures or social institutions, social factists accord them the status of material entities. Such a status leads the social factist to be primarily concerned with the interrelationship between structures, between institutions, and between individuals and structures and/or institutions. This leads into the sociological theories included within the social facts paradigm. The sociological theories differ in terms of the way they conceptualize the relationship between institutions, structures, and individuals.

THEORIES

The dominant theory within the social facts paradigm is, by far, structural-functionalism.* In fact, one observer (Davis, 1959) took the position that it is, for all intents and purposes, coterminous with sociology. More recently, Alvin Gouldner (1970) took a similar position when he attacked western sociology by criticizing the functional theory of Talcott Parsons. While there is much more to contemporary western sociology than structural-functionalism, it is preeminent in the social facts world of sociology.

To the functionalist, society is a social system. This means that society is composed of a series of interrelated parts and these integrated parts are in a state of equilibrium. Each part of the social system contributes to the maintenance of other parts. They are in a state of equilibrium because changes in one part will, because of these systemic linkages, lead to changes in other parts of the system. Society is believed to be in a kind of balance with a change in one part necessitating changes in other parts. The equilibrium of the social system is therefore not static, but a moving equilibrium. Parts of society are always changing, and these changes lead to sympathetic changes in other parts of the social system. Thus, change is basically orderly, rather than catyclysmic, as it often is to conflict theorists.

Early functional theories went far beyond this view to take some positions that left them open to severe criticism. They focused on the question of why society is orderly and ignored the question of conflict in social life. They tended to look only at the contribution one system or event made to other systems or events and therefore ignored the possibility that an event or system could operate against the functioning of the rest of the system. At the extreme, functionalists argued that all events and structures were functional for the social system. If they were not functional, they would not have existed or

* I will use the terms functionalism and structural-functionalism interchangeably in this discussion.

occurred.   This led to the conclusion that all structures that existed were indispensable to the social system.

There is obviously a conservative bias in this kind of position. It argues that all structures that exist should continue to exist.   Thus, by extention, war, social inequality, racial inequality, and poverty are "needed" by the social system.   This is obviously the view of those who profit from the status quo rather than those who suffer at its hands.   Victims of racism, war, or poverty are unlikely to hold to the view that their fate is inevitable.   To the vulgar functionalists, change could only be a slow process that occurs solely *within* the system.   When conflicts occur, the vulgar functionalist focuses on how they can be resolved so the social system will be re-equilibrated.   The focus on resolution and re-equilibration obviously holds out little possibility of meaningful change within a social system.

This brief overview of structural-functionalism, raises the question of how I will cover structural-functional theory, as well as every other theoretical perspective.   This is not a theory book and I therefore do not intend to give a complete picture of each theory.   Instead, I intend to present some very selective highlights of each theory. These will be selected on the basis of their theoretical significance as well as their relevance to the paradigm under discussion.   This discussion of structural-functionalism is particularly difficult because more has been written about it than any other theoretical perspective (*see* Demerath and Peterson, 1967).   Instead of trying to cover the entire theory, in the remainder of this section I will concentrate on two pieces of work by Merton (1968) and Gans (1972) that are representative of modern structural-functional theory and are most relevant to the social facts paradigm.

Contemporary structural-functionalism has moved beyond its early vulgar stage largely through the work of Robert Merton.   He makes it clear from the outset that structural-functional analysis is subsumed under the social facts paradigm.   He states the objects that can be subjected to structural-functional analysis must "represent a *standardized* (i.e. patterned and repetitive) item."   (Merton, 1968: 104)   He offers the following examples of these items, all of which are clearly social facts: "social roles, institutional patterns, social processes, cultural pattern, culturally patterned emotions, social norms, group organization, social structure, devices for social control, etc." (Merton, 1968:104)

Early structural-functionalists tended to focus almost entirely on the *functions* of one social fact for another social fact. However, in Merton's view, early analysts tended to confuse subjective motives with functions. The focus of the structural-functionalist should be on functions rather than motives. Functions are defined as "those observed consequences which make for the adaptation or adjustment of a given system." (Merton, 1968:105) There is, however, a clear ideological bias when one only focuses on positive consequences. After all, one social fact can clearly have negative consequences for another social fact. To rectify this serious omission in early structural-functionalism, Merton developed the idea of a *dysfunction*. Just as structures or institutions could contribute to the maintenance of other social facts, they could also have negative consequences for them. Take the example of slavery in the southern United States. Slavery clearly had functions for white Southerners such as cheap labor, support for the cotton economy, and a source of social status. It also had dysfunctions such as making them overly dependent on an agrarian economy and therefore unprepared for industrialization. The continuing disparity between the North and the South in terms of industrialization can be traced, at least in part, to the dysfunctions of the institution of slavery in the South.

Once you possess the dual concepts of function and dysfunction, the question arises of their relative weight. Merton developed the concept of *net balance* to help answer the question of whether functions outweigh dysfunctions or vice versa. Even with the concept, this is never an easy question to answer. One can never simply add up functions and dysfunctions and objectively determine which outweighs the other. The utility of the concept is in orienting the theorist to the question of their relative weights. Thus, to return to the example of slavery, we must orient ourselves to the question of whether, on balance, slavery was more functional or more dysfunctional to the South. While this question can be studied, it is too broad and obscures a number of issues.

Recognizing the abstractness of functionalism, Merton added the idea that there must be *levels of functional analysis*. It is clear that one could conduct a functional analysis of a society as a whole as well as an organization, an institution, or a group. Functionalists had generally restricted themselves to the most macroscopic questions, but Merton made it clear that this need not be so. Returning to the issue of the functions of slavery for the South, it may be necessary to further refine our level of analysis and ask about the functions and dysfunctions of slavery for black families, white families, black political organizations, white political organizations, etc. In net balance terms, slavery was probably more functional for certain social units and more dysfunctional for other social units. Addressing the issue at these more specific levels is an aid in answering the question of the functionality of slavery for the South as a whole.

Merton's concepts of *manifest* and *latent* functions have also been an important asset to functional analysis. Manifest functions are intended while latent functions are unintended. For example, the manifest function of slavery was to increase the economic productivity of the South, but it had the latent social function of providing a vast underclass that served to increase the social status of southern whites, both rich and poor. This idea is related to another of Merton's concepts—*unanticipated consequences*. Actions have both intended and unintended consequences. While everyone is aware of the manifest consequences, it takes a sociologist to uncover the latent functions (and dysfunctions). To some, the very essence of sociology is the uncovering of unintended consequences. Peter Berger (1963) has called this *debunking* or looking beyond stated intentions to real effects.

As further clarification of functional theory, Merton pointed out that all events and structures are not necessarily functional for the entire social system. A given structure can be functional for one subsystem and dysfunctional for another. Furthermore, a structure that is dysfunctional for the system as a whole may well continue to exist. For example, a good case can be made that discrimination against blacks, females, and other minority groups is dysfunctional for American society, yet it continues to exist. Discrimination continues precisely because it is functional for a part of the social system, e.g. discrimination against females is functional for males. It is important to point out that these forms of discrimination are not without dysfunctions for the group which benefits. Males do suffer from their discrimination against females and whites similarly are hurt by their discriminatory behavior toward blacks.

Although Merton has made several other important contributions to functional theory, one further point will suffice for our purposes. Merton contends that all events and structures are not indispensable to the workings of the social system. There are parts of our social system which can be eliminated. This helps functional theory overcome another of its conservative biases. By recognizing that some structures are expendable, the neo-functionalist opens the way for meaningful social change. Our society could continue to exist (and even be improved) by the elimination of discrimination against various minority groups.

At this point it would be useful to go into a detailed example of the utility of modern-day functionalism, specifically Robert Merton's model of functional analysis. That example is provided by Herbert Gans (1972) in his functional analysis of a rather interesting social fact—poverty. It is Gans' thesis that although poverty obviously has all sorts of dysfunctions, it has not been exposed to a systematic functional analysis that seeks to uncover its positive functions. In so doing, Gans is not trying to be an apologist for poverty. He is not saying that because poverty has functions for various segments of society it should or must persist. He is arguing, following Merton, that functional analysis is (when used correctly) ideologically neutral. Someone can use the results of a functional analysis to either help or hurt the poor, but the analysis itself can and should be as value-neutral as possible. Gans even notes that his effort to point out the positive functions of poverty can be used by those who are inclined to improve the lot of the poor. How? By providing alternate sources of similar rewards to those who gain from the existence of poverty. This, in Merton's terms, exemplifies the existence of functional alternatives. I shall examine some of these functional alternatives as well as the implications of Gans' work, but first let us turn to the essence of his thesis—the fifteen functions he sees poverty performing. These fifteen functions can be subdivided into four categories: economic, social, cultural, and political.

Economic

1. The existence of poverty provides society with a group of people (the poor) who are willing (or unable to be unwilling) to perform the "dirty work" in society. Gans (1972:278) defines such work as that

which is "physically dirty or dangerous, temporary, dead-end, and underpaid, undignified, and menial . . ." Perhaps most importantly, these occupations command low pay. Furthermore, certain sorts of enterprises such as hospitals, restaurants, and industrial agriculture often depend for their very existence on the availability of poor people to fill these jobs.

2. The fact that the poor receive so little money is a kind of subsidy to the rich, allowing them to use the money they save to further their own ends. This saved money can be used to further their personal ends or, through saving and investment, the ends of the entire capitalistic economy. This subsidy function can also take a variety of noneconomic forms. For example, poor people who work as domestics free wealthy women for other activities; or the poor who serve as paid volunteers in medical experiments pave the way for the wealthier who can afford the treatments when, and if, they are proven to be safe and useful.

3. A whole series of occupations exist because there are poor people. If poverty were to disappear, many middle and upper class people would be out of work. In Gans' opinion, examples of occupations dependent on the poor are the policeman, the penologist, the numbers runner, the Pentecostalist minister, and the heroin pusher. In addition, Gans claims the peacetime army exists mainly because the poor are willing to serve in it.

4. Poor people also purchase goods and use services that otherwise would go unused. Day-old bread and quack doctors find a market in depressed areas.

Social

5. The existence of the poor validates dominant societal norms. Although the poor probably do not deviate more, they can be more easily labelled as deviant. For example, if a middle class and a poor youth commit the same deviant act, it is far more likely that the poor youth will be labelled a juvenile delinquent than the middle class adolescent. Norms such as hard work, honesty, and monogamy need some violators so that they can be reaffirmed and thereby retain their potency. The poor perform the very valuable function of enabling society to keep its norms powerful.

6. There is a subgroup among the poor that is defined as deserving. These may be people who are poor because they are suffering from a disability or have experienced some bad luck. Whatever the cause,

this group provides upper classes with psychic gratification by providing an outlet for their altruism, pity, and charity.

7. More affluent people can also live vicariously by imagining that the poor engage in, and enjoy more, "uninhibited sexual, alcoholic, and narcotic behavior."

8. Since social status is so important in our society, the poor provide a measuring rod for other classes. Thus, the working class knows where they are and, more importantly, that they stand above some group in the hierarchy of society.

9. Poor people also aid other groups in ascending the stratification ladder. "By being denied educational opportunities or being stereotyped as stupid or unteachable, the poor thus enable others to obtain better jobs." (Gans, 1972:281) Furthermore, the poor provide those who are rising in the stratification system the goods and services they need to make it to the next rung on the ladder.

10. The poor provide a reason for existence for some members of the aristocracy who can serve the poor through various charitable agencies. Similarly, the middle classes derive a great deal of satisfaction out of doing volunteer work for the needy.

Cultural

11. The poor have provided the physical labor needed to construct some of our more impressive cultural monuments (e.g. the Egyptian pyramids) and the excess capital that goes to the support of various types of intellectuals and artists.

12. The culture of the poor (e.g. jazz) is frequently adopted by those above them in the stratification system and some members of the poor (e.g. the hobo, the prostitute) become heroes and subjects of study by other members of society.

Political

13. The poor serve as the rallying cry or enemy of various political groups. The political left rallies around the poor while the right attacks the poor with such epithets as "welfare chiseler."

14. The burden for change and growth in American society can be placed on the shoulders of the poor. Gans (1972:283) gives the following examples:

During the 19th century, they did the back-breaking work that built the cities; today, they are pushed out of their neighborhoods to make room for "progress". . . . The major costs of the industrialization of agriculture in America have been borne by the poor, who are pushed off the land without recompense, just as in earlier centuries in Europe, they bore the brunt of the transformation of aggrarian societies into industrial ones. The poor have also paid a large share of the human cost of the growth of American power overseas, for they have provided many of the foot soldiers for Vietnam and other wars.

15. Since the poor vote less and participate less in the political process, they have been a less potent force in the political system than their number would indicate. In Gans' view this has made American politics more "centrist" than it would otherwise have been and it has made the political system more stable.

At this point it is important to repeat that Gans is not in favor of poverty. In fact, one of the implications of Gans' work is that if we really want to do away with poverty we must find *alternatives* to a variety of these functions currently being performed by the poor. For the first function he suggests that automation would be an alternate way of doing some of society's dirty work and the rest could be performed at higher wages. Similarly, he suggests that instead of the third function, professionals could perform other useful chores. Social workers could help the ulcer-ridden business executive instead of the skid row bum. For functions five through seven he suggests that we reserve our pity and charity for the disabled and leave the poor alone. He continues with this type of analysis, but the point is when we examine poverty functionally, we see there are alternatives that could perform some of the same functions as the poor. Those who "profit" from the existence of poor people would be more likely to accept changes among the poor if they knew their own gains would continue, but from other sources and in other ways.

Despite the existence of alternatives to some functions, Gans finds that for others there are no suitable alternatives. These appear mainly in political functions thirteen through fifteen, where Gans finds it hard to think of suitable alternatives. Furthermore, in many cases he finds that the alternative would be more costly, particularly to more affluent members of society. He concludes that poverty persists for three basic reasons:

1. It is functional to a variety of units in society. Entrepreneurs, executives, welfare workers, and many others profit from poverty.
2. There are no alternatives to some of these functions performed by the poor.
3. Where there are alternatives, they are costlier to the affluent than retaining the poor as a source of these satisfactions.

These sources of the persistence of poverty lead Gans to a conclusion that he regards as very similar to a radical sociologist's, even though he arrived at it using what is considered the most conservative sociological orientation—functionalism. He concludes that social phenomena such as poverty persist when they are functional for the affluent and dysfunctional for the poor. Similarly, they will continue to persist as long as their elimination creates dysfunctions for the affluent. This leads him to conclude that poverty can only be eliminated under two conditions. First, it will die when it becomes sufficiently dysfunctional for the affluent. Second, it will die when the poor achieve enough power to change the dominant system of social stratification. On this radical note, we can conclude this analysis of poverty and turn to a discussion of the criticisms of contemporary functionalism, one of which is its supposed conservative orientation.

Functionalism has frequently been accused of ignoring the significant variables of conflict and change. The tendency to focus on what holds society together has often blinded it to what tears society apart. Although this criticism is true of much of functional theory, it is more deserved by early functional theory. Contemporary functionalism, armed with such concepts as dysfunctions, latent functions, and net balance is more attuned to conflict in society. Functionalists have generally ignored the question of social change in favor of an analysis of social structure. In fact, Talcott Parsons (one of functionalism's prime spokesmen) has often said we cannot hope to study social change until we have an adequate understanding of social structure. Even Parsons seems to have shifted, since his recent work is almost exclusively devoted to social change. His shift reflects the fact that contemporary functionalists are less guilty than their predecessors of ignoring the change factor. Nevertheless, it continues to be true that functionalists, even when they deal with change, tend to see it as a relatively slow process occurring within the system. Few functionalists seem to want anything to do with revolutionary change (Gans is one of the exceptions). They often find it difficult to deal with analytically, and repugnant ideologically.

Emphasis on order in society and de-emphasis of conflict and change (especially revolutionary change) has led to the charge that functionalism is ideologically conservative. Functionalists are viewed by many as establishment sociologists serving to justify the status quo. Given our overview of the functional perspective, it should be clear to the reader that functionalism need not *necessarily* be conservative, but that does not deny the fact that, as frequently used, functionalism has been conservative in orientation. Functionalism as used by many sociologists often serves to support the establishment. More radical sociologists go even further and contend that functionalism is a theoretical tool for, and functional theorists are agents in, the maintenance of the status quo (see Szymanski, 1972).

It is in this context that we must look at the major opposition to functionalism—conflict theory. Keep in mind, however, that both orientations are subsumed under the social facts paradigm. Although conflict theory has a long and distinguished tradition of its own dating back to the work of Karl Marx* (some would even trace its origins further back), much of its contemporary rebirth can be viewed as a reaction to the real and imagined failings of functional theory. In the late 1960s, young, militant sociologists, dissatisfied with the work of their mentors, turned outside of establishment sociology and identified with conflict theory. Unfortunately, much of conflict theory is simply a series of positions directly antithetical to functional ideas, although they both share the basic social facts paradigm. Thus, conflict theorists, like functionalists, are oriented toward the study of social structures and institutions. Instead of developing their own distinctive theoretical position, conflict theorists are, in the main, content to allow this theory to be little more than a series of contentions that are direct opposites of functionalist positions. This is best exemplified by the work of Ralf Dahrendorf (1959) in which the basic tenets of conflict and functional theory are juxtaposed.

Society is static or, at best, in a state of moving equilibrium to

---

* In my view, conflict theory has not been true to Marxian principles. I believe that critical theory, to be discussed briefly in Chapter 5, is the true inheritor of Marxian ideas.

functionalists, but to Dahrendorf and the conflict theorists, every society at every point is subject to processes of change.

Where functionalism emphasizes the fact that society is orderly, conflict theorists see dissension and conflict at every point in the social system.

Functionalists (or at least early functionalists) argue that every element in society contributes to stability, while the exponents of conflict theory see each societal element contributing to disintegration and change.

Functionalists tend to see society as being held together informally by norms, values, and a common morality. On the other hand, conflict theorists see whatever order there is in society stemming from the coercion of some members by those at the top. Where functionalists focus upon the cohesion created by shared societal values, conflict theorists emphasize the role of power in maintaining order in society.

Dahrendorf is the major exponent of the position that society has two faces (conflict and consensus) and, therefore, sociological theory should be divided into corresponding camps of conflict and integration theory. While consensus theorists should focus on value integration in society, the conflict theorist's task is examination of conflict of interests and the coercion that holds society together in the face of these stresses. He recognizes that society could not exist without both conflict and consensus. In fact, each is a prerequisite for the other. For example, he argues that conflict cannot exist without some measure of integration. Thus French housewives are highly unlikely to conflict with Chilean chess players since there is no prior integration to serve as a basis of conflict. Despite the interrelationship between the process of consensus and conflict, Dahrendorf (1959: 164) is not optimistic about the possibility of developing a single sociological theory encompassing both processes: "It seems at least conceivable that unification of theory is not feasible at a point which has puzzled thinkers ever since the beginning of Western philosophy." Eschewing a singular theory, Dahrendorf sets out on the task of constructing a conflict theory of society.*

---

* It might be noted in passing that Dahrendorf (1959:164) calls conflict and coercion "the ugly face of society." One can ponder whether a man who regards them as "ugly" can develop an adequate theory of conflict and coercion.

Dahrendorf begins with, and is heavily influenced by, structural-functionalism. He notes that to the functionalist the social system is held together by voluntary cooperation and/or general consensus. However, to the conflict (or coercion) theorist society is held together by "enforced constraint." This means that some positions in society are delegated power and authority over others. This fact of social life leads Dahrendorf (1959:165) to his central thesis that the differential distribution of authority "invariably becomes the determining factor of systematic social conflicts."

It is important to note that the basic focus for Dahrendorf is social facts. Central to his thesis is the idea that differential *authority* is an attribute of various *positions* within society. The central concepts here are "authority" and "positions," both of which are social facts. Authority does not reside in individuals but in positions and it is positions and the differential distribution of authority among them that should be the concern of sociologists: "The *structural* origin of such conflicts must be sought in the arrangement of social roles endowed with expectations of domination or subjection." (italics mine) (Dahrendorf, 1959:165) The first task of conflict analysis to Dahrendorf is identification of various authority roles within society. In addition to making the case for social factism, Dahrendorf is also aware of the other paradigms (social definitionism and social behaviorism) and demonstrates their inadequacies in contrast to social factism. In fact, he implies that the varying degrees of psychological reductionism of the other paradigms disqualifies them as sociological paradigms. This kind of political attack on other paradigms is a disturbing and pervasive reality in sociology. We will return to this theme throughout this book.

Authority attached to positions is the key to Dahrendorf's analysis. Authority always implies both superordination and subordination. Those who occupy positions of authority are *expected* to control subordinates. It is not their psychological characteristics that impel them to dominate, but the expectations of those who surround them. These expectations, like authority, are attached to positions, not people. Authority is not a generalized phenomenon; those who are subject to control, as well as permissible spheres of control, are specified. Finally, because authority is legitimate, those who do not comply can be sanctioned.

Authority is not a unilinear concept for Dahrendorf. He argues that society is composed of a number of units that he labels "imperatively coordinated associations." Within *each* of these associations there are authority positions as well as positions which are subject to domination. Since there are a number of such associations, an individual can occupy a position of authority in one and a position of subordination in another.

Authority within each association is dichotomous and therefore two, and only two, conflict groups are formed within any association. Those in positions of authority and those in positions of subordination hold certain *interests* that are "contradictory in substance and direction." We are encountering here another key term in Dahrendorf's theory of conflict—*interests*. Groups on top as well as those at the bottom are defined by common interests, but even these interests that sound psychological are basically social facts:

> For purposes of the sociological analysis of conflict groups and group conflicts, it is necessary to assume certain *structurally generated* orientations of the actions of incumbents of defined *positions*. By analogy to conscious ("subjective") orientations of action, it appears justifiable to describe these as interests . . . The assumption of "objective" interests associated with social positions has no psychological implications or ramifications; it belongs to the level of sociological analysis proper. (italics mine)   (Dahrendorf, 1959:175)

In every association there is both domination and subordination. Those at the top seek to maintain the status quo while those at the bottom seek change. A conflict of interests is at least latent at all times and this means that the legitimacy of authority is *always* precarious. This conflict of interest need not be conscious in order for both groups to act. The interests of a given group are objective in the sense that they are expectations (roles) attached to positions. An individual does not have to internalize these expectations or be conscious of them in order to act in accord with them. The occupation of a given position insures that he will behave in the expected manner. An individual is "adjusted" or "adapted" to his role when he contributes to conflict between the groups. Dahrendorf uses the term *latent interests* to stand for these unconscious role expectations. On the other hand, manifest interests are latent interests that have become conscious. Dahrendorf sees as one of conflict theory's major tasks the analysis of the systematic connection between latent and manifest interests. Nevertheless, it is important to reiterate that a group need not be conscious of its interests in order to act in accord with them.

Next Dahrendorf differentiates two broad types of conflict groups. The first are *quasi-groups* or "aggregates of incumbents of positions with identical role interests." (Dahrendorf, 1959:180) These are the recruiting grounds from which emerge the second type of conflict group—the *interest group.* "Common modes of behavior are characteristic of *interest groups* recruited from larger quasi-groups. Interest groups are groups in the strict sense of the sociological term; and they are the real agents of group conflict. They have a structure, a form of organization, a program or goal, and a personnel of members." (Dahrendorf, 1959:180)   Out of all of the many interest groups emerge *conflict groups* or those that actually engage in group conflict.

Dahrendorf feels that the concepts of latent and manifest interests, quasi-groups and interest groups, are the basic elements of an explanation of conflict group formation. Under *ideal* conditions no other variables are needed to explain the emergence of conflict groups. However, conditions are never ideal, so there are a variety of factors that intervene in the process of conflict group formation. Among others, Dahrendorf mentions such technical conditions as adequate personnel, such political conditions as the overall political climate, and such social conditions as the existence of communication linkages. Another social condition of importance to Dahrendorf is the way people are recruited to the quasi-group. If the recruitment is random and determined by chance, he feels that a conflict group is unlikely to emerge. Thus, in contrast to Marx, Dahrendorf does not feel that the *lumpenproletariat* will form a conflict group since people are recruited to it by chance. On the other hand, quasi-groups, to which recruitment is structurally determined, provide fertile recruiting grounds for interest groups.

The final aspect of Dahrendorf's conflict theory is the linkage of conflict to change. Here Dahrendorf recognizes the importance of Coser's work (to be discussed shortly) that focuses on the functions of conflict in maintaining the status quo. He feels, however, that this is only one part of the problem; conflict also leads to change and development.

Briefly, Dahrendorf argues that once conflict groups emerge they engage in actions that lead to changes in social structure. When the conflict is intense the changes that occur are radical ones. When conflict is accompanied by violence, structural change will be sudden. Whatever the nature of conflict, sociologists must be attuned to the relationship between conflict and change as well as conflict and the status quo.

Conflict theory is subject to many of the same kinds of criticisms as functionalism, as well as some others. It can be criticized for ignoring order and stability, just as the functionalists have been criticized for being oblivious to conflict and change. Conflict theory can also be criticized for being ideologically radical while functionalism was similarly lambasted for its conservative orientation. Beyond these parallel criticisms, conflict theory is far less developed than functional theory. It is not nearly so sophisticated, perhaps because it has arisen as a response to another perspective rather than being a truly innovative perspective. Its attenuated development can also be explained by the fact that many of the best sociologists have historically devoted their attention to functional theory, leaving relatively few oriented toward developing conflict theory. Recently this trend has changed as many high quality young sociologists have adopted a conflict perspective.

As they now stand, both functionalism and conflict theory are inadequate. The reason for their inadequacies in addition to previously discussed criticisms is the reality that each, in itself, is only useful for explaining a portion of all social facts. Obviously, sociology must be able to explain order as well as conflict, structure as well as change. It is this last fact that has motivated several efforts to reconcile conflict and functional theory. Although none of these efforts at reconciliation are totally satisfactory, they suggest at least some sociological agreement that what is needed is a theory explaining both consensus and dissension. Yet not all theorists seek a reconciliation of these conflicting perspectives. Dahrendorf, for example, sees them as alternative perspectives to be used situationally. According to Dahrendorf, when we are interested in conflict, we are to use conflict theory, and the issue of order necessitates a functional perspective.

In my opinion, this seems to be an unsatisfactory position. Social facts are social facts and we need a theoretical perspective that enables us to deal with conflict and order *simultaneously.*

To date, Pierre van den Berghe (1963) has provided the major effort at reconciling the two perspectives. As a start toward that reconciliation he has pointed out several commonalities in the two approaches. Both perspectives are *holistic,* looking at societies as interrelated parts with a concern for the interrelationships between the parts. Secondly, theorists of each persuasion tend to focus on their variables while at the same time ignoring variables of concern to the other perspective. They should recognize, however, that conflict can contribute to integration and, conversely, that integration can be a cause of conflict. Many have written on the functions of social conflict at a variety of levels. Coser (1956) has written on this theme at the broad level while others, such as Himes (1966) and Coleman (1971), have tried to reconcile the two views at a more microscopic level. Third, van den Berghe notes that both share an evolutionary view of social change. That is, in both theories society is moving forward and upward. Society may be viewed by a conflict theorist as advancing irrevocably toward a utopian society. To a functionalist such as Parsons, society is becoming increasingly differentiated and ever better able to cope with its environment. Finally, van den Berghe sees both as basically equilibrium theories. We have already discussed the emphasis on societal equilibrium in functional theory. In Marxian* theory the dialectical process of thesis-antithesis-synthesis leads inevitably to a new state of equilibrium in the synthesis stage. Thus, in Marxian theory the end result (communism) is in equilibrium despite the emphasis on disequilibrating forces in earlier stages. Ultimately, van den Berghe's work is a step forward, but unsatisfying. Demonstrating commonalities between theories is a long way from reconciling them. Despite the commonalities, many outstanding differences remain.

Let us examine the work of Coser and Himes, with their focus on the functions of social conflict. These are basically functional theories of conflict and very provocative leads toward the ultimate

---

* Although Marx is discussed here as a conflict theorist, this is an oversimplification. As will be discussed in the last chapter, Marx is one of the few remarkable sociologists who have been able to bridge paradigms.

resolution of conflict and structural-functional theory. What is needed is parallel work discussing the disequilibrating effects of order (which, as we will see, Coleman does begin). It is clear that certain kinds of order, or too much order, leads to disequilibrium in the social system. A good example is the destructive effects a totalitarian ruler can have on the stability of a society despite his emphasis on order. Lacking much work of this sort, I focus primarily on the functions of social conflict.

The early seminal work on the functions of social conflict was done by Georg Simmel, but it has been expanded more recently by Lewis Coser. Coser argues that in a loosely structured group, conflict may serve as a solidifying agent. A society which seems to be disintegrating may be well advised to engage in conflict with another society in order to restore its integrative core. The seeming disintegration of the United States over, among other things, the Vietnam War may be traced to the warming of the cold war with the Soviet Union and the lack of a real outside threat to our society. Conversely, the cohesion exhibited by Israel may be attributed, at least in part, to its continuing conflict with the Arab world. One might predict that the end of the war with the Arabs might well cause underlying strains in Israeli society to become more prominent. This idea has long been recognized by propagandists who may construct an enemy where none exists or seek to fan antagonisms toward an inactive opponent (e.g. southern race-baiting politicians).

Conflict with one group may serve to produce cohesion by leading to a series of alliances with other groups. For example, conflict with the Soviet Union has led to American involvement in such groups as NATO and SEATO. It should be noted that the cooling of the Soviet-American conflict also seems to have weakened the bonds that held those groups together.

Within a society, conflict can bring some individuals into an active role where they were ordinarily isolated. The protests over the Vietnam War motivated many young people to take an active role in American society for the first time. Those who worked on Eugene McCarthy's and George McGovern's ill-fated campaigns for the presidency exemplify these processes. Conversely, many young people who have alienated themselves from American society would quickly become reintegrated were there a real threat to American society.

Conflict also has a communication function. Prior to conflict, groups may be unsure of their adversary's position, but as a result of conflict, positions and boundaries between groups often become clarified. Individuals and groups know exactly where they stand in relation to their adversary and are therefore better able to decide on a proper course of action.

The act of conflict also allows the parties to get a better idea of their relative strengths and may well increase the possibility of rapprochement.

Although most Americans are socialized to have a negative view of conflict, it is clear that conflict can perform many functions in the social system. More importantly, from a theoretical perspective, it is possible to wed functional and conflict theory when one looks at the functions of social conflict. However, this discussion should not be misconstrued—conflict also has dysfunctions. In any case, we should not be quick to try to eliminate conflict. We should look at the balance sheet of functions and dysfunctions before deciding whether or not conflict should be eliminated.

Himes' task is similar to Coser's, although he focuses specifically on the functions of racial conflict. Himes specifies that he is discussing only *rational* group action by American blacks. His concern is with deliberate collective behavior designed to achieve predetermined social goals. It involves a conscious attack on overtly defined social abuses. Examples include legal redress (e.g. achievement of voting rights, educational opportunities, and public accommodations), political action (actions such as voting and lobbying), and nonviolent mass action. The kind of conflict with which Himes is concerned involves *peaceful* work *within* the system; his analysis excludes violence such as race riots and lynching. Although Himes ignores violent collective conflict, one could perform a functional analysis of these forms just as easily as one analyzes peaceful conflict. The race riots of the late 1960s clearly had functions for American blacks, such as demonstrating their power and the weakness of the white power structure. They certainly had dysfunctions (i.e. white backlash), but that does not detract from the fact that it is possible for violence to have positive functions.

As Himes sees it, racial conflict has structural, communication, solidarity, and identity functions. Structurally, conflict can limit the power advantage of the dominant white majority and increase the power of blacks so that whites will meet with them to discuss issues of mutual importance. Racial conflict can perform such communications functions as the following: increasing attention to racial matters, increasing coverage of racial matters by the mass media, allowing uninformed people to get new information, and changing the content of interracial communication. The old, standard social amenities between the races (the etiquette of race relations) no longer suffice and there is a greater likelihood of an honest dialogue over substantive issues. Racial conflict also serves solidarity functions such as unifying the blacks involved and establishing a conflict relationship between the races that ultimately may form the basis of a more peaceful and long lasting relationship. Finally, racial conflict has several identity functions, including giving blacks a greater sense of who they are, enhancing group solidarity, and clarifying group boundaries. Perhaps the most important identity function is the sense the black participants can get of their identity as true Americans fighting for the United States' basic, but forgotten, principles of freedom and country.

Coleman's work is somewhat different. While Coser and Himes have looked at the functions of conflict, Coleman examines both the sources of integration and the conflict within a local community. The significance of this work is Coleman's ability to look *simultaneously* at integrative and disintegrative processes. The ultimate reconciliation of functional and conflict theory (if it is to occur) is most likely to lie in this direction.

Let us look at just a few of Coleman's points. He states that dissimilar activities leading to different attitudes, values, and beliefs can be a source of disintegration within the community. Conversely, similar activities carrying with them similar attitudes, values, and beliefs can aid in community integration. Integration is also likely to be aided by common problems requiring joint action while it is likely to be adversely affected by idiosyncratic problems and solutions. Yet not all differences necessarily lead to disintegration. Coleman argues that dissimilar activities can often result in integration. This is similar to Durkheim's concept of organic solidarity, in which a community is held together because each person performs specialized tasks and therefore needs many others with their specialties in order to survive. The butcher needs the tailor who needs the grocer who needs the truck driver, etc. A community can be held together by the very force of its differences. Coleman's work does not prescribe the conditions that will lead to disintegration where there are dissimilar activities or the factors conducive to integration; these are obviously questions that need to be answered if conflict and functional theory are to be reconciled. In the meantime, Coleman and the others have aided in an effort that may result in a true reconciliation.

This concludes our very selective excursion into two theories subsumed under the social facts paradigm—structural–functionalism and conflict theory. There are other, less notable, theories that could be included in the paradigm. One is systems theory (Buckley, 1967), although much of systems theory can be subsumed under structural-functionalism. Another is macrosociology, which is generally traced to the work of Amitai Etzioni (1970).

METHODS

Those who accept the social facts paradigm *tend to* use questionnaires and/or interviews when they do empirical research. The correspondence is far from exact; some who subscribe to the social facts paradigm use other methods while some who use these methods accept other paradigms. Nevertheless, in general, those who study social facts are most likely to use questionnaires and interviews. Since their interest is in social facts, it is difficult for them to use the other major methods. The observation method is not well-suited to the study of social facts. One cannot actually see most social facts. The process information obtained by observation is often seen as different from the structural information required by those who accept the social facts paradigm. Those who accept the social facts (and social behavior) paradigm tend to be more "scientific" than their social definitionist colleagues (who prefer the observation technique) and therefore reject observation as a "crude" technique. Social factists are equally apt to reject the experimental method preferred by behaviorists as a methodological tool, although for a different reason.

Social factists reject the experiment primarily because they feel experiments are too microscopic for their interests. Those who accept the social facts paradigm tend to be macroscopic sociologists interested in broad societal questions that are not easily studied in the laboratory. Rejecting experiments and observations, most social factists find themselves using interviews and questionnaires in their research. Yet, do interviews and questionnaires actually generate the data needed by the adherents of the social facts paradigm?

The interesting, ironic feature of the major methods used by the supporters of the social facts paradigm is that they do not really serve to gather information on social facts, but on individuals. After all, the interview or the questionnaire is answered by an individual. The individual replies may be summed, but this "sum of the parts" does not yield a social fact in the sense intended by the adherents of this paradigm. Alternatively, the individual may be asked to give information about a social fact, but the information is determined through his eyes; therefore, is his definition of what the social fact is, not necessarily what it "really" is.*

The renown social factist and student of the interview/questionnaire method, James Coleman (1970:115–116), recognizes the fact that these methods do not tap social facts:

> Survey research methods have led to the neglect of social structure and of the relations among individuals. . . . The *individual* remained the unit of analysis. No matter how complex the analysis, how numerous the correlations, the studies focused on individuals as separate and independent units. The very techniques mirrored this well: Samples were random, never including (except by accident) two persons who were friends; interviews were with one individual, as an atomistic entity, and responses were coded onto separate IBM cards, one for each person. As a result, the kinds of substantive problems on which such research focused tended to be problems of "aggregate psychology," that is, *within*-individual problems, and never problems concerned with relations between people.

Thus, the interview/questionnaire usually gathers data on individuals, not social facts.

---

* Charles Warriner makes the useful point that this is the way the social definitionist uses the interview/questionnaire technique, but as we will see in the next chapter social definitionists tend to prefer the observation technique.

Coleman thinks this need not be the case. He follows his critique of the usual interview/questionnaire strategy with a variety of suggestions designed to produce more information about social facts. For example, he suggests that the interview/questionnaire utilize *relational questions* designed to gather sociometric data and thereby get at group structure. He also suggests asking individuals questions about the social unit itself. It seems that both are ultimately unsatisfactory ways of gaining information on social facts. Coleman's first suggestion assumes that individual descriptions of their social relations give an accurate portrayal of that social fact. The second suggestion assumes that the sum of the individuals is equal to the whole. Both of these assumptions are highly questionable, especially from the social fact perspective.

Coleman also suggests a variety of sampling techniques to overcome the problems attached to the interview/questionnaire methodology. He calls each of these strategies an effort to obtain information from individuals "with reference to social structure." The first is *snowball sampling,* which Coleman (1970:118) sees as involving "first interviewing a small sample of persons, then asking these persons who their best friends are, interviewing these friends then asking their friends, interviewing these, and so on." By such a strategy we would ultimately be able to study all of the individuals within a given social group. In a second technique, which Coleman labels *saturation sampling,* an effort is made to survey everyone within a group using sociometric questions. There is also *dense sampling,* a compromise version of saturation sampling. Finally, there is *multi-stage sampling,* in which given units are sampled and then individuals within those units are sampled. For example, one could take a sample of all the universities in the country and then a sample of teachers within those universities included in the sample. Although these may be useful sampling strategies, they still assume that the whole is equal to the sum of the parts and that we can gain information about social facts by asking people. Again, these are questionable assumptions given the social facts paradigm.

Coleman himself (1970:120) recognizes the weaknesses in his suggestions for improving the questions and sampling techniques when he says: "The *real innovations* in this new kind of research are in the techniques of analysis." (italics mine) He therefore minimizes the significance of his suggestions for bringing the nature of the questions and the sampling techniques more into line with the social facts paradigm. He does, however, see four major techniques of data analysis as effective ways of enabling the interview/questionnaire to measure social facts.

Contextual Analysis

The basic premise of contextual analysis is that an attribute of the respondent's social context is related to an attribute of the respondent himself. This is useful, of course, in that an individual characteristic is related to a social fact. The question arises as to how the researcher gathers information about the social fact. Ultimately, it must be gathered by a method other than the interview/questionnaire, thereby pointing out once again the inability of those methods to gather data on social facts. At best these methods can collect individual data that can be related to data on social facts collected by other methods.

Boundaries of Homogeneity

This method seeks to establish group boundaries by ascertaining the beliefs and attitudes, and then differentiating groups in terms of homogeneity of belief or attitude. Coleman (1970:121) suggests that we utilize such research questions as: "In a medical school, for example, are a student's attitudes toward medicine more like those of his fraternity brothers or more like those of his laboratory partners?" Although such a technique may prove useful in enabling us to get indirectly at some social facts, it is not likely to be used in the study of others. For example, how would this method help us in studying the question of the relationship between the religious and familial institutions?

Pair Analysis

Here the focus shifts from individuals to dyads. Instead of studying a single person, the individual and, let's say, a friend of his choice become the unit of analysis. Here is the way Coleman (1970:124) describes this technique in operation: "In the study . . . of drug introduction by doctors, these pair relations were used as the major aspect of the analysis. By examining how close in time a doctor's first use of a new drug was to the doctor he first mentioned as a friend, it was possible to infer the functioning of friendship networks in the introduction of this drug." Instead of inferring the existence of a social fact (in this case a friendship network) from the responses of one individual, we are inferring its existence from the replies of a dyad. Nevertheless, we are still inferring the existence of a social fact from individuals rather than directly examining the social fact.

Partitioning into Cliques

This involves utilization of sociometric questions to divide a group into its cliques. This, again, merely allows us to identify (and very tentatively) one social fact—a clique. It still involves inference from individual replies rather than direct examination of a social fact.

Coleman makes an effort to more closely align the interview/questionnaire method with the social facts paradigm, but, as the previous discussion indicates, his degree of success in this effort is problematic.

How, then, can one actually study social facts? It seems that the only effective methods are historical and/or comparative research. Max Weber, for example (whose work, ironically, is an exemplar for the social definition paradigm), engaged in cross-cultural, historical research on the relationship between religion and economics. He found the Protestant Ethic contained characteristics that, in part, led to the development of the spirit of capitalism. Individuals were the dependent variables in this research, affected by changes at the level of social facts. Individuals were clearly the mechanism by which one idea system was transformed into another idea system.   Nevertheless, the focus was on social facts, not individuals.

One can conduct historical and/or comparative research using any of the methods discussed in this book: interviews, question-naires, observation, and experiments.   The point is that the data, however it is collected, must be *compared* either over time, between groups, or cross-culturally.   It is the comparison that allows us to infer that differences in the data are attributable to differences in social structures or institutions.

The problem with the interview/questionnaire technique as it has been used traditionally by social factists is that no effort is made at comparison.

The idea of the social fact is a clear example of a "black box." We know something is there and we know it has certain character-istics, but most often we cannot see it.   What we can see (but barely) are generally the least important things about a social fact.   We can sometimes see its boundaries as, for example, the boundaries of a community.   Sometimes we cannot even see the boundaries.   For example, what are the boundaries of a university?   The tentacles of almost all structures stretch so far and become so amorphous at the edges that it is difficult to tell where they begin or end.   We can tell the size (physical, numerical) of the social fact, if the boundaries are clear.   In the end, we can actually see very little, even of a trivial nature.   Furthermore, we can only see a little of a few social facts that are physically tangible.   We cannot see a norm, a value, a role, an institution, etc.   We can hear the way respondents describe these social facts and we can see their effects on individuals, but we can never actually see them.

Because we can see little or nothing of a social fact, we must, when we use the interview/questionnaire, rely on our respondents to tell us about them, to represent them, or to demonstrate their effects. We can use interviews and questionnaires to ask people about their perceptions of existing social facts.   They can describe the parameters of their social group, its normative structure, or its stratification pat-tern.   We can then survey all of our responses and let the most com-mon reply stand for the social fact—be it a group, its norms, or its hierarchial structure.   Second, we can let the sum of the individuals be the social fact.   Next, we can ask people about (or observe) their feelings, attitudes, and behaviors and from their responses (or our observations) infer the nature of the social fact that determined the response or behavior.

No matter which of the three approaches we choose, it appears that we are hard-pressed to demonstrate that we are actually studying a social fact. We are most frequently studying *social definitions* of social facts not the social facts themselves, or we are taking the sum of the individuals to be the social fact, or we are inferring the existence of social facts from the reports of individuals and our observations of them. I think it is safe to conclude that when he uses interviews or questionnaires, the social factist is not really studying social facts. This is nowhere clearer than in the sociological study of the professions.

Individuals interested in the sociology of occupations have great interest in the question of what characteristics differentiate a profession from all other occupations. This interest stems from a variety of sources. In American society many occupations such as nursing, social work, and teaching are clamoring for recognition as professions—a demand that has created the need to identify those characteristics they need to acquire this status. Impelled by such demands, sociologists have spent a good deal of time investigating the distinguishing characteristics of the professions.

In our schema a profession is clearly a social fact. It is more than simply the sum of all the individual professionals within it; the medical profession consists of more than all of the doctors in the United States. A profession is a constellation of structures, groups, values, norms, and the like. Given that a profession is a social fact, how have sociologists sought to study it? Not surprisingly, they have most frequently done so by surveying individual professionals (by interviews or questionnaires) concerning their attitudes toward such things as altruism, autonomy, and control over clients. From these questions asked of *professionals*, they have deduced that *professions* have strong norms of altruism, autonomy, and client control. Those people who have sought to ascertain the nature of professions in this way have clearly made the kinds of errors discussed in this section.

I argue elsewhere (Ritzer, 1972) that sociologists have frequently confused the study of professionals with the study of professions.   These are clearly separate areas of study.   The "professional-ism" of individuals is related to the degree of "professionalization" of the occupation, but the two are not conterminous.   It is legitimate to study individual professionals, if we are interested in them, but not if we are interested in professions in general.   Studying professions as social facts requires the use of very different techniques.   Some sociologists use methods appropriate to the study of professions as social facts.   They look at the historical sequence of stages through which an occupation goes en route to professional status.   (Caplow, 1963; Wilensky, 1964)   They generally find that a profession goes through a sequence of stages, such as the development of a training school, the acquisition of a code of ethics, and public and legal recog-nition of their privileged status.   An occupation that successfully negotiates these stages is, in this schema, a profession.   By studying professions in terms of historical stages the sociologist is truer to the social facts paradigm than if he generalizes from the replies of indi-vidual professionals.

Despite criticisms of the lack of congruity between the social facts paradigm and the interview/questionnaire method, those who accept the social facts paradigm use this method most frequently. The alternatives at their disposal, such as historical and comparative studies, although truer to the paradigm, are more expensive, more difficult, and more time-consuming than the interview/questionnaire. Furthermore, such methods of study are not applicable to a wide range of questions of interest to the social factist.   Finally, historical and comparative methods often do not produce the kind of data amenable to the rigorous statistical and computer analysis that the social factist, in this age of scientism, uses.   With observation and experiments even less suitable to the study of social facts, the social factist is left with little in the way of methodological alternatives—he utilizes the interview/questionnaire.*

Whether or not the interview/questionnaire actually taps social facts, the social factist argues that it has several assets and liabilities. Let us examine some of the claims made by social factists of the assets and liabilities of the interview/questionnaire in light of the political criticisms by those who subscribe to other methods and paradigms.

* There are, of course, exceptions to this generalization.   I have already discussed Weber's work as an exception and I would also include under this heading work such as Merton's study of science, the studies of many ecologists, etc.

Most interviews employ a questionnaire and we can group structured interviews and questionnaires together for purposes of most of this discussion.*   It should be pointed out that questionnaires may be used in other than interview situations.   For example, a mail questionnaire is frequently used and this obviously employs no interview. The subject is asked to answer the questionnaire on his own and return it to the sender.   We will discuss interviews (including most questionnaires) first, and then turn to mail-type questionnaires.

Interviews

Interview techniques have, in the eyes of social factists, a variety of assets as research instruments.   Of primary importance is the fact that almost all who are approached by an interviewer will participate in the study.   This is particularly important in descriptive studies where generalizations are being made about a total population.   High response rates in interview studies allow the construction of an almost perfect sample of the population as a whole.   This takes on added importance when we see later that one of the basic problems with the mail questionnaire technique is the high number of nonrespondents typical of such research.   In contrast to observation techniques, the interviewer can collect a variety of information on the background of the respondent that may be useful in testing hypotheses and analyzing results.   The interviewer can also return for more information or to correct errors he might have made initially.

The social factist argues that when the observation technique is used, we can only see what is going on at the moment and we cannot usually observe a number of forms of action (such as sexual behavior).   But when we use an interview, we can ask about the past as well as the present (and even the future), and we can ask about things we would be unable to observe.   Although the interviewer can ask about these issues, the social definitionist and social behaviorist often disagree over the validity of the information he gets verbally from his respondents.   Is what the subject tells us the truth?   Can we be certain a respondent is telling us the truth when he tells us that

* This does not include exploratory interviews which will not be dealt with in this discussion.

he has sexual intercourse fifteen times a week?   Or is the subject telling the interviewer what he thinks the researcher wants to hear or what society regards as its ideal?   Responses from interviews (and similarly from questionnaires) have always been attacked on this basis.

When used on its own, the interview technique is assailable.   It is attacked (by devotees of the two other paradigms) on the grounds of the validity of its findings.   The social definitionist often argues that the interview yields distorted data.   In some cases the respondent may distort what he tells us and in others he may be simply unable to tell us what has really occurred.   He may suppress his real feelings or forget past occurrences.   Although it cannot overcome these problems, the interview technique is stronger in this situation than the mail questionnaire.   In the interview, the researcher can adjust when he feels he is getting misinformation and ask additional questions.   He can also observe the individual as he is responding and assess the validity of the response from his actions.   Finally, he is usually interviewing in the respondent's own milieu and can use what he observes around him to assess the validity of verbal responses. The great asset, therefore, of the interview over the mail questionnaire is its flexibility.

Although it limits subjectivity (at least in comparison to observation), the interview has been attacked by the social behaviorists for not being objective enough.   Subjective factors enter into the interview at a variety of points.   The kinds of questions used and the way they are phrased are affected by the interviewer's biases.   During the interview itself, the intonation and facial cues used by the interviewer enter the picture.   More importantly, the answers given by the respondent are filtered, in most cases, through the interviewer.   The interviewer may find his own attitudes affecting how he transcribes what the subject says.   This is less of a problem when the interviewer takes notes as the respondent is talking and is exacerbated when the interviewer is in a situation in which he cannot write down what has transpired until after the interview is over and he has left the research site.   When interviews take place at field sites (e.g. while the respondent is on the job), notes frequently cannot be taken and the interviewer must rely heavily on his memory to record the responses at a later time.   Since he must rely on memory, there is a greater likelihood that his biases will affect what he transcribes.

Supporters of the interview approach (and the social facts paradigm) respond that although they cannot eliminate subjectivity, they do much to reduce it. Furthermore, they point out that their approach is far less subjective than observation methods. One way interviewers meaningfully reduce subjectivity is to tape record interviews and transcribe them after the actual interview is completed. Unfortunately, there are some interviewees who refuse to allow researchers to use tape recorders.

In general, the social factist argues that the interview technique is far more objective than observation. Although the personal biases of the researcher enter at many points, they are claimed to be a less significant factor in the interview. A uniform set of questions is usually asked of all respondents and attempts are made to have them phrased in the same ways. Thus, there is some assurance that the same information will be gathered in each interview. The social factist contends that this is not true of observation. The observer rarely even has a set series of things to look for. In fact, if he did, the great asset of the observation approach—its ability to uncover information that the researchers had not thought of—would be lost. What he looks for, how he sees it, and how he records it are very likely to be affected by the observer's personal biases. Because it is more structured, the interview is less likely than observations to uncover unanticipated information. Yet it is not as structured as the approach we will turn to next. Because it is more flexible than the mail questionnaire, it is more likely to uncover unforeseen attitudes, opinions, and behaviors.

Mail Questionnaire

The mail questionnaire is even more structured than the interview. We encounter an expansion of the defense of its strengths by the social factist and attacks on its weaknesses by, in particular, the social definitionists. One such criticism is the continuing decline in ability to make unanticipated discoveries. There are frequently a number of open-ended questions in the interview, but they are infrequently found in mail questionnaires. In both cases open-ended questions are employed for a specific purpose, but it is possible for them to yield information that leads to a number of unanticipated insights. In an interview the researcher is actually present and he can therefore observe things that may lead him in some uncharted directions. This is impossible in a mail questionnaire since the researcher is not present when the questionnaire is being completed.

The use of the mail questionnaire is defended by the social fact-ist on a number of counts, as has already been pointed out, although it is questionable whether this technique actually elicits information on social facts since it is individuals who reply. By using a mail questionnaire a larger number of people can be reached in widely dispersed geographic areas for relatively little money. The use of the observation technique restricts the researcher to an in-depth look at a much smaller number of objects. Of course, a large number of observations can be simultaneously conducted at a variety of locations, but the cost may be prohibitive. In addition, there would be the problem of certainty that each observer was gathering comparable information. Similarly, interviews can be conducted with as many respondents as in a mail questionnaire study, but again, the cost would be far greater. In the mail questionnaire, efficiency is maximized and the respondents do a lot of work for the researcher, but, as we will see, this efficiency is not without its costs.

Observations and interviews require highly skilled personnel, but since the mail questionnaire is self-administered, the need for such skilled people is minimized. A relatively few researchers skilled in questionnaire construction can be substituted for the large number of interviewers or observers needed to do a comparable study with these other techniques. The use of a mail questionnaire also enables the researcher to contact subjects located in areas whose distance from the research site would make interviews or observation very costly. Because of the ability to reach these people, a more representative sample of the total population can be achieved using mail questionnaires.

The social factist argues that the effect of the researcher's presence is minimized in the mail questionnaire. The researcher has affected the nature of the replies by the way he constructs the questions, but he is not interacting with, and thereby affecting the replies of, the respondents. In a mail questionnaire study the questions are the same for all respondents and their replies are not affected by differences in wording or intonation that frequently occur in interview studies. The mail questionnaire also gives the respondent a sense of privacy and he may, therefore, answer ticklish questions more comfortably. Finally, because he can retain the questionnaire for a period of time, the respondent can obtain whatever additional information is needed to answer a particular question. (Of course, conversely, it may give him time to think of an appropriate distortion.)

Despite its relative efficiency, the mail questionnaire method is criticized by the devotees of methods associated with the other paradigms. They contend that we have no way of knowing in a mail questionnaire whether the respondent has misinterpreted a question and responded inappropriately. We are less able to assess the validity of his responses since there is no opportunity to probe, to assess his surroundings, and to examine his physical mannerisms as he responds. Questionnaires themselves are designed by highly literate researchers and they frequently assume that the responding population is almost as literate. Thus the wording of questions in mail questionnaires frequently baffles respondents.

Another major difficulty is response rate. Although the number of people responding will vary greatly depending on length of the questionnaire, types of questions used, and topics asked, a response rate of 50 percent is generally considered good in large-scale mail questionnaire surveys. The fact that half of the subjects frequently do not respond poses very difficult problems of interpretation of results, especially when the researcher is engaged in a descriptive study in which he is trying to make generalizations about a population as a whole. (A low response rate is less of a problem when the researcher is testing theoretical hypotheses and need only have enough variation to test the hypotheses.) It may well be that the 50 percent who do not respond in a descriptive study are very different from the 50 percent who do respond. For example, if we are doing research on sex behavior, the half who respond may be liberal sexually while the half who do not may be conservative. We would jump to the erroneous conclusion that the group we were studying was liberal sexually, but the results have been skewed by the fact that the conservatives could not bring themselves to answer questions on sex behavior.

Perhaps the most damaging critique (most often made by those who use experimental methods) of the mail questionnaire method is that it, too, is subject to the biases of the researcher. The difference between the questionnaire, and interviews and observation is where this subjectivity manifests itself.   In interviews and observation, personal biases intrude primarily during the process of collecting information.   While these are reduced through use of mail questionnaires, biases manifest themselves instead during the process of forming the questions to be asked.   The personal inclinations of the researcher affect the issues he is interested in, the kinds of questions he asks, the way they are phrased and ordered, and the choices he provides the respondent (if choices are provided) .   Critics note that mail questionaires are not more objective, they simply manifest their subjectivity at a different phase in the research process.

The social factist believes that observation lends itself best to exploratory research and the generation of hypotheses.   However, he feels that interviews and questionnaires are far more amenable to hypothesis-testing and theory development.   This is not to say that all interviews and questionnaires are used in this way.   Some, most notably surveys of voting patterns and consumer behavior, are simply used to collect information in much the same way as observation. Some of these tell us about such issues as premarital sexual behavior, but they contribute little to the development of sociological theory.

Most sociologists who interview or use mail questionnaires begin with hypotheses they are interested in testing.   (It should be pointed out that in many cases these hypotheses are derived from research conducted using the observation approach.)   With an hypothesis, or hypotheses, in mind, the researcher sets out to construct his research instrument.   The questions to be included and even their wording and order are determined by the information needed to test the hypothesis.   The groups to which the instrument is applied and how the results are analyzed and interpreted are also shaped by the hypothesis being tested.   In the end, the researcher has very focused data that can confirm, or fail to confirm, the hypothesis in question. Repeated tests of this kind on different populations and in different settings lead to progressive refinement of hypotheses.

Conclusion

In this chapter I have examined the first of the three sociological paradigms—the social facts paradigm—in terms of the four components of a paradigm outlined in Chapter 1. I have discussed the work of the exemplars of the social factist, Emile Durkheim a, Charles Warriner. In the process I pointed out the difficulties in volved in categorizing Durkheim as a social factist even though hᵉ coined the term "social facts." I discussed the image of the subject matter of the social factist—social structures and social institutions. I analyzed the two major theories encompassed by the social facts paradigm—structural-functionalism and conflict theory. Finally, I discussed the interview/questionnaire as the major method of the social factist.

In the discussion of this first paradigm, I have been concerned primarily with describing its parameters. I have not spent a great deal of time in this chapter discussing the political conflict that rages between paradigms, although some of it did surface in the discussion of the methods associated with the social facts paradigm. In the next two chapters the theme of political conflict will be brought out much more strongly, although I will continue to be concerned with describing the sociological paradigms.

BIBLIOGRAPHY

Berger, Peter. *Invitation to Sociology.* New York: Doubleday, 1963.

Bierstedt, Robert. *The Social Order.* 3rd ed. New York: McGraw-Hill, 1970.

Blau, Peter. "Structural Effects." *American Sociological Review* 25 (1960) :178–93.

Broom, Leonard, and Selznick, Phillip. *Sociology.* 3rd ed. New York: Harper and Row, 1963.

Buckley, Walter. *Sociology and Modern Systems Theory.* Englewood Cliffs, New Jersey: Prentice-Hall, 1967.

Caplow, Theodore. *The Sociology of Work.* New York: McGraw-Hill, 1963.

Coleman, James. "Relational Analysis: The Study of Social Organizations with Survey Methods." *Sociological Methods.* Edited by Norman Denzin. Chicago: Aldine, 1970.

———. "Community Disorganization and Conflict." *Contemporary So-*

cial Problems. 3rd ed.   Edited by Robert Merton and Robert Nisbet. New York: Harcourt Brace Jovanovich, 1971:657–708.

Coser, Lewis.   *The Functions of Social Conflict.*   New York: The Free Press, 1956.

Dahrendorf, Ralf.   *Class and Class Conflict in Industrial Society.*   Stanford: Stanford University Press, 1959.

Davis, Kingsley.   "The Myth of Functional Analysis as a Special Method in Sociology and Anthropology."   *American Sociological Review* 24 (1959):757–72.

Demerath, Nicholas, and Peterson, Richard, eds.   *System, Change and Conflict.*   New York: The Free Press, 1967.

Durkheim, Emile.   *Suicide.*   New York: The Free Press, 1951.

———.   *The Rules of Sociological Method.*   New York: The Free Press, 1964.

Etzioni, Amitai.   "Toward a Macrosociology."   *Macrosociology: Research and Theory.*   Edited by James S. Coleman, Amitai Etzioni, and John Porter.   Boston: Allyn and Bacon, 1970:107–43.

Gans, Herbert.   "The Positive Functions of Poverty."   *American Journal of Sociology* 78 (1972):275–89.

Gouldner, Alvin.   *The Coming Crisis in Western Sociology.*   New York: Basic Books, 1970.

Himes, Joseph.   "The Functions of Racial Conflict."   *Social Forces* 45 (1966):1–10.

Mauss, Marcel, and Fauconnett, Paul.   *Sociologie.*   Paris: La Grande Encyclopedie, 1901.

Merton, Robert.   "Manifest and Latent Functions."   *On Theoretical Sociology.*   New York: The Free Press, 1968:73–138.

Parsons, Talcott.   *The Social System.*   New York: The Free Press, 1951.

Ritzer, George.   *Man and His Work: Conflict and Change.*   New York: Appleton-Century-Crofts, 1972.

Szymanski, Albert.   "Toward a Radical Sociology."   *Issues, Debates and Controversies: An Introduction to Sociology.*   Edited by George Ritzer.   Boston: Allyn and Bacon, 1972.

van den Berghe, Pierre.   "Dialectic and Functionalism: Toward Reconciliation."   *American Sociological Review* 28 (1963):695–705.

Vera-Godoy, Hernan.   "Marcel Mauss' Sociological System: An Essay in Method Interpretation."   Master's thesis, Notre Dame, Indiana: University of Notre Dame, 1971.

Warriner, Charles.   "Groups Are Real: A Reaffirmation."   *American Sociological Review* 21 (October, 1956):549–54.

Wilensky, Harold.   "The Professionalization of Everyone?"   *American Journal of Sociology* 70 (1964):136–58.

3

The
Social
Definition
Paradigm

EXEMPLAR

The exemplar for the social definition paradigm is a very specific aspect of the work of Max Weber, that is, his analysis of social action. (Freund, 1968:88–89)   Weber's position stands in stark contrast to Durkheim's conception of social facts*: "The originality of Weber's contribution lies in the fact that he did not sever social structures and institutions from the multifarious activities of man, who both builds them and endows them with significance. . . . He took the view that to study the development of an institution *solely* from the outside, without regard to what man makes of it, is to overlook one of the principal aspects of social life.   The development of a social relationship can also be explained by the purposes which man assigns to it, the benefits he derives from it and the different meanings he attaches to it in the course of time. . . ."   (Freund, 1968:88–89) Although Weber makes the case for looking at social definitions, he does not, in Freund's view, downgrade the importance of looking at social facts as well.   There are times, however, when Weber almost unconsciously slips into a polemic against the social facts paradigm: "In this approach the individual is also the upper limit and sole carrier of meaningful conduct. . . . In general, for sociology, such concepts as 'state,' 'association,' 'feudalism,' and the like, designate certain categories of human interaction.   Hence, it is the task of sociology to reduce these concepts to 'understandable,' action, that is, *without exception,* to the actions of participating individual men." (italics mine)   (Gerth and Mills, 1958:55)   The paradox here,

---

* Durkheim is obviously being set up as a straw man here. Even Parsons (1937:717) recognizes that Durkheim knew social facts could only reside in the minds of men. "The crucial importance . . . resides in the paradox of a society as a phenomenon *sui generis,* with a specific type of causality, which is nevertheless present in the minds of individuals and only there."

as we will see later, is that much of Weber's work deserves the label of social factism.

In criticizing the social factists, Weber alluded to the essence of his action approach (and social definitionism) —the meaningful action of individuals. In fact, Weber (1947:88) defines sociology as the study of social action: "Sociology . . . is a science which attempts the interpretative understanding of social action in order thereby to arrive at a causal explanation of its course and effects." There are two key phrases in this definition: *social action* and *interpretative understanding*.

Weber (1947:88) defines social action as "all human behavior when and insofar as the acting individual attaches a subjective meaning to it. Action in this sense may be overt, purely inward, or subjective; it may consist of positive intervention in a situation, of deliberately refraining from such intervention, or passively acquiescing in the situation. Action is social insofar as by virtue of the subjective meaning attached to it by the acting individual (or individuals), it takes account of the behavior of others and is thereby oriented in its course." Thus, the subject matter of sociology (from the perspective of Weber's action theory) is as follows:

1. Human behavior to which the actor attaches subjective meaning. This obviously excludes some forms of human behavior, but we will get to that shortly.
2. Action may be either overt or purely inward and/or subjective.
3. Action includes positive intervention, deliberate refraining from behavior, and passive acquiescence.
4. It may refer to one or more individuals.
5. Action takes account of the behavior of others and is oriented by this concern with others.

In addition to characteristics derivable from the definition, social action has a number of other distinguishing characteristics. While it may be oriented to the present behavior of others, it can *also* be oriented toward their past or future behavior. Furthermore, the "other" to which the actor is orienting his action may be either an individual or a collectivity.

By defining certain behaviors as social action, other behaviors are excluded from Weber's sociology. For example, "overt action is non-

social if it is oriented solely to the behavior of inanimate objects."
(Weber, 1947:173)   A child idly tossing a rock into a river is of
no concern to the action theorist, although he is, by the way, of concern to the behaviorist who argues that the same principles that explain social interaction explain interaction with inanimate objects
such as rocks.   However, Weber even excludes some social interaction from action theory (and, therefore, his brand of sociology).
Weber, for example, excludes such behavior as two cyclists inadvertently crashing.   Prior to their collision they were *not* orienting their
behavior to one another, hence, they were not engaging in social
action.   Other examples of action Weber excludes from sociology are
people opening their umbrellas at the same time because it has started
raining.   They are orienting their behavior to the rain (an inanimate
object), not to other people.   Mass or crowd hysteria and pure imitation are also excluded by Weber because they constitute pure reaction without any *meaningful* orientation to other people.

Given this view of social action, how can one possibly study such
things as an actor's meaningful orientations, especially since Weber
was very much interested in scientific sociology?   At this juncture
Weber's idea of "interpretative understanding" (Verstehen) is crucial.   It is clear that one cannot simply look at behavior and study
Weber's brand of social action.   If one attempts to merely examine
behavior, he can never be sure that it has subjective meaning and is
oriented toward others.   The sociological researcher must seek to
interpretatively understand his subject's behavior.   This basically
means that the sociologist must understand the "motives" of the
actor.

How do you study motives?   Weber suggests two ways—through
empathy, and by reliving the experience of subjects.   The researcher
is urged to put himself in the place of the subject and "understand"
things as he sees them.   Weber, however, does not devote all of his
attention to understanding; he also urges that the sociologist engage
in the causal research of the social factist and the behavioral sociologist.   Nevertheless, the addition of the idea of understanding served
to set Weber apart from those who accept the other paradigms: "by
emphasizing the understandability of human conduct, as opposed to
the mere causal explanation of 'social facts' as in natural science,
Weber draws the line between his interpretative sociology and the

'physique sociale' in the tradition of Condorcet, which Comte called *sociologie* and Durkheim worked out in such an eminent manner." (Gerth and Mills, 1958:57)

Weber realized that all social action was not of one piece and proceeded to divide social action into four types based on the degree to which they were amenable to interpretative understanding. In general, the most rational type of action is the most easily understood, while the least rational is most difficult to understand. The purest form of rational action is labelled by Weber (1947:175) *Zweckrational* action. In this type of action, the actor assesses not only the best means of achieving an end, but also determines the value of the end itself. Thus, the end in Zweckrational action is not absolute; it can be a means to another end. When an actor behaves in this highly rational manner, it is very easy to "understand" his action.

Not quite as pure is Weber's second type of action, *Wertrational* action. Here, the actor cannot assess whether the means he chooses is the most efficacious, nor is it possible for the end to be the means to another end. It is viewed as an end in itself. In Wertrational action (such as in a religious ritual) the end and the means tend to become indistinguishable. Nevertheless, it is rational because the choice of means will presumably lead to the desired end. While this second form of action is still rational and therefore amenable to "understanding," it is not as rational as Zweckrational action and a Weberian would, therefore, not be as successful analyzing Wertrational action.

The final two forms of action, while still amenable to understanding, frequently fall outside the scope of action theory because actors are not meaningfully orienting themselves to each other. *Affectual* action is dominated by feelings, emotions, and affects of the actor. *Traditional* action is based on doing things habitually on the basis of lengthy past practice. Affectual and traditional action are frequently only automatic responses to external stimuli and therefore involve no meaningful action orientation. At other times, there is meaningful orientation in these two types and they are therefore, at these times, amenable to interpretative understanding.

Although Max Weber started at the level of action, he soon left it for more macroscopic fields. The next step up is the *social relationship* defined by Weber (1947:176) as "the behavior of a plurality of actors insofar as, in its meaningful conduct, the action of each takes account of that of others and is oriented in these terms." Not all collectivities qualify as having social relationships. Where there is no mutual orientation to one another, there is no social relationship, even if a group of people are found together. Weber does not stop here. He goes on to discuss empirical uniformities of social action and social relationships. Thus, sociologists should devote at least some of their attention to patterns of action and social relationship. It is not a very great leap from here to social groups, social institutions, and social organization. In other words, it is not a very great leap to the level of social facts.

Despite his great concern with social action, Max Weber spent most of his life studying social facts. Although he would reject the label of social factist, he was one of its most able practitioners. His historical and comparative studies of the effect of religion on economics (both social facts) stand as models of a method of studying social facts. Emile Durkheim, the prototypical social factist, was not nearly as good at social fact analysis as was Weber. The paradox is that Weber starts with social action but works at the level of social facts. Gerth and Mills (1958:57) echo this view:

> Were one to accept Weber's methodological reflections on his own work at their face value, one would not find a systematic justification for his analysis of such phenomena as stratification or capitalism. Taken literally, the "method of understanding" would hardly allow for Weber's use of structural explanations; for this type of explanation attempts to account for the motivation of systems of action by their functions as going concerns rather than by the subjective intentions of the individuals who act them out. According to Weber's method of understanding, we should expect him to adhere to a subjective theory of stratification, but he does not do so.

Weber's orientation is far from totally congruent with the paradigm for which his work is the exemplar. As you will remember, the same was true of the relationship between Durkheim's work and social factism. Both Weber and Durkheim were far too wide-ranging to be placed within the confines of a single paradigm. They, along with others like Marx and Parsons, are what I call "paradigm bridgers." The great sociological theorists seem to be capable of integrating and/or moving between paradigms with relative ease. Despite his ability to bridge paradigms, Weber and his work on social action is considered the exemplar for the social definition paradigm.

IMAGE OF THE SUBJECT MATTER

All three of the theories to be discussed in this chapter (action theory, symbolic interactionism, and phenomenology) clearly have a number of differences, but there are also several overarching commonalities in terms or image of the subject matter of sociology that far outweigh the differences. The fact that the similarities more than compensate for the differences allows us to include all three under the heading of the social definition paradigm.

Perhaps the major theme that is consistent for all three theories is the idea that man is an active creator of his own social reality. The converse of this is another consistent theme in the social definition paradigm: social reality is *not* a static set of coercive social facts. In action theory, this shows up most clearly in Talcott Parsons' concept of voluntarism. Among the symbolic interactionists, we find people like Herbert Blumer (1962:189) saying: "The organization of a human society is the framework inside of which social action takes place and is *not the determinant of that action*." (italics mine) Even here, however, we begin to see differences between the theories as Blumer admits that there is some social framework that has a real existence separable from the actions of men. Supporters of a branch of phenomenological sociology, ethnomethodology, take issue with this even though they, too, see man as the creator of his own reality. But they go further and deny the existence of any social reality beyond that created by man at the moment. Dreitzel (1970:XV) describes ethnomethodology in this way: "Ethnomethodologists, on the other hand, maintain that social order, including all its symbols and meanings, exists not only precariously but has no existence at all

independent of the members accounting and describing practices."
Although this is clearly an important difference, it remains true that
all three theories are united in an active, creative view of man. In
this they stand in stark contrast to the social factist who views man as
controlled by such things as norms, values, and social control agencies.
They are also, as we will see, at variance with the social behaviorists
who see man as being controlled by "contingencies of reinforcement."
In fact, the high priest of behaviorism, B. F. Skinner, goes so far as
to call for the ouster of the view of man as active and creative (what
he calls "autonomous man") from the social sciences.

Although they cannot examine it directly, those who accept each
of these three theories are interested in what takes place within the
mind of man. Something occurs in a man's mind between the time
a stimulus is applied and the response is emitted and it is this creative
activity that is the concern of the social definitionist. To the social
factist, external social constraints determine behavior, while to the
behaviorist there is no room for creative responses since contingencies
of reinforcement determine behavior.

United in their interest in the creative "minding" process, the
social definitionists are divided on the ways of studying this "invisible
process." Action theory, while committed to observation, has not
had much research conducted under its aegis, while symbolic interactionism and phenomenology are united in their support for, and
use of, observation, particularly participant observation. Yet even
here a significant split has developed as phenomenologists identified
within the ethnomethodological school have opted for methods that
serve to disrupt the assumptive rules by which people operate in
order to gain a better understanding of them.

A third concern running through all three theories is with social
process. This is most fully developed among the symbolic interactionists, many of whom are also labelled processualists. They tend
to focus on the process of social interaction rather than on static
structure or behavior. This interest can also be found among action
theorists and phenomenologists, albeit in a less well-developed form.

Finally, I believe that there is an ideological theme that can be
found in all of the social definitionist theories, although it is certainly
not explicit. Sociologists of both liberal and radical persuasion *tend*
to gravitate toward social definitionism (as well as critical theory

which will be discussed in Chapter 5). Social definitionism allows these sociologists to see man as a relatively free creator of his social world. He is not simply a victim of the social world, as he is to the social factist, nor is he little more than a set of behaviors as he is to the social behaviorist. A free, active, creative view of man and his relationship to society is clearly attractive to liberal-left sociologists. Politically more conservative sociologists are more likely to be attracted to the social fact/facts and social behavior paradigms.

There are a number of minor commonalities and differences that could be reiterated at this point, but the above suffice to give you a feel for the image of the subject matter of the social definitionists.

THEORIES

There are three major theories included within the social definition paradigm: action theory, symbolic interactionism, and phenomenological sociology.

Action Theory

Action theory is, of course, directly traceable to the work of Max Weber. In fact, contemporary action theory has not progressed much beyond Weber's groundbreaking work. Action theory, in my opinion, has proven to be a virtual dead-end, and its significance lies in the role it played in the development of symbolic interactionism and modern phenomenological sociology. It is because of this role that it is worth spending a few pages analyzing the basic tenets of action theory.

Action theory enjoyed something of a heyday in sociology in the 1930s and 1940s with the publication of a number of works that adopted its orientation. Among them are Florian Znaniecki's *The Method of Sociology* (1934) and *Social Actions* (1936); Robert M.

MacIver's *Society: Its Structure and Changes* (1931) and *Social Causation* (1942); and Talcott Parsons' *The Structure of Social Action* (1937). All of these men had European backgrounds and were responsible for bringing the action orientation to American sociology. Hinkle (1963) argues that they were heavily influenced by the action orientation in Pareto, Durkheim, and most importantly, Weber. Pre-depression American sociology, however, was not heavily influenced by Pareto, Durkheim, and Weber. In these early years theorists, such as Comte, Spencer, Gumplowicz, Ratzenhofer, Tarde, and Simmel were far more influential. Despite this fact, Hinkle sees a number of ideas in early American sociology that were precursors of action theory.

Drawing from the work of MacIver, Znaniecki, and Parsons, Hinkle (1963:706–707) offers the following as the fundamental assumptions of action theory:

1. Men's social activities arise from their consciousness of themselves (as subjects) and of others and the external situations (as objects).
2. As subjects, men act to achieve their (subjective) intentions, purposes, aims, ends, objectives, or goals.
3. They use appropriate means, techniques, procedures, methods, and instruments.
4. Their courses of action are limited by unmodifiable conditions or circumstances.
5. Exercising will or judgment, they choose, assess, and evaluate what they will do, are doing, and have done.
6. Standards, rules, or moral principles are invoked in arriving at decisions.
7. Any study of social relationships requires the researcher to use subjective investigative techniques such as *verstehen,* imaginative or sympathetic reconstruction, or vicarious experience.

Of course, these premises are not novel to action theory. According to Hinkle (1963:707) "they were present in many classical Greek works, St. Thomas Aquinas, eighteenth century essayists, and in much of modern literature, philosophy, psychology and sociology."

There is some evidence that the action approach was anticipated by pre–World War I sociologists such as Lester Ward, E. A. Ross, Franklin Giddings, Albion Small, and Charles H. Cooley. The linkages to modern action theory for most of these people were tenuous.

Most of these early sociologists were preoccupied with the macroscopic question of societal evolution. Although they discussed an active, creative view of man, their emphasis on society tended to give it coercive power over the individual.

The exception to this was Charles H. Cooley. Although he accepted some of the tenets of his contemporaries and their interest in evolution, "what became ultimately significant in social life [were] subjective consciousness and personal feelings, sentiments, ideas, or ideals in terms of which men initiate and terminate their actions toward one another." (Hinkle, 1963:709)   Methodologically, therefore, Cooley accepted an approach that allowed the sociologist to understand the personal experience of each actor. He objected to the application of the methods of the natural sciences to sociology because they implied a mechanistic conception of man. He also opposed statistical analyses because they concentrated on outer behavior rather than inner consciousness. Cooley, like most of those associated with social definitionism, urged the use of *verstehen*.

Except for Cooley, the pre–World War I sociologists showed only minor linkages to later action theory. Those sociologists who worked between the end of World War I and the depression exhibited far greater congruence with later action theory. Among the more important of these sociologists were Robert Park, Ellsworth Faris, W. I. Thomas, and George Herbert Mead.

It should be noted that all of these figures were important in the Chicago school of sociology and the development of symbolic interactionism. George Herbert Mead was, of course, the major figure in the development of that theoretical orientation. The linkages between action theory and these men buttresses the case that both of these theoretical perspectives are part of the same paradigm—social definitionism. We need not be detained at this point discussing the linkages between these men and action theory. We will turn to symbolic interactionism in the next section, and the linkages will be clear in that discussion.

Let me conclude this brief discussion of action theory by turning to the action approach taken by Talcott Parsons. Parsons was the major inheritor of the Weberian orientation and his use of action theory in his early work gave that approach its widest audience.

Parsons, like all other social action theorists, was anxious to differentiate action theory from behaviorism. In fact, the term *action* was chosen because it had a different connotation than behavior. Behavior implied mechanical conformity to stimuli, while action implied an active, creative, "minded" process. Parsons (1937:77–78) was careful to differentiate action theory from behaviorism: "A theory which, like behaviorism, insists on treating human beings in terms which exclude his subjective aspect, is not a theory of action."

From the beginning, Parsons made it clear that action theory could not explain all of social life. While action theory dealt with the most elementary form of social life,* he recognized in his first major work that it could not deal with the entire social structure. Parsons' equivocation at this early point in his career foreshadows his later work in which many people feel he almost totally abandoned action theory (and therefore social definitionism) for the social facts paradigm.

The basic unit in Parsons' action schema is the *unit act* which has the following characteristics:

1. There must be an actor.
2. The act must have an end, "a future state of affairs toward which the process of action is oriented." (Parsons, 1937:44)
3. Action occurs in a situation that must differ in one or more ways from the ends to which it is oriented. The situation can be subdivided into the following:
   a) conditions-elements of the situation over which the individual has no control
   b) means-elements of the situation over which he has control
4. There are norms that orient the actor in terms of his choice of means to an end.

The image here is of an actor seeking a goal in a situation in which there are norms that orient his choice of means. Yet, these norms do *not* determine his choice of means to the ends. This ability to choose is Parsons' well-known notion of *voluntarism*. In fact, it is this concept of voluntarism that allows us to place action theory within the social definitionist paradigm. The actor, in behaving voluntaristically, "is essentially an active, creative, evaluating crea-

---

* Parsons' conception of the most elementary unit of social analysis does not coincide with such social behaviorists as George Homans.

ture." (Parsons, 1934:282)   However, the actor is never seen by Parsons as being totally free, as having free will. Ends, conditions, and norms, as well as other situational exigencies, all serve to restrict the freedom of the actor. Man, in Parsons' action theory, is voluntaristic, but far from totally free. Whatever his degree of freedom, Parsons' actor is active, creative, and evaluative.

This type of orientation leads Parsons to a methodological position similar to Weber's interpretative understanding: "the schema is inherently subjective . . . This is most clearly indicated by the fact that the normative elements can be conceived of 'existing' only in the mind of the actor." (Parsons, 1937:733)   Despite this methodological contention, it plays almost as small a role in Parsons' later work as it did in Weber's. Most of Parsons' later work is at the level of social facts and an examination of them *as if* they are separable from the minds of men. Although Parsons pays lip-service to action theory in his later works, it is relatively insignificant.

As early as *The Structure of Social Action* (1937) Parsons was laying the groundwork for his defection to social factism. He talked of the interrelationships between unit acts as well as the emergent properties of interacting unit acts. Parsons soon abandoned unit acts for the domain of systems that are composed of, and emerge from, unit acts.

Many people have criticized Parsons for abandoning action theory. John Finley Scott (1963) was one of the first to accuse Parsons of abandoning action theory and, specifically, the voluntaristic thesis. Tiryakian (1965:684) notes Parsons' later adoption of many Freudian ideas, and laments the fact that this orientation tends to undermine his earlier voluntarism. Buckley (1967:19) argues that Parsons "has tended to backtrack in his later works by stressing structure at the expense of action." However, in a recent paper Turner and Beeghley (1972) have attacked these critics, arguing that Parsonian theory has been continuous, especially in terms of its voluntaristic thesis. Among other things, they point to the fact that in many of Parsons' later works, voluntaristic action theory tends to reappear. While it is true that Parsons is almost always careful to touch base with action theory, it has had little effect on his later work. He merely mentions action theory and then proceeds to work within the social facts paradigm as a structural-functionalist. More importantly,

Parsons drops the commitment to interpretative understanding implicit in his early statements on action theory. In his later, more macroscopic work, we no longer need to understand the actor but must instead study the relationship between abstract systems. These abstract systems, such as the social and cultural system, seem to have a life of their own separable from the minds of men. They may be analyzed structurally rather than subjectively.

The tendency of both Parsons and Weber to ignore subjective analysis in their later work sets them apart (at that point) from the social definitionist paradigm. Nevertheless, in its basic formulation, action theory lies squarely within the social definitionist camp.* Because it was abandoned by its founders, action theory has not developed as fully as other theories within the social definitionist paradigm. Let us, therefore, turn to the more fully developed orientations.

Symbolic Interactionism

While action theory has not, in my view, been well developed theoretically, or extensively used in empirical research, a very similar perspective (*symbolic interactionism*) has become a major force in sociology, both theoretically and empirically. It is important to note that Max Weber and his action orientation is recognized, probably erroneously, by most symbolic interactionists as congenial to their

---

* This section is based on the traditional interpretation of action theory, in particular, traditional views of the work of Weber and Parsons on action. There is, however, another interpretation of action theory that would place it squarely within the social facts paradigm. From this perspective, Weber and Parsons are seen as never being interested in such microscopic issues as minding, intrasubjectivity, and intersubjectivity. Their interest in action and the unit act are seen as merely the base on which their focal interest in social structure is built. This view holds that Parsons and Weber were consistently interested in more macroscopic questions. Verstehen is also seen in a different light. Instead of a method aimed at grasping the minding process, *verstehen* is seen as a method of examining macroscopic phenomena from the point of view of the actor. Such a view of *verstehen* is more consistent with its basic formulation by Dilthey. My sympathies lie with this interpretation, although I have outlined the traditional interpretation of action theory in this section. I have done so because I think it is more important to understand the way modern sociologists interpreted action theory, than to understand the intentions of action theory's founders. I would like to thank Jill Quadagno and Richard Bell for helping me see this point.

own approach. Although symbolic interactionism developed before Weber was well known in the United States, symbolic interactionists have come to see Weber's action theory as a forerunner of their own approach. In contrast, Parsons' action theory which is virtually indistinguishable from Weber's in many ways, receives almost no recognition from symbolic interactionists. The neglect of Parsons' work by symbolic interactionists, despite a number of similarities, stems from several sources. For one thing, Parsons taught and developed his theoretical orientation at Harvard and his major initial impact was in the Ivy League and on the East Coast. In contrast, symbolic interactionism blossomed at the University of Chicago and was associated with the Midwest for a long time. The philosopher John Dewey and the sociologist Charles Horton Cooley, important contributors to the development of symbolic interactionism, were at the University of Michigan. Dewey later moved to the University of Chicago and there influenced such crucial figures in the development of symbolic interactionism as W. I. Thomas and George Herbert Mead. Later Robert Park arrived at Chicago. Park had studied philosophy at Harvard under two other figures associated with symbolic interactionism, William James and Josiah Royce. Park also brought with him the influence of the German formalist, George Simmel, as well as experience with education and the news media—backgrounds that were to help give symbolic interactionism its strong empirical orientation. Thus, the Chicago orientation was far more philosophical and empirical than the Ivy League orientation, which under Parsons moved increasingly in the direction of the development of abstract sociological theory. In addition, by the time Parsons' work was becoming widely known, the Chicago school was in full swing and much of its direction was already set. The abstract theories being developed by the Parsonians were antithetical in many ways to the needs and interests of the Chicagoans, who were out in the field using their "theory" to orient their research. Despite the fact that Parsons' work was ignored by the Chicagoans for these and other reasons, his early work on action theory was highly relevant to the symbolic interactionism being developed by them.

Of all of the schools of sociological thinking, symbolic interactionism is one of the most difficult to summarize. Glimpses of it can be derived from a variety of sources, but no single source or person can provide a self-contained single statement on it. Perhaps the place to start in trying to provide some idea of the nature of this position is in terms of what it is reacting against—behaviorism. In fact, the central figure in symbolic interactionism, George Herbert Mead, labelled the subject of focal concern to him, "social behaviorism."* He intended to differentiate this from the "radical behaviorism" of J. B. Watson.

Radical behaviorists of Watson's persuasion were concerned with the *observable* actions of individuals. While Mead recognized the importance of observable action, he also felt that there were *covert* aspects of behavior that were ignored by the radical behaviorists. This interest in covert behavior led Mead to a methodological difference with the behaviorists. Behaviorists studied behavior objectively from without. Mead's orientation required that symbolic interactionists apply introspective techniques and be able to see and understand things from the point of view of the actor. Behaviorists also tended to see human behavior as similar to animal behavior while Mead saw a qualitative difference between the two. A good portion of this difference is attributable to the human capacity to acquire and use language. Learning to the behaviorists was equated with conditioning and they generally ignored the role of language.

Stemming from this early orientation, symbolic interactionism has had a running feud with the behaviorist paradigm to be discussed in the next chapter. The prime antagonist, to the symbolic interactionists, is anyone who seeks to reduce human behavior to stimulus-response. That antagonism is clear in the following definition of symbolic interactionism by its greatest contemporary exponent, Herbert Blumer (1962:180):

> The term "symbolic interaction" refers, of course, to the peculiar and distinctive character of interaction as it takes place between human beings. The peculiarity consists in the fact that human beings interpret or "define" each other's actions instead of *merely reacting* to each other's actions. Their response is *not* made directly to the actions of one another but instead is based on the meaning which they attach to such actions. Thus, human interaction is mediated by the use of symbols, by interpretation, or by ascertaining the meaning of one another's actions. This mediation is equivalent to

---

* This is not to be confused with the social behaviorism discussed in this book which resembles what Mead calls *radical behaviorism*.

inserting a process of interpretation between stimulus and response in the case of human behavior.

I think the key to the symbolic interactionist position lies in this process of interpretation that mediates between stimulus and response. It is true that they are also interested in stimulus and response, but it is the interest in the interpretative process that sets them apart. But they are not alone in this interest. It was certainly of prime concern to the action theorist with his interest in the "orientation" of the actor and the use of the method of *verstehen*, as well as to the phenomenologists to be discussed later in this chapter.

Despite similar interests, the action theorist never really did much with this process of interpretation, while the symbolic interactionists made it the center of their work. Similarly, social behaviorists, such as George Homans, are certainly aware that there is something that intervenes between stimulus and response, but they do not feel that it is necessary to examine this interpretative process. Furthermore, they are adamanantly opposed to the subjective approach that one must take if he is interested in studying an actor's orientation or interpretation.

Just as symbolic interactionism is interested in distinguishing itself from social behaviorism, it is also eager to set itself apart from social factism. There is a decided disinclination to deal with society as if it is a set of "real" structures distinct from people. "Human society is to be seen as consisting of acting people, and the life of the society is to be seen as consisting of their actions." (Blumer, 1962: 187)   There is a disinclination, therefore, on the part of symbolic interactionists to, in Marxian terms, *reify society*. To the symbolic interactionists, social facts are not "things" that control or coerce man, but are little more than the framework within which the truly important aspect of society, symbolic interaction, takes place:

> From the standpoint of symbolic interaction, the organization of a human society is the framework inside of which social action takes place and is not the determinant of that action. Second, such organization and changes in it are the product of the activity of acting units and not of forces which leave such acting units out of account.* . . . People—that is, acting units—do not act toward cul-

---

* It is important to note here that acting units can be individuals, collectivities, and organizations.

ture, social structure or the like; they act toward situations . . . One should bear in mind that the most important element confronting an acting unit in situations is the actions of other acting units.†

The acting units and the way they orient themselves to each other are central to symbolic interactionists. Actors fit their actions to those of others through a process of interpretation. When, through this process, actors form groups, the action of the group is the collective action of the individuals involved. Individuals, interaction, and interpretation are key terms here, but not to the social factists, who in Blumer's (1962:186) view stand in stark opposition to this position:

> As opposed to this view, sociological conceptions generally lodge social action in the action of society or in some unit of society. Examples of this are legion. Let me cite a few. Some conceptions, in treating societies or human groups as "social systems," regard group action as an expression of a system, either in a state of balance or seeking to achieve balance. Or group action is conceived as an expression of the "functions" of a society or of a group. Or group action is regarded as the outward expression of elements lodged in society or the group, such as cultural demands, societal purposes, social values, or institutional stresses. These typical conceptions ignore or blot out a view of group life or of group action as consisting of the collective or concerted actions of individuals seeking to meet their life situations. If recognized at all, the efforts of people to develop collective acts to meet their situations are subsumed under the play of underlying or transcending forces which are lodged in society or its parts. The individuals composing the society or the group become "carriers," or media for the expression of such forces; and the interpretative behavior by means of which people form their actions is merely a coerced link in the play of such forces.

In contrast to the social factist, the social definitionist sees man as far more "voluntaristic," far less coerced by society, and far more a creator of the society in which he lives. Further, social facts are seen as far less static structures that emerge in situations rather than simply lying in wait "out there" preparing to coerce the next person who comes along.

† Herbert Blumer, "Society as Symbolic Interaction," *Human Behavior and Social Processes,* ed. Arnold Rose (Boston: Houghton Mifflin, 1962) .

The symbolic interactionist rejects the social factist and the social behaviorist for essentially the same reason—neither recognizes the importance of the individual.   To the social factist, the individual is seen as responding to such external forces as culture, norm, and role.   This view tends to deny the fact that man has a self.   On the other hand, the social behaviorist sees external stimuli determining the behavior of man.   The fact that man *creates* his own world is either ignored or denied in both paradigms, but not by the symbolic interactionists.   Symbolic interactionists share a voluntaristic conception of man with action theorists, but they do far more with that view, by focusing to a much greater extent on the actor's process of interpretation or orientation.

This introduction to symbolic interactionism has sought to demonstrate its position relative to the other two paradigms as well as its companion within the social definition paradigm (action theory) but I have yet to give you a systematic summary of symbolic interactionism.   It is time I do that by focusing on the efforts of Arnold Rose (1962) to lay out symbolic interactionism in terms of a series of assumptions and derived general propositions.   In so doing, it will become apparent that it is the concept of a *symbol,* and its role in symbolic interactionism, that sets this theoretical orientation apart from action theory.

Assumption 1.   "Man lives in a symbolic environment as well as a physical environment and can be 'stimulated' to act by symbols as well as by physical stimuli."   (Rose, 1962:5)

The important point here is that man responds to *symbols* as well as to mere physical stimuli.   The reaction of a man dying of thirst is strictly physical and hence is not learned.   More precisely, the need for the water is not learned, although such variables as how or when it is consumed are learned.   Few of our stimuli are of this physical character; most are learned and are therefore symbolic.   That is, the meaning and value of a symbol are learned and we respond to them in terms of their learned meaning, not as physical stimuli.   We, therefore, react to a police uniform, Afro hairdo, and a home run because we have learned their meaning and value.   Symbols can be visual as in the examples above, but what truly distinguishes man is his capacity to communicate symbols verbally through a highly developed language. Man is possessed with the vocal apparatus that enables him to make a wide range and a large number of sounds. Furthermore, his nervous system (in particular, his brain) is capable of storing millions of values and meanings of symbols. Man's capacity to communicate, learn, store, understand symbols, and reason is what sets him apart from other animals and is what makes symbolic interaction to those of this persuasion the essential focus of sociological analysis.

Assumption 2. "Through symbols, man has the capacity to stimulate others in ways other than those in which he is himself stimulated." (Rose, 1962:7)

In understanding this assumption, as well as Assumption 1, it is important to introduce Mead's differentiation between *natural signs* and *significant symbols*. Natural signs are those that instinctively evoke the same reaction in another person as they evoke in you. For example, water (assuming some degree of thirst) will evoke the same reaction in both you and another person. Conversely, significant symbols do not necessarily evoke the same reaction in both parties. The actor who uses a significant symbol has a given meaning in mind, but the receiver of that symbol does not necessarily attribute the same meaning to it. This accentuates the point that symbolic communication is a two-way process with both parties giving each symbol meaning.

When I say "how are you" to a co-worker, I really mean hello. Although I know what I mean by "how are you," it is possible that the receiver does not know that I mean hello and actually proceeds to give me a fifteen minute discourse on his various maladies. If everyone were to give such discourses every time someone said "how are you," much of the world would come to a standstill.

How, then, is this avoided? Why is it that people do not reply with their health record every time they are asked how they are? Mead outlines two processes by which such inappropriate replies are avoided. The first involves "role-taking." That is, as we are about to say "how are you," or to reply to that question, we take the role of the person to whom we are speaking. If the person who asks how you are is rushing past you on the street, you know (if you have successfully taken his role) that he desires nothing more than a smile, a hello, or a nod.   If, on the other hand, he is visiting your bedside in the hospital, you can feel relatively sure by taking his role that he really does want to know about the state of your health.   The second is taking the role of the "generalized other."   Thus, instead of putting yourself in the place of the other person involved, you try to understand how the group as a whole would respond to the symbol in question.

Assumption 3.   "Through communication of symbols, man can learn huge numbers of meanings and values—and hence ways of acting—from other men."   (Rose, 1962:9)

Since symbols are such a central part of life and since symbols are by definition learned, man must and does learn the meaning of innumerable symbols.   Furthermore, because knowledge can be communicated in symbols, man can acquire an enormous amount of information.   In learning symbols and to symbolize, man learns to act. Learning to communicate symbolically occurs in a three-stage process in childhood.   (Meltzer, 1972)

1. Preparatory stage.   At this stage the child is simply engaged in meaningless imitation of those around him.
2. Play stage.   At this point the child learns to take roles, but only one at a time.   The child plays mommy or daddy and may even view himself from their perspective. However, he vacillates between discrete roles, and therefore, lacks a unitary conception of himself.
3. Game stage. Here the child begins to take the roles of several people simultaneously and to respond to the expectations of several people at once. In so doing, the child ultimately builds up a generalized other and a generalized standpoint with which to view himself.

General Proposition (Deduction) 1.   "Through the learning of a culture (and subcultures, which are specialized cultures found in particular segments of society) men are able to predict each other's behavior most of the time and gauge their own behavior to the predicted behavior of others."   (Rose, 1962:9–10)

Society, in order to exist, must provide through its culture a set of common meanings for its symbols.   This is necessary in order for interaction to proceed.   If such common meanings were not provided, society would disintegrate into chaos and cease to exist.   A set of common meanings need not always exist between actors; some inappropriate responses can be accommodated. Society, however, would cease to exist if man could rarely, or never, be certain of how others would respond. This leads Rose (1962:10) to a definition of society: "In this sense and only in this sense, society is more than a collection of individuals: it is a collection of individuals with a culture. . . ." Rose, like Blumer and other symbolic interactionists, is not inclined to emphasize the structural aspects of society. Some symbolic interactionists deny that such structures exist while others downgrade their importance.

Assumption 4. "The symbols and other meanings and values to which they refer do not occur only in isolated bits, but often in clusters, sometimes large and complex."

It is under the heading of clusters of symbols that Rose seeks to deal with some of the concerns of social factists. In fact, he sees two basic types of meaning (value clusters) *roles* and *structures*. A role is defined by Rose (1962:10) as "a cluster of related meanings and values that guide and direct an individual's behavior in a given social setting," while a structure is "a cluster of related meanings and values that govern a given social setting." Thus, structures and roles are the same thing looked at from the perspective of the individual and the social setting.

General Proposition (Deduction) 2. "The individual defines (has meaning for) himself as well as other objects, actions, and characteristics."

Mead saw man as having a self and therefore having the ability of being the object of his own actions. Man can act toward himself just as he can act toward external objects. Blumer (1962:181) describes the operation of the self in this way: "Each of us is familiar with actions of this sort in which the human being gets angry with himself, rebuffs himself, tries to bolster his own courage, tells himself that he should 'do this' and not 'do that,' sets goals for himself, makes compromises with himself, and plans what he is going to do." It is this ability to relate to one's self that gives man much of the freedom he has in the eyes of the symbolic interactionist. Yet, how can man have freedom when what he learns comes from the culture of the society that encapsulates him? In order to give man this capacity for freedom, Mead endows the self with two components—an "I" and a "me." The "me" represents the conformist aspect of the self: "In any given situation, the 'me' comprises the generalized other and, often, some particular other." (Meltzer, 1972:10) When the individual responds to others, however, he responds as an "I". The "I" may reflect some aspects of the others involved in the specific situation, but it is also composed of attitudes imposed by the individual upon himself. The "I" never fully conforms to surrounding expectations and is the spontaneous, unorganized, impulsive force in Mead's thinking. The "I" is the motor force in the self, giving propulsion, while the function of the "me" is to channel the "I" in the direction of the expectations of others. The fact that the "me" is not totally successful makes man free in the view of symbolic interactionists.

Now the concepts of "I" and "me" are as unrealistic as Freud's concepts of id, ego, and superego. We need not accept the idea of "I" and "me" literally. For our purposes, it is sufficient to note that despite the pressures from role-senders and the generalized other, man is not totally controlled by these constraints.*

Assumption 5. "Thinking is the process by which possible symbolic solutions and other future courses of action are examined, assessed for their relative advantages and disadvantages in terms of the values of the individual, and one of them chosen for action." (Rose, 1962:12)

Although much of what has been said up to this point on symbolic interactionism has separated it from behaviorism, it is at this point that the difference is clearest. It is the thought processes and the mind of man that the behaviorist leaves out:

> They failed to take full account of the social character of the act, and what was worse yet, they limited analysis to fragmentary portions of the act. A thorough-going behaviorism would include within its purview the *complete* act, and particularly that portion of it which goes on in the central nervous system as the beginning of the individual's act and as the organization of the act. This larger

---

* Charles Warriner argues that Mead never made the "I" and "me" the fixtures or substances that his followers did. He treated them as phases or stages in the process of action, stages in the act, not as part of the personality.

inclusiveness would necessarily take the investigator beyond the field of direct observation, Watson's starting point." (Troyer, 1972:321)

To Mead, the individual has the complete act in his mind before he begins it and tries out various alternatives mentally. Hence, the act is broadened by Mead from the overt behavior to the covert mental processes that precede the actual behavior.

The mind is defined by the symbolic interactionists as a *process* in which the individual interacts with himself, employing significant symbols. By interacting with himself, the individual is able to select, from all of the stimuli aimed at him, those that he will respond to. He is not simply responding to stimuli, but determining which stimuli he will respond to. Furthermore, even after he has selected the stimuli, he can try out various responses in his mind before he actually responds to them. The actor is looking into the future and ascertaining the effects of the different courses of action he could choose. He is temporarily inhibiting his response to a stimuli in order to choose the response he wants. All of this serves to downgrade the importance of the environment or the external stimuli which are emphasized by the behaviorists. Because of "minded behavior," man's behavior is not reducible to stimulus-response.

The image of a thinking man replaces the behaviorist's image of a hedonist or one who learns by trial and error. Rose argues that thinking is far more efficient than learning by trial and error. In the first place, one can conduct imaginative trials of courses of behavior far more quickly than actually trying them out behaviorally. Secondly, an individual need not be tied to choosing the first alternative that works during trial and error. He can choose the course of action that is the best of all he knows. In addition, imaginative exploration is far less risky than actual experimentation. "Through thinking, man brings the imagined or expected future into the present, so that present behavior can be a response to future expected stimuli, and courses of action can be laid out for quite some time into the future." (Rose, 1962:12–13)   Not only can thinking bring in the future, it can also bring in the past, thereby increasing the efficiency over mere trial and error.

All of this leads us to the distinctive conception of the "act" in symbolic interactionism: "The act, then, encompasses the total process involved in human activity. It is viewed as a complete span of action. Its initial point is an impulse and its terminal point some objective which gives release to the impulse. In between, the individual is in the process of constructing, organizing his behavior." (Meltzer, 1972:16)   It is in the last sentence of the preceding quotation that we return to the essence of symbolic interaction—the process that intervenes within the neurological structure of man between stimulus and response. The major goal of symbolic interaction is an understanding of this process. Since it does occur within the minds of men, it leads the symbolic interactionist to a very different methodological position than social factists and social behaviorists. He must use the method of *verstehen,* putting himself at further odds with supporters of the other paradigms which extol the virtues of what they believe to be more scientific methods. We will have more to say about this issue in the methods section.

A caveat is in order before proceeding. The preceding discussion of symbolic interactionism, although drawn from several sources, attempts to give a coherent image of the theory. Since the theory is lacking a single overarching perspective, I have had to piece one together myself. Many symbolic interactionists are likely to take issue with at least one of the points made above. Nevertheless, given the purposes of this book, I thought it necessary to communicate a singular image of symbolic interactionism. I cannot continue, however, without at least briefly mentioning one division that exists among symbolic interactionists.

While most of symbolic interactionism arose in Chicago, a rather maverick brand of it emerged at the University of Iowa under Manfred Kuhn. The basic difference between Kuhn and more traditional symbolic interactionists, such as Herbert Blumer, lies in Kuhn's efforts to make symbolic interactionism more quantitatively empirical. While Blumer seeks simply to make modern society intelligible, Kuhn is concerned with universal predictions of human conduct. Methodologically, Blumer is a devotee of "feeling one's way inside the experience of the actor," or sympathetic introspection (Verstehen). Conversely, Kuhn is oriented toward operationalizing and using in empirical, scientific research the concepts of symbolic interactionism. Kuhn is still interested in covert aspects of action, but paradoxically only through the use of "objective overt-behavioral

indices (chiefly verbalizations by the actor) of the covert aspects."
(Meltzer and Petras, 1972:47)   In terms of concepts, Blumer
favors what he labels "sensitizing concepts." These are concepts that
only impose enough structure to the research to *suggest* in which directions the researcher might look. On the other hand, Kuhn supports operational concepts that serve to prescribe what the researcher
will see. Blumer is opposed to studies that seek to test the relationship between variables, while Kuhn sees little wrong with them. Because of his acceptance of the Meadian concept of "I", Blumer sees
much indeterminance and unpredictability in social behavior. In
Kuhn's hands the self becomes solely "me" with the source of inde-
terminancy, "I", dropping from the picture. Finally, Blumer, like
all of the Chicago school, focuses on process while Kuhn is forced by
his orientation more in the direction of the analysis of structure. Although Kuhn maintains many positions that keep him within the
social definitionist paradigm, he still has a number of ideas in common with social behaviorists. In any case, this little aside on the debate between Blumer and Kuhn is intended to illustrate that the
nature of symbolic interactionism is far more complex than the
limited sketch presented above.

Phenomenological Sociology*

In recent years, an increasing number of sociologists have come to
describe their work as "phenomenological." In the relatively short
period of time since this word was introduced into the vocabulary of
sociologists, it has come to represent an approach that is supposed to
provide an "alternative" to more traditional modes of sociological
inquiry. However, few terms in sociology have generated more
confusion. Its staunchest adherents sometimes have difficulty in
explaining whether it constitutes a particular theory, method, or
general approach. Phenomenological sociology seems to defy clear
categorization when one examines the literature that supposedly
gives the area definition. The confusion is exacerbated by two

* This contribution on phenomenology was written by Professor Robert J. Antonio.

further factors: first, under the rubric of phenomenological sociology, studies with varied types of research designs are listed;* and
secondly, some phenomenological sociologists (especially the ethnomethodologists) write in a rather abstruse fashion.   Many sociologists who are upset with the seeming obfuscation of some of the
self-identified phenomenologists, claim that they have made little substantive contribution to either theory or method and represent little
more than a cultish reaction to mainstream sociology.

Regardless of the existing confusion, analysis of the sociological
work considered phenomenological, reevals a particular type of sociological imagination.   By this, is meant that it represents a rather
unique way of approaching the constitution of social reality.   However, its defining qualities are elusive and are probably more easily
tapped in stating what the approach is not, rather than what it is.
Phenomenological sociology is not *objectivist, static,* or *abstractly
empirical.*   Although it represents a rather unique orientation, it
combines theoretical and methodological approaches not really foreign to more traditional sociology.   In the following, I will consider
some of the basic ideas of three of the most important thinkers in this
area and conclude with a discussion of what I think to be the basic
attributes of phenomenological sociology.

Husserl and the Foundations of
Phenomenological Sociology

The origins of the phenomenological movement in philosophy can
be traced to the work of Franz Brentano, a nineteenth century philosopher.   However, Edmund Husserl (1859–1938) is considered the
real father of phenomenology, and it is his philosophical system that
provides the impetus for phenomenological sociology.   Even though
many contemporary sociologists claim to be working in his tradition,
the relationship is tenuous and even nonexistent at certain crucial
points.

---

* Even in Harold Garfinkel's *Studies in Ethnomethodology* (1967), which is thought by
many to lay the groundwork for contemporary phenomenological sociology, there is a
confusing amalgam of research styles: a case study, participant observation, survey research, analysis of census data, and both statistical and naturalistic analysis.

Husserl (1969:74–75) recommends that philosophers return "to the facts themselves." This statement derives from an argument in which Husserl stresses that there is no way of knowing objects in themselves. Instead, we must concern ourselves with the objects as they are presented in experience. Thus, to the extent that philosophy represents the rational inquiry into the nature and development of knowledge, it is consciousness, the field in which experience occurs and on which knowledge is based, that must be brought under philosophic inquiry (*see* Spiegelberg, 1969:82). This idea represents a radical departure from, and is in a sense a reaction to, the naturalistic-empiricism that has come to dominate both the science and philosophy of the past two centuries (*see* Husserl, 1965:79–122). According to Husserl, naturalistic-empiricism treats objects (behavior or social facts) that exist in nature as if they could be known objectively (as they exist in themselves) through the senses. Translated into method, it suggests that science should proceed by the accumulation of information drawn from measurements aimed at divulging the empirical dimensions of objects in nature. Husserl (1965:87–88) attacks the very assumptions on which this approach is based:

> How can experience as consciousness give or contact an object? How can experiences be mutually legitimated or corrected by means of each other, and not merely replace each other or confirm each other subjectively? How can the play of a consciousness whose logic is empirical make objectively valid statements, valid for things that are in and for themselves? Why are the playing rules, so to speak, of consciousness not irrelevant for things? How is natural science to be comprehensible in absolutely every case, to the extent that it pretends at every step to posit and to know a nature that is in itself— in itself in opposition to the subjective flow of consciousness?

Husserl (1965:85) argues that the empiricism of natural science is "naive" or pre-datum, meaning that it is prior to scientific reflection. He opposes this to phenomenology that attempts to examine the data of *experience* as they appear in consciousness with the theoretic tools of philosophic science.

To those of you who have not been exposed to the language of philosophy, and specifically philosophy of science, the discussion above may seem obscure. However, it refers to what is perhaps one of the most common expressions in contemporary social science, *scientific objectivity*. This is a crucial element in the method of modern empirical science. Husserl's argument represents a broadside against this idea (at least as it was carried to its extreme by social factists and behaviorists to exclude consciousness from scientific inquiry). It is directed toward legitimating inquiries into consciousness.

Prior to Husserl, consciousness was hopelessly lodged in the subjective realm and therefore believed to be beyond the scope of scientific study. Later in this discussion it will be shown that Husserl's ideas about this issue are used by phenomenological sociologists in their criticism of mainstream sociology, which they see dominated by the logic of naturalistic empiricism and its method of radical scientific objectivity. To avoid much unnecessary discussion, it is simply asserted that this represents the *basic* tie between Husserl and phenomenological sociology. Certain techniques and conceptual tools utilized by this school of sociology can also be traced ultimately to Husserl, but these are too numerous and complex to be discussed here. However, these all evolve out of the critique of naturalistic-empiricism and are constructed for use in the subjective analysis of consciousness and *intersubjectivity*.

I need to explicate a few of Husserl's ideas on phenomenology even though you will see that these ideas do not resemble, and are in fact contradictory to, what is today called phenomenological sociology. It is important to do this because contemporary phenomenologists who cite Husserl as their precursor often neglect to recognize these differences. First and most importantly, although the thrust of his new philosophy deals with consciousness, it does not suggest that sympathetic introspection (*verstehen*) be used as a methodological tool. Quite the opposite, Husserl (1965:115) asserts specifically that the phenomenological method should *not* be confused with introspection. I mention this because introspective description is (as it is in symbolic interactionism) one of the main tools of phenomenological sociology. To Husserl, introspection, albeit subjective, is still a form of empiricism for it involves merely reporting and recording the data of consciousness. Husserl asserts that empiricism is not a science. Instead, it is at best the method for providing the facts that a theoretical science attempts to explain. He wants to develop a philosophy of consciousness that is nonempirical and contradictory to natural science. This necessitates the development of abstractive concepts, discovered through theoretical reflection, that are interrelated in absolute fashion and presented in theoretical form. In short, Husserl envisions phenomenology as the basis for a pure and cumulative scientific philosophy (*see* Husserl, 1965:71–148).

It will be seen later in this discussion that this position is antithetical to phenomenological sociology, for the latter is characterized by introspection, descriptive empiricism (although generally not quantitative), and a lack of any formal theory. Phenomenological sociologists should be aware of these differences before they claim to be doing research in the tradition of Husserl.

Alfred Schutz: The Father of
Phenomenological Sociology

Alfred Schutz (1899–1959), a social philosopher, provided the real grounds for the development of phenomenological sociology. As a student of Husserl's philosophy, he performs the same functions for social science that Husserl did for philosophy. That is, subjective analysis of things in consciousness replaces objective analysis of things in the world. This version of social definitionism (as do the others) stands in opposition to the social facts and behaviorist paradigms. Again, to the social factist and behaviorist there are objective entities (social facts, behaviors) existing in the world. These can be revealed *objectively* through the empirical techniques construed to constitute the scientific method. The conception of social science expounded by Schutz differs radically from this position.

Because of his sociological orientation, Schutz focuses particularly upon one form of subjectivity, that is intersubjectivity. This refers literally to shared subjective states, or simply the dimension of consciousness common to a particular social group or group of interactants. It is intersubjectivity that makes social intercourse possible, for the patterning of interaction depends on the knowledge of *rules* that are shared, yet experienced subjectively. The concept of intersubjectivity refers to the fact that groups of men come to interpret and even experience the world similarly. Such mutual understanding is necessary for cooperative tasks on which most social organization is predicated. Schutz is concerned with the conscious structures necessary for such mutual activity and understanding. The broader question underlying his concern should be a primary issue for all serious social scientists: How is society possible?

Schutz begins with the work of Max Weber, attempting to criticize and extend his ideas. Weber, as we have seen, believes sociology should be geared toward the explanation of social action. Human behavior becomes a social relationship when man attributes meaning to it and *other men* understand it as meaningful. Subjective meaning becomes crucial to interaction, both for the actor intending the behavior and for the others who must interpret it and react accordingly. Weber, in fact, sees social relationships as being no more than actors sharing a common context of meaning, who are oriented to each other on the basis of this context. Weber's methodological concept (*verstehen*) suggests that social scientists must involve themselves in a form of sympathetic introspection with interactants in order to understand their meaning contexts that serve as the impetus to action.

It is important to point out here that Weber's ideas apply very nicely in some respects and are contradictory in others, to Husserl's conception of phenomenology. Obviously, Weber, like Husserl, takes a subjectivist orientation. It is also important to note that Husserl concerns himself with the problem of intersubjectivity (how actors come to share certain subjective states), but is never able to work out the riddle of its occurrence satisfactorily within his philosophical system. Part of this difficulty results from his methodology which requires treating the individual in radical abstraction from his interpersonal world (the pure phenomenologist performs "epoche," bracketing or suspending interest in all social and personal existence) .* Schutz finds Weber's work seriously flawed and in need of

---

* Husserl argues that pure phenomenology attempts to establish the essential structures of consciousness (for all men for all times). These structures must be ahistorical and theoretical; to determine them the subject must be treated in abstraction from the empirical world. To perform "epoche," or to bracket, means to hold constant the empirical contingencies of existence so the subject can be studied theoretically.

extension. However, it provides Schutz with a starting point and in-spiration for his work on the problem of intersubjectivity.

Schutz, in his Weberian moment, became acquainted with the Chicago School of Sociology, and its theoretical orientation—symbolic interactionism. He considers the work of several of the scholars in this school (e.g. Mead and Thomas—*see* Schutz, 1964, 1970, 1971) although not nearly with the depth and concern he shows for Weber and action theory. As we have seen, the symbolic interactionist ori-entation is consistent with Weber's approach since it also focuses on the subjective understanding of meaningful action. Symbolic inter-actionists attempt to explain how actors become intersubjective be-ings, in other words, how actors are socialized to internalize and share socially-determined contexts of meaning that are experienced sub-jectively and serve as the basis for social action. Schutz sees in these ideas the basis of intersubjectivity, actors being socialized to collec-tively "typify" repetitive social encounters as objective externalities. However, these "typifications" are experienced in consciousness as a subjective reality.*

Schutz, besides taking the subjectivist approach of Husserl's phe-nomenology, also makes extensive use of Husserlian concepts, remolded to fit his more socially based phenomenology. Most impor-tantly, Schutz represents a synthesis of phenomenology with action theory (extended by some symbolic interactionist concepts). How-ever, in performing the synthesis, Schutz abandons Husserl's assertion of the need for a nonempirical, nonintrospective subjectivism to serve as the method used to forge a cumulative philosophy of phenome-nology. In taking an action theory approach he abandons these goals (with the exception of subjectivism). Action theory is founded upon a method of introspection (*verstehen*), which although subjective, still results in a form of descriptive empiricism (but nonquantitative) that Husserl condemns. Introspective understanding of meaningful action certainly could not lead to the development of the pure and timeless knowledge that Husserl believes necessary for cumulative

---

* Schutz uses the word "typify" in discussing intersubjective consciousness. This refers to the ability to establish a situation or object as being part of a socially significant category of situations and objects. Actors sharing common sets of "typifications" are able to structure their experience of the world similarly by applying common mean-ings to significant regions of experience.

philosophy.   The results of Schutzian inquiry are introspective and empirical and thus must be profoundly influenced by history and setting.   This inquiry would not fit Husserl's definition of the rigorous philosophic science of phenomenology.

It is Schutz's modified brand of phenomenology that serves as the basis of much of what is labelled today as phenomenological sociology.   This form of subjectivism involves usage of introspective techniques geared toward providing empirical (though usually nonquantitative) description of the conscious structures of meaningful social action.   Obviously, this is not foreign to some long-standing sociological approaches and certainly sounds almost synonymous with the positions of contemporary, qualitatively, and naturalistically inclined sociologists and anthropologists.   Its independence from these traditions is only partial, owing to its stricter concern for consciousness and its conceptual apparatus that has its origins in the heritage of Husserl.

Garfinkel and the Ethnomethodologists

There are many sociologists who today consider their work to be phenomenological.   It would take a book or more to sort out this work, analyze it, and then fix the degree to which the person is following the model of Husserl, Schutz, or one of the other variants of phenomenology (e.g. Merleau-Ponty, Heidegger).   Instead, it is easier, and probably more important, to consider an already influential and still rapidly growing sociological school, ethnomethodology, that purports to be phenomenological in the Schutzian sense.*

The person most often associated with the word ethnomethodology is Harold Garfinkel, who wrote the first major treatise under the rubric.   However, this book, *Studies in Ethnomethodology* (Garfinkel, 1967), is so abstrusely written that it created as much confusion as it did popularity for the approach.   Garfinkel suggests that

---

* Although there are many variants of phenomenology, the Schutzian brand (due to its social focus) is most often adhered to by phenomenological sociologists, even those not calling them ethnomethodologists.

ethnomethodology is concerned with the routine activity of everyday life and the modes of consciousness through which it is maintained. This concern has its origins in the work of Husserl, as well as Schutz, who had reinterpreted Husserlian concepts in terms of his own system. Garfinkel follows in the tradition of Schutz's phenomenology, applying this approach in sociological inquiries on the microscopic level. Ethnomethodology implies that basic to achieving an understanding of man must be an analysis of the intersubjective structures that order his everyday life and make his interaction predictable. These structures are so ingrained in the interactive process that man normally tends not to be aware of them as his self creations. Rather, he takes them to be a segment of his natural environment. Garfinkel sees these to constitute a set of assumptive rules that are constantly maintained, validated, and even altered in the process of everyday activity of mundane life.

Garfinkel considers all men to be practical theorists engaging in forms of rational action through which they manage the settings and processes of everyday affairs. This all takes place in a social context requiring mutual definition and understanding of each other's activity. Garfinkel (1967:77–78) suggests that such understanding is predicated on what he refers to as *documentary interpretation,* where actors constantly interpret and reinterpret each other's behaviors as expressions of an underlying pattern (of deeply held normative expectations).

> The method consists of treating an actual appearance as "the document of," as "pointing to," as "standing on behalf of" a presupposed underlying pattern. Not only is the underlying pattern derived from documentary evidences, but the individual documentary evidences in their turn are interpreted on the basis of "what is known" about the underlying pattern. Each is used to elaborate the other. (Garfinkel, 1967:78)

Thus, both the external behavior and the assumed pattern are related in such a systematic way that alterations in the former lead to reinterpretation of the latter. The social rules that structure everyday life have a rather tenuous existence since they are constantly in the process of being constituted and reconstituted. According to Garfinkel, the normative structure or appearance of normative structure lives, grows, dies, and is reborn in the context of everyday, face to face, interactive behavior.

Ethnomethodologists depart drastically from the objectivist conception of normative structure that dominates the social facts paradigm. That is, the idea that norms are social facts, with an objective existence, which are deeply internalized, are coercive on man, and narrowly channel his activities.

> This is where ethnomethodologists radically depart from the established approaches in sociology, including symbolic interactionism which still concentrates on the shared symbols and meanings of everyday activities, even if these symbols are seen as the result of negotiations and interpretations and, therefore, have a precarious, constantly shifting existence. Ethnomethodologists, on the other hand, maintain that social order including all its symbols and meanings, exists not only precariously but has no existence at all *independent* of the members accounting and describing practices. (Dreitzel, 1970:XV)

As is stressed in the quotation above, the ethnomethodologist is even more radically subjectivist in orientation than the symbolic interactionist. According to the ethnomethodologist, the symbolic interactionist still attributes too much independence to a quasi-objective set of symbols and pre-established meanings. On the other hand, the ethnomethodologist refuses to admit the significance of practically anything outside of the constitutive practices of actors. Ethnomethodology's approach stands almost as a negation of social factism, or even to any traces of social factism that may exist in subjectivist approaches like symbolic interactionism. Instead of depicting intersubjective reality as static, overarching, and radically objectified, ethnomethodology sees it as a modifiable, partially individuated process that has an existence no deeper than the interpretive procedures of the actors who experience it. Ethnomethodology focuses upon the ongoing process of reality construction that is constantly emerging from the activity of actors in carrying on their everyday life. Furthermore, it is in the accounts (actor's explanations of their action) of these actors that the experience and maintenance of social structure is revealed. Thus, sociologists must also rely on "documentary interpretation" to understand this process. In other words, the social scientist must depend on the actor's (practical theorists) definitions, not his own constructions, to faithfully depict this living reality.

One of the most widely known elements in Garfinkel's approach is the "ethnomethodological experiment." These experiments are calculated attempts to upset the reality of the participants in an interactive situation. The experimenter enters or even brings about such situations and then grossly violates some or many of the subtle rules that govern the event. Most importantly, the actors are ignorant of his machinations.

Garfinkel (1967) gave several examples of these experiments, most of which his students carried out in settings involving peers or family. All involved radical departures from the "normal" routines of face-to-face interaction. For example, each of the students engaged acquaintances in conversation insisting on great clarity and detail of information not normally revealed. Cues usually used to communicate unwillingness to give this information were systematically ignored by the experimenters (students). The experimenter said to person A: "How do you feel?" Person A replied, "very well." The experimenter said "why?" Person A replied, "I don't know." The experimenter insists on more information saying "you must know why!" Well, the scenario intensifies as the experimenter insists relentlessly for information that the person does not know how to give or does not want to give. Finally, the point is reached where the normal, taken for granted reality of the situation is destroyed along with the expected communicative routine. Garfinkel (1967:54–55) said in this respect:

> In short, the member's real perceived environment on losing its known-in-common background should become "specifically senseless." Ideally speaking, behaviors directed to such a senseless environment should be those of bewilderment, uncertainty, internal conflict, psycho-social isolation, acute and nameless anxiety along with various symptoms of acute depersonalization. Structures of interaction should be correspondingly disorganized.

The type of experiment discussed above may seem quite senseless and even inhuman, but the ethnomethodologist sees it as basic to his inquiries. He argues that actors are often unaware of the rules that govern interaction. As mentioned earlier, these rules reside in the ongoing process of reality construction. One way of uncovering them is by radically upsetting this process. It is at the point of dissolution that interactants are likely to express revealing accounts concerning the rules that structure the overturned routines. Furthermore, such disruptions can also indicate alternative modes of reality construction that the disturbed interactant uses to reestablish a definition of the situation. In any respect, such experiments are done to expose both the structure and flexibility that characterize human interaction.

Ethnomethodologists emphasize the necessity of trust and confidence among interactants so that each will uphold the reality (or illusion of reality) of joint activity. If an interactant exhibits an unwillingness to abide by the routines that promote the prescribed definition of situation, joint activity along with the experience of reality begins to dissolve and may even eventually collapse. The ethnomethodologist studies the forces that maintain or dissolve this reality. This inquiry is microscopic. He sees social order emerging from the agreements that exist between actors in joint activity, and being upheld in a series of negotiations that crystallize in mutual expectations.

Phenomenological Sociology:
Principal Elements

The discussion of Husserl, Schutz, and Garfinkel only touches upon some of the major aspects of phenomenological sociology. As I mentioned earlier, there are many sociologists, too numerous to discuss, now working in this tradition. It would be a burdensome task to discuss the diverse research and writing of these individuals. Instead, at the risk of oversimplification, I will attempt to analyze what I believe to be the principal elements of this approach.

Concern for the Subject. The reader is reminded of Husserl's attack on the founding idea of natural science; there is a discoverable objective reality governed by natural law. According to the natural scientist, this reality and its laws must be approached by means of the scientific method involving a systematic empiricism governed by the rules, procedures, and techniques of objective observation and validation. Those using this method attempt to minimize the effects of subjectivity, for they see subjectivity to be the source of distorted, biased, and inaccurate information. Remember, according to the natural scientist, the subject does not constitute reality, instead he provides the lens through which reality (although somewhat distorted) can be seen. The natural scientist's main concern is to peer through the haze of this lens, attempting to minimize the violence that the subject does to reality. Needless to say, the approach of natural science differs radically from that of phenomenological sociology.

The objectivist approach in sociology is characterized by Durkheim's (1964) insistence that we treat social facts as things. Carried to its extreme, this approach suggests that we objectively gather data about social facts while minimizing the importance of man's perceptions and ideas about social reality. Such an extreme objective empiricism focuses upon ecological information and data on observable behavior rather than social definitions. Few sociologists of this type are so pure in their objectivity. However, many social factists attempt to be as objective as possible and often treat their data as if they were the taproot of objective reality. They imply that the attitudes of actors provide interiorized pictures (however imperfect) of the external reality that they desire to study. The goal of *objectivist* sociology is to study empirical regularities that are taken to be reflections of the external laws of an objective social reality independent of man's constitutive activity.

The phenomenologically oriented sociologist does not accept this conception of reality. Instead of one natural, objective order independent of man, he sees multiple, shifting realities that are profoundly dependent upon man. The phenomenological sociologist believes that it is man who constitutes and reconstitutes these realities. Therefore, his consciousness is no longer viewed as a necessary impediment to study, but instead becomes the focus for study itself. It should be stressed, however, that he does not negate the existence of external reality. Instead, he brackets it (not arguing for or against its existence), suggesting that there is no way of knowing it. To the phenomenological sociologist, the dictim of W. I. Thomas—to define a situation as real makes it real in its consequences, becomes a pervasive concern. Holding to this idea, he attempts to uncover the subjective definitions of social actors. To return to "the facts themselves" the social phenomenologist must have the utmost respect for such definitions and must take great care not to distort them through the lenses of his own deductive concepts.   In fact, he works from the ground up, constantly shaping his concepts to fit the realities as seen through the eyes of those he is observing.   The social phenomenologist attempts, in a sense, to break down barriers that establish distance between himself and his subjects.   Psathas (1972:132–133), a well-known phenomenological sociologist, states this position well.

> The distinction between natural science and social science, as Natanson, Schutz and others clearly point out, is based on the fact that men are not only objects existing in the natural world to be observed by the scientist, but they are creators of a world, a cultural world, of their own.   In creating this world, they interpret their own activities.   Their overt behavior is only a fragment of their total behavior.   Any social scientist who insists that he can understand all of man's behavior by focusing only on that part which is overt and manifested in concrete, directly observable acts is naive, to say the least.   The challenge to the social scientist who seeks to understand social reality, then, is to understand the meaning that the actor's act has for him.   If the observer applies his own categories or theories concerning the meanings of acts, he may never discover the meanings these same acts have for the actors themselves. Nor can he ever discover how social reality is "created" and how subsequent acts by human actors are performed in the context of *their* understandings.

Some scholars react to this kind of description by arguing that phenomenological sociology does not sound any different from some traditional modes of sociological inquiry.   Indeed, there are similarities.   Severyn Bruyn (1966:12), states, "The interests of the phenomenologist and the participant observer are remarkably similar. . . ."   This similarity exists because the origins of phenomenological sociology lie not only in philosophy but also in symbolic interactionism, which has utilized participant observation as a basic tool.   Furthermore, it owes a huge debt to Max Weber and his method of *verstehen*.

Focus on Paramount Reality and the Natural Attitude.   In their studies, phenomenological sociologists generally focus upon the taken-for-granted world of everyday activity.   This is what Schutz calls "paramount reality"—a reality so basic and mundane that we are often not directly cognizant of it.   We live in this reality in the "natural attitude," a mode of consciousness through which we come to experience the world of everyday life to be a natural realm in the world. In this state, man is oblivious to the fact that it is he who constitutes the social world. He loses sight of the fact that it is he who is engaged in constant interaction and negotiation from which reality emerges.

The phenomenological sociologist desires not to study social facts, but instead, the process through which social facts are created by man. He desires to study the ongoing process of reality construction in society. He does not grant social facts objective existence; instead, he argues they only have the appearance of objective facticity. They are in reality the extensions of man's own social existence. They are the products that result from man's unique ability to objectify this existence. He is in the constant process of building a network of communications that mirror his social life. This network of communications has a *sui generis* reality separate from the consciousness of any one individual, and thus can be experienced by man as an objective facticity.

Berger and Luckmann (1967:61) state that *"society is a human product. Society is an objective reality. Man is a social product."* This means that man externalizes his existence in objectifications, he experiences these objectifications as objective reality and is himself emergent from within the parameters of these objectifications. Thus, while the social factist studies social facts as coercive on man, the phenomenological sociologist studies how men engage in the process of creating the maintaining social facts that are coercive on him.

To do this, the phenomenological sociologist must uncover the processes through which social order emerges from the negotiative behaviors of everyday settings. It is from these settings that the appearance of paramount reality is constructed, upheld, and through which constraint is experienced.

The Microscopic Focus.   The phenomenological sociologist tends to work on the microscopic level.* He focuses on this level

---

* There are some significant deviations from this point. There have been several European social scientists (e.g. Gurvitch, Scheler, and Vierkandt) who have applied phenomenological approaches to more macroscopic issues, especially in the area of sociology of knowledge. Today some macroscopic phenomenological inquiry is being carried out by European scholars, several of whom are identified with the "Frankfort school of neo-Marxism."

because of his concern with the reality construction and reality maintenance processes that take place at the level of face-to-face interaction. Remember, he desires to discover the interactants' definitions of the situation. To uncover these definitions the phenomenological sociologist often engages in the activities he is, at the same time, observing. To increase his understanding, he may try to experience the activities that he is observing for himself. Finally, he not only respects the accounts of actors involved in the activities, he seeks out *their* accounts of the situation. All this requires a microscopic orientation that puts the observer in as close touch as possible with the subjective experience of those actors he is observing.

Emergence, Change, Process, Activity. The phenomenological sociologist has a processual view of man and society. Both are constantly being constituted, changed, and reconstituted. The phenomenological sociologist sees social order not as a static entity but instead as a dynamic process. He is not simply interested in describing social order, but desires to understand how it is created and maintained in daily interaction. Dreitzel (1970:XV) describes this emphasis in his discussion of ethnomethodology.

> Thus the focus of interest is not the members' everyday activity but rather the process by which members manage to produce and sustain a sense of social structure. In this view, the norms and rules that govern social behavior and provide for orderly structure and sequence of events are an accomplishment of the interpretation which actors give to such events.

Men, according to the approach of phenomenological sociology, are not passive receptacles into which norms are deposited. The behaviorist and social factist assumption that man is basically a complex, normatively programmed automaton is abandoned in favor of an active, voluntaristic conception in which man manipulates and molds norms in accordance with his activity. The phenomenological sociologist never takes norms and roles for granted. Their existence is problematic since they are constantly being altered through activity and reinterpreted in *accounting* practices. According to this orientation, man is continually "becoming." He is emerging from his activity and his struggle to impose order and meaning on an essentially meaningless world and absurd existence (*see* Lyman and Scott, 1970).

123

Due to the subjectivist approach of the phenomenologist, orde and meaning cannot have an objective existence in the world. Instead, the phenomenologist sees order and meaning as being imposed on the empirical world by man. It is exactly in this ability to constitute reality from a mass of undifferentiated, meaningless sense datum, that man's defining quality, his ability to constantly transcend his condition, emerges. A reality created by man is potentially a reality that can be altered in terms of the needs of man.

Through the eyes of the phenomenological sociologist, order ceases to be a "given," the world is characterized by conflict and disorder as much as harmony, and change hangs over the social world (no matter how *reified*) * as a perpetual possibility. As Garfinkel's ethnomethodological experiments reveal, order and social reality have a tenuous existence that can be overturned by violation of the assumptive rules of routine activities. The individual then takes on enormous proportions, since he has within his power the ability to maintain or destroy (at least temporarily) the social world of those with whom he comes in contact. Goffman (1961:80–81) describes this power beautifully:

> The process of mutually sustaining a definition of situation in face-to-face interaction is socially organized through rules of relevance and irrelevance. These rules for the management of engrossment appear to be an insubstantial element of social life, a matter of courtesy, manners and etiquette. But it is to these flimsy rules, and not the unshaking character of the external world, that we owe our unshaking sense of realities. To be at ease in a situation is to be properly subject to these rules, entranced by the meanings they generate and stabilize; to be ill at ease means that one is ungrasped by immediate reality and that one loosens the grasp that others have to it. To be awkward or unkempt, to talk or move wrongly, is to be a dangerous giant, a destroyer of worlds. As every psychotic and comic ought to know, any accurately improper move can poke through the thin sleeve of immediate reality.

* To reify means literally to make real. In applying this to social facts it means to give them an existence like physical facts separate from man's productive ability. By treating social facts in this way one attributes to them a timeless quality and implies that they must be adjusted to, rather than altered or changed. For example, when we attribute the causation of war to any timeless source whether it be God, biological nature, social nature, or the requisites of social organization, we put war beyond man's willful activity. When war is conceptualized in this fashion, it is not likely that man's willful activity can eliminate it.

METHODS

Those who accept the social definition paradigm tend to use the observation method in their research. This choice of method is, of course, made necessary by the nature of the social definition paradigm. The social definitionists, as has already been pointed out, are primarily concerned with understanding intrasubjective and intersubjective reality by studying social action and interaction. Social definitionists are interested in examining such issues as: the way a taxi driver deals with his fare, how a group comes to define an individual as deviant, or how a person's failure to follow conventional rules of behavior disrupts the group. This research is used as an aid in understanding man's conscious processes as well as how man is able to share in subjective states of consciousness with other men. This focus on intrasubjective and intersubjective *processes* discourages the questionnaire/interview type of research because this technique is best suited to gathering information on static variables. The laboratory experiment technique would seem to be amenable to process-oriented research, but it is infrequently used by social definitionists. I think that the reason lies in the fact that they are interested in spontaneous, "natural" processes and the structure of sociological experiments militates against such spontaneity and naturalness. The technique best suited to the demands of social definitionist research is observation because it allows the researcher to examine process over time in a natural setting.

One of the questions I will be raising is whether the observation technique actually fits (i.e. is congruent with) the social definitionist paradigm. Similarly, in Chapter 2 I have questioned whether interviews and questionnaires really tell us about social facts, and in Chapter 4 I will discuss whether experiments really tell us about behavior.

Does observation of people in their natural setting tell us anything about the social definitions by which they orient their actions? It seems to me that the best we can do with the observation method is *deduce* the intrasubjective and intersubjective social definitions that led to the actions we have observed. After all, we cannot see social definitions which exist within and between the minds of the people we are observing. We could ask about the social definitions by which an individual operates, but are we likely to get an accurate reply from an individual? Can a respondent give us an accurate description of his social definition? Will what he tells us be distorted either consciously or unconsciously? I think distortion is likely because most people are either unaware of, or distort, the real social definitions behind their actions. Social definitions are largely unconscious; thus, we cannot rely on how they are described by respondents.

Social definitionists are forced back to observing action and interaction and deducing operating definitions from them. In addition, phenomenologists seek to disrupt everyday behavior in order to observe operant social definitions. Nevertheless, we do not actually *see* social definitions when we are doing observational studies, but we do gather information that allows us to make deductions on the nature of the operant social definitions.

The observation technique requires systematic surveillance and reporting of social behavior by trained researchers. Several things serve to make sociological observation more rigorous than lay observation. The sociologist is trained to be aware of realities of life that might pass unnoticed were the observer a layman. When he ventures into the field, the sociological observer is looking for a number of specific things and is therefore much more likely to uncover some subtleties of social action that would escape the layman. Despite this focus, the sociological observer frequently happens on one thing when he is looking for something else. Although he is doing his research for a specific purpose, the sociological observer must always be open to unforeseen, but significant, occurrences. One of the great strengths of sociological observation is its flexibility, which allows for a variety of unforeseen contingencies. Sociological observation is also superior to the lay variety because data is systematically recorded rather than being haphazardly accumulated. Because they are systematically recorded, one is better able to verify the results of sociological studies using the observation technique. We can be more certain of the validity of these studies because they are ultimately published and subjected to the critical review of fellow professionals. All in all, sociological observation, although it is the "softest" of the sociological methods, is far more rigorous than lay observation.

Types of Observation
Techniques

The "softest" of the observation techniques can be termed *exploratory* observation. This is the most subjective of these techniques and the closest to lay observation. This technique is employed by the sociologist prior to the actual conduct of the research project. He uses exploratory observation techniques to uncover issues or questions he will study when he undertakes the actual research. Exploratory observation helps to define the nature of a research project soon to be undertaken. Since this is really not a research tool, but a pre-research tool, I will concentrate on the research techniques actually used during the course of a study.

There are four types of observation techniques. Categorization of these types is based on the way the sociologist participates in the group he is studying. (Gold, 1969) When the researcher becomes a member of the group being studied, but does not tell the group that he is doing research, the technique is labelled *participant observation*. It is important to underscore the point that those who use this technique do not tell the subjects that they are doing research. The researcher may purposely mislead the subjects or simply fail to mention that in addition to belonging to the group, he is also doing research. This technique has been used on a wide variety of occasions by sociologists, most frequently when they are studying specific occupations. Sociologists have spent a good deal of time being participant observers in business organizations, taxi cabs, and at race tracks.

The second type of observation technique is labelled *participant-as-observer*. The major difference between this method and participant observation lies in the fact that in this method subjects are informed that they are being studied. This technique is more frequently used than participant observation because it avoids most of the ethical questions that arise when one disguises his true identity or intent. Ethical purity is gained at the expense of lost information because the researcher's intent and identity are known. However, devotees of this approach reply that the participants soon forget that they have a researcher in their midst and behave as they would under normal circumstances. This technique is used to answer many of the same research questions as participant observation and although some information may be lost, a number of the ethical dilemmas are avoided.

The third technique of this genre is labelled *observer-as-participant*. This method is differentiated from participant-as-observer by the fact that it is most frequently used in single visit studies and does not require multiple visits. The researcher spends an hour or a day observing his subjects rather than the weeks, months, or even years required in the two previously discussed observation techniques. Because of time limitations, this technique must, of necessity, be more structured than those discussed above. The researcher must have a fairly clear idea of what he is looking for and focus his observations on those issues. This is a more efficient method but it is also more restricted than the other two methods; the researcher is therefore less likely to make unexpected discoveries.

The final observation technique is called *complete observer*. This is the only observation method in which the researcher does not participate in the group in any way. The researcher is a total outsider and the subjects are unaware that they are being observed and studied. The researcher simply observes interaction and records what he sees without being part of the group. Or, more controversially, the researcher might use a one-way mirror to observe a group without their knowledge. This sort of observation can be carried on for long or short periods. It has the asset of most observation techniques of allowing for the discovery of unforeseen events. It can be structured or unstructured. Its major drawback lies in the fact that as an outsider the researcher is not privy to the kinds of information he would obtain as an insider.

Each observation technique is open to specific criticism and all of the techniques taken together are subject to some common attacks. Examples of specific criticisms are the attacks on participant observation for deceiving the subjects and the participant-as-observer method for distorting behavior. These criticisms exist because the subjects know a researcher is present and may wish to convey the kind of impression they think the researcher wants or that society deems appropriate. Other criticisms are aimed at all observation techniques but are not of central concern here. For example, it is argued that it is difficult to accurately record events while one is observing, events of importance may occur while the researcher is "off duty," and certain kinds of events (e.g. sex behavior, crime) are difficult, if not impossible, to observe.

The most important criticisms, however, come from devotees of the other two methods (and paradigms) discussed in this book. Many of these attacks tend to focus on the so-called "softness" of the observation technique. One thing that particularly bothers the critics is that all of the information reported in observational studies is filtered through the eyes of the researcher. They wonder how much of the data reported by observers happened only in the minds of the researchers? Thus, supporters of "harder" experimental techniques attack observational studies on the validity of their findings.

The most important criticisms by devotees of the other paradigms of the observational techniques surround the issue of the inability of the methods to lead to a cumulative body of knowledge. Observational studies are typically aimed at adding a quantum of information to the existing body of knowledge rather than building a cumulative body of knowledge. The observer is prone to gathering data in a previously unexamined tribe, culture, gang, or occupation. Collection of additional discrete bits of information is characteristic of this type of sociological research. The development of empirical generalizations, the testing of hypotheses, and the development of "theory" are frequently missing. These prerequisites to the development of a cumulative body of knowledge are possible using observation, but rather difficult. Users of the observational technique tend to become immersed in a particular setting, organization, or culture and lose sight of generalizations that have been, or could be, tested or developed. Another factor is the kind of data collected by the observer. It is more difficult to see and test common themes running through a number of studies because they are unlikely to be quantitative and most likely to be qualitative. Although theoretical development is possible using observational methods, most observers have been guilty of many of the charges levelled at them by disciples of "harder" techniques. They have frequently been satisfied with collecting esoteric tidbits of knowledge and have had little concern with the cumulative development of sociology.

Devotees of the observational technique (and the social definition paradigm) have replied to these criticisms in a variety of ways. Some maintain that cumulation is possible using the observational technique. They argue that it is occurring, although not through the "pseudoscientific" rigor of those who support other paradigms and methods. Most typically, however, the observers reply in a different manner. Many of them do not aspire to scientific status, or at least the kind of scientific status desired by those who support other paradigms and methods. To observers, sociology has at least as much in common with the humanities as the sciences. While many do not deny the possibility of becoming a science, they see it as a future goal that should not interfere with their immediate humanistic concerns. They argue that the only way to truly understand human behavior at this point in the development of the social sciences is by observing it *in vivo*. Through this technique, they can (in addition to gathering data useful to sociology) see things that might be hidden to the layman who is untrained in sociology. This is Peter Berger's (1963) *debunking* process. The goal is to uncover the myths that abound in social life and serve to deceive people. By uncovering these myths and laying bare the realities of social life, the sociologist can provide laymen with new information and insights that they can use to improve the quality of their life.

Although the cumulation of knowledge using observational techniques is difficult, it is not impossible. Let me illustrate by using a field close to my heart—the sociology of occupations. No sociological subfield has been more dominated by the observation method than the sociology of occupations. With its origins in the Chicago school of sociology (which was dominated by the theoretical approach of symbolic interactionism), this field has been dominated by one man, Everett Hughes (1971). Hughes was a major supporter of the observation approach and urged his students to use it in studies of literally hundreds of occupations. Speaking of Hughes, one of his students reminisces: "Many years ago, in a course on methods of field research, he taught us that it was fun to sally forth with pencil and notebook, like newspaper reporters to observe and to question." (Roy, 1968:49)   Using this technique, the sociology of occupations has amassed an unprecedented number of insights into life in the work world. We know that there is stress between the taxi driver and his fare and this stress focuses on the size of the tip. (Davis,

1959)   We know that janitors conflict with tenants over whose responsibility it is to perform certain tasks around the apartment building.   (Gold, 1965)   We know there is stress between the prostitute and her "john" over such issues as duration of the sexual encounter, amount of fee, and techniques to be used.   (Bryan, 1965) Similarly, we know that the jazz musician is in conflict with his "square" audience over the kinds of music he should play.   (Becker, 1951)   These and other studies of the same kind illustrate the best and the worst in the observation method.   On the positive side, we have accumulated a massive number of rich and important insights into occupational life.   On the negative side, these findings are discrete and have not, until recently, led to the development of hypotheses to be tested, let alone a theory of occupational life.

It is true that there has been little theoretical development in the sociology of occupations (as well as all other fields dominated by the observation method), but this need not necessarily be so.   It is difficult to build hypotheses and theory from observations, but it is not impossible.   Devotees of the observation approach have been guilty of not developing theory, but it can be done.   In a recent book (Ritzer, 1972), I have tried to move the sociology of occupations beyond simply a collection of interesting insights into the work world. I have attempted to develop a number of hypotheses derived from observational studies, thereby following Glaser and Strauss' (1967) advice to develop "grounded theory."   A series of discrete hypotheses is a long way from a theory of occupations, but it is a step in that direction.   The next step (although certainly not imminent) would be the interrelation of these hypotheses and the construction of a general theory.*

To take one example that relates to some occupational findings discussed above, I hypothesize that those who are employed in low status and deviant occupations that are not in organizations ("free" occupations) are most likely to be confronted with conflicts with customer/clients.   This hypothesis stems from the examples discussed above of taxi drivers, janitors, prostitutes, and jazz musicians, as well

---

* Although I opt for an inductive approach to theory development here, I am really ambivalent about the debate between deductivists and inductivists.   We currently have, in my opinion, no theory (in a formal sense) in sociology.   It is an open question as to which group, if either, will be the first to develop a theory.

as the results of many other observational studies of low status occupations not in organizations.   In contrast, I hypothesize that low status occupations found in organizations are most likely to be faced with alienation, not conflict with clients.   Examples of low status occupations in organizations include assembly-line workers, machine-tenders, and the like.   The next step is the utilization of these hypotheses (and the many others I develop in *Man and His Work*) in additional studies of these occupations.   As these studies progress, some hypotheses will be refined, others proved useless, and new ones will arise to replace those discarded and to supplement those that are retained.   The essential point is that the occupational sociologist now has hypotheses to guide his research, rather than simply a general interest in a particular occupation.   Furthermore, I hope that the groundwork is laid for a theory of occupations.*

Although the methods of the social definitionists have been criticized by those who accept other paradigms and methods, the social definitionists have not stood by idly.   They are particularly upset by the *scientism* and pseudo-scientism of those who use the harder methods of interviews, questionnaires, and experiments.   Herbert Blumer (1969) exemplifies the position taken by the social definitionist vis-à-vis these other methods. As a social definitionist, Blumer seeks to build sociology by immersing the researcher in the real world consisting of what human beings "experience and do, individually and collectively, as they engage in their respective forms of living; it covers the large complexes of interlaced activities that grow up as the actions of some spread out to affect the actions of others; and it embodies the large variety of relations between participants."   (Blumer, 1969:35)

The observation technique and those who use it are obviously in Blumer's favor, but those who use the more "rigorous" techniques are not.   In Blumer's view, they have forgotten the mandate to immerse themselves in the real, empirical world   They have substituted, instead, requirements that are met by

> . . . formulating and elaborating catchy theories, by devising ingenious models, by seeking to emulate the *advanced procedures* of

---

* Despite the course I outline here, I do not believe that theory comes from a simple pyramiding of propositions.   I think propositions are useful, but the creative sociologists must make a quantum leap from propositions to the "invention" of sociological theory.

physical sciences, by adopting the newest mathematical and statistical schemes, by coining new concepts, by developing more precise *quantitative techniques,* or by insisting on adherence to the canons of research design. (italics mine)   (Blumer, 1969:34)

Blumer is clearly opposed to these forms of scientism that serve to remove the sociologist further and further from the real world. His criticisms of more rigorous methods (and the rest of their accompanying scientific paraphernalia) , as well as his support for the social definitionist paradigm and the accompanying observational method, are clear in the following quotation:

To begin with, most research inquiry (certainly research inquiry modeled in terms of current methodology) is not designed to develop a close and reasonably full familiarity with the area of life under study. There is no demand on the research scholar to do a lot of free exploration in the area, getting close to the people involved in it, seeing it in a variety of situations they meet, noting their problems and observing how they handle them, being party to their conversations, and watching their life as it flows along. In place of such going on, reliance is put on starting with a theory or model, posing a problem in terms of the model, setting a hypothesis with regard to the problem, outlining a mode of inquiry to test that hypothesis, using standardized instruments to get precise data, and so forth. I merely wish to reassert here that current designs of "proper" research procedure do not encourage or provide for the development of firsthand acquaintance with the sphere of life under study. Moreover, the scholar who lacks the firsthand similarity is highly unlikely to recognize that he is missing anything. Not being aware of the knowledge that would come from firsthand acquaintance, he does not know that he is missing that knowledge. Since the sanctioned scheme of scientific inquiry is taken for granted as the correct means of treatment and analysis, he feels no need to be concerned with firsthand familiarity with that sphere of life. In this way, *the established protocol of scientific inquiry becomes the unwitting substitute for a direct examination of the empirical social world.* (italics mine) The questions that are asked, the problems that are set, the leads that are followed, the kinds of data that are sought, the relations that are envisioned, and the kinds of interpretations that are striven towards—all of these stem from the scheme of research inquiry instead of from familiarity with the empirical area under study.

There can be no question that the substitution of which I write takes place. The logical question that arises is, "So what?" Why is it important or necessary to have a firsthand knowledge of the area of social life under study? One would quickly dismiss this as a silly question were it not implied so extensively and profoundly in the social and psychological research of our time. So the question should be faced. The answer to it is simply that the empirical social world consists of ongoing group life and one has to get close to this life to know what is going on in it. . . .

The metaphor that I like is that of lifting the veils that obscure or hide what is going on. The task of scientific study is to lift the veils that cover the area of group life that one proposes to study. The veils are not lifted by substituting, in whatever degree pre-formed images for firsthand knowledge. The veils are lifted by getting close to the area and by digging deep into it through careful study. Schemes of methodology that do not encourage or allow this betray the cardinal principle of respecting the nature of one's empirical world.

How does one get close to the empirical social world and dig deeply into it? This is not a simple matter of just approaching a given area and looking at it. It is a tough job requiring a high order of careful and honest probing, creative yet disciplined imagination, resourcefulness and flexibility in study, pondering over what one is finding, and a constant readiness to test and recast one's views and images of the area. It is exemplified among the grand figures of the natural sciences by Charles Darwin. It is not "soft" study merely because it does not use quantitative procedure or follow a pre-mapped scientific protocol.* (Blumer, 1969:37–40)

It has been pointed out earlier and is clear in Blumer's contentions that political motives affect the battle between adherents of the methods that parallel the three paradigms. Supporters of one method often engage in an effort to elevate the importance of "their" method while, at the same time, they seek to denigrate the significance of other methods. The political character of this phenomenon is nowhere more clear than in the debate between Howard Becker and Blanche Geer (1957) and Martin Trow (1957). That debate is dealt with at this point because the debate began with Becker and Geer's effort to elevate the importance of the observation technique.

Let me simply quote from the original article by Becker and Geer in which they make the case *for* observation and *against* the interview method. In reading these remarks, the reader should keep in mind the fact that Becker and Geer are closely tied to symbolic

* Herbert Blumer, *Symbolic Interactionism: Perspective and Method*, © 1969, pp. 37–40. Reprinted by permission of Prentice-Hall, Inc., Englewood Cliffs, New Jersey.

interactionism and the Chicago school of sociology. Furthermore, they have made extensive use of the observation technique in their own research.

> The most complete form of the sociological datum, after all, is the form in which the participant observer gathers it: An observation of some social event, the events which precede and follow it, and explanation of its meaning by participants and spectators, before, during, and after its occurrence. Such a datum gives us *more information* about the event under study than data gathered by *any other* sociological method. (italics mine) Participant observation can thus provide us with a yardstick against which to measure the completeness of data gathered in other ways, a model which can serve to let us know what orders of information escape us when we use other methods.
>
> We have no intention of denigrating the interview or even such *less precise* (italics mine) modes of data gathering as the questionnaire, for there can always be good reasons of practicality, economy, or research design for their use. We simply wish to make explicit the difference in data gathered by one or the other method and to suggest the differing uses to which they can legitimately be put. In general, the shortcomings we attribute to the interview exist when it is used as a source of information about events that have occurred elsewhere and are described to us by informants. Our criticisms are not relevant when analysis is restricted to interpretation of the interviewees conduct *during* the interview, in which case the researcher has in fact observed the behavior he is talking about. (Becker and Geer, 1957:28)

Naturally, such a highly partisan statement was not left unanswered. Martin Trow replied to the Becker and Geer polemic and, in the process, made a plea for a more balanced approach to sociological research. Trow admits that participant observation is a useful method of collecting data, but he objects to Becker and Geer's implication that one method is inherently superior to any other method. Instead, he argues that the method to be used should be dictated by the problem being studied. Furthermore, most sociological problems are so complex that they require the use of multiple methods. He recognizes that each of the major sociological methods is best suited to collecting different types of data, and that these multiple types of data can then be brought to bear on the issue in question. To Trow (1957:34–35), the danger of Becker and Geer's paper "lies in the kind of exclusive preoccupation with one method that leads to a systematic neglect of the potentialities, even the essential characteristics of another."

Trow (1957:35) concludes his critique of Becker and Geer with a plea for multiple methods:

> Every cobbler thinks leather is the only thing. Most social scientists, including the present writer, have their favorite research methods with which they are familiar and have some skill in using. And I suspect we mostly choose to investigate problems that seem vulnerable to attack through these methods. But we should at least try to be less parochial than cobblers. Let us be done with the arguments of "participant observation" *versus* interviewing—as we have largely dispensed with the arguments for psychology *versus* sociology —and get on with the business of attacking our problems with the widest array of conceptual and methodological tools that we possess and they demand. This does not preclude discussion and debate regarding the relative usefulness of different methods for the study of specific problems or types of problems. But that is very different from the assertion of the general and inherent superiority of one method over another on the basis of some intrinsic qualities it presumably possesses.

In the face of the logic of Trow's argument, Becker and Geer were forced to retreat. They argued that Trow misunderstood them and that they did not say that participant observation is the best method for all sociological problems. They contended that all they said was that participant observation gives us the most complete information about social "events." By events they mean only "specific and limited events which are observable." (Becker and Geer, 1958: 39)   They now make it clear that they fully subscribe to the notion that different questions are best studied in different ways with the nature of the question determining the choice of the problem.

Despite the retreat by Becker and Geer, this debate underscores the political character of the debates between the paradigms, and more specifically, the debates between adherents of each of the major methods.

While they retreated in the face of Trow's criticisms, Becker and Geer continued to adhere to the idea that for things that we can see, participant observation is the best method. This, of course, reflects the interest of those identified with the social definition paradigm in the observation method. *If* you are interested in studying natural social processes, *then* the best method is observation. Since Becker and Geer are major exponents of the social definition paradigm, it is little wonder that they see observation (particularly participant observation) as the method best suited to the issues studied by the social definitionist.

Conclusion

In this chapter I have outlined the basic components of the social definition paradigm as well as some of the political conflicts that swirl around it. The exemplar for the social definitionist is Max Weber's work on action. It is interesting to note that Weber, like Durkheim in the social facts paradigm, does not fit neatly into the social definition paradigm. In fact, much of his work is a model of social facts analysis. He is one of the group I have labelled "paradigm bridgers." The image of the subject matter of sociology to the social definitionist is the process of social definition and the ensuing action. Put another way, it is intrasubjectivity and intersubjectivity as well as social action. The theories subsumed under the social definition paradigm are action theory, symbolic interactionism, and phenomenology. Methodologically, the social definitionists tend to prefer the observation technique.

BIBLIOGRAPHY

Becker, Howard S. "The Professional Dance Musician and His Audience." *American Journal of Sociology* 57 (1951):136–44.
Becker, Howard S., and Geer, Blanche. "Participant Observation and Interviewing: A Comparison." *Human Organization* 16 (1957):29–32.
————. "Participant Observation and Interviewing: A Rejoinder." *Human Organization* 17 (1958):39–40.

Berger, Peter. *Invitation to Sociology.* Garden City, New York: Doubleday Anchor, 1963.

Berger, Peter, and Luckmann, Thomas. *The Social Construction of Reality.* Garden City, New York: Doubleday Anchor, 1967.

Blumer, Herbert. "Society as Symbolic Interaction" in *Human Behavior and Social Processes.* Edited by Arnold Rose. Boston: Houghton Mifflin, 1962.

————. *Symbolic Interactionism: Perspective and Method.* Englewood Cliffs, New Jersey: Prentice-Hall, Inc., 1969.

Bruyn, Severyn. *The Human Perspective in Sociology.* Englewood Cliffs, New Jersey: Prentice-Hall, Inc., 1966.

Bryan, James. "Apprenticeships in Prostitution." *Social Problems* 12 (1965) :287–97.

Buckley, Walter. *Sociology and Modern Systems Theory.* Englewood Cliffs, New Jersey: Prentice-Hall, Inc., 1967.

Davis, Fred. "The Cabdriver and His Fare: Facets of a Fleeting Relationship." *American Journal of Sociology* 65 (1959) :158–65.

Dreitzel, Hans Peter. *Recent Sociology.* New York: Macmillan, 1970.

Durkheim, Emile. *The Rules of Sociological Method.* New York: The Free Press, 1964.

Freund, Julien. *The Sociology of Max Weber.* New York: Pantheon Books, 1968.

Garfinkel, Harold. *Studies in Ethnomethodology.* Englewood Cliffs, New Jersey: Prentice-Hall, Inc., 1967.

Gerth, Hans, and Mills, C. Wright, eds. *From Max Weber: Essays in Sociology.* New York: Oxford University Press, 1958.

Glaser, Barney, and Strauss, Anselm. *The Discovery of Grounded Theory.* Chicago: Aldine, 1967.

Goffman, Erving. *Encounters.* Indianapolis: Bobbs-Merrill, 1961.

Gold, Raymond. "In the Basement—The Apartment Building Janitor" in *The Human Shape of Work.* Edited by Raymond Gold. New York: Macmillan, 1965.

————. "Roles in Sociological Field Observations" in *Issues in Participant Observation.* Edited by George McCall and J. L. Simmons. Reading, Massachusetts: Addison-Wesley, 1969.

Hinkle, Roscoe. "Antecedents of the Action Orientation in American Sociology Before 1935." *American Sociological Review* 28 (1963) : 705–15.

Hughes, Everett. *The Sociological Eye.* Chicago: Aldine, 1971.

Husserl, Edmund. *Phenomenology and the Crisis of Western Philosophy.* New York: Harper and Row, 1965.

————. *Ideals.* London: Collier-Macmillan, Ltd., 1969.

Lyman, Stanford, and Marvin Scott. *A Sociology of the Absurd.* New York: Appleton-Century-Crofts, 1970.

MacIver, Robert. *Society: Its Structure and Changes.* New York: Ray Long and Richard R. Smith, Publishers, 1931.

————. *Social Causation.* Boston: Ginn, 1942.

Meltzer, Bernard. "Mead's Social Psychology" in *Symbolic Interaction.* 2d ed. Edited by Jerome Manis and Bernard Meltzer. Boston: Allyn and Bacon, 1972.

Meltzer, Bernard, and Petras, James. "The Chicago and Iowa Schools of Symbolic Interaction" in *Symbolic Interaction.* 2d ed. Edited by Jerome Manis and Bernard Meltzer. Boston: Allyn and Bacon, 1972.

Parsons, Talcott. *The Structure of Social Action.* New York: The Free Press, 1937.

Psathas, George. "Ethnomethods and Phenomenology" in *Symbolic Interaction.* 2d ed. Edited by Jerome Manis and Bernard Meltzer. Boston: Allyn and Bacon, 1972.

Ritzer, George. *Man and His Work: Conflict and Change.* New York: Appleton-Century-Crofts, 1972.

Rose, Arnold. "A Systematic Summary of Symbolic Interaction Theory" in *Human Behavior and Social Processes.* Edited by Arnold Rose. Boston: Houghton Mifflin, 1962.

Roy, Donald. "The Union Organizing Campaign as a Problem of Social Distance" in *Institutions and the Person.* Edited by Howard S. Becker, *et al.* Chicago: Aldine, 1968.

Schutz, Alfred. Collected Papers. Vol. I. The Hague: Martinus Nijhoff, 1964.

————. Collected Papers. Vol. III. The Hague: Martinus Nijhoff, 1970.

————. Collected Papers. Vol. I. The Hague: Martinus Nijhoff, 1971.

Scott, John Finley. "The Changing Foundations of the Parsonian Action Schema." *American Sociological Review* 28 (1963) :716–35.

Spiegelberg, Herbert. *The Phenomenological Movement.* The Hague: Martinus Nijhoff, 1969.

Tiryakian, Edward A. "Existential Phenomenology and Sociology." *American Sociological Review* 30 (October, 1965) :674–88.

Trow, Martin. "Comment on 'Participant Observation and Interviewing: A Comparison.'" *Human Organization.* 16 (1957) :33–35.

Troyer, William. "Mead's Social and Functional Theory of Mind" in *Symbolic Interaction.* 2d ed. By Jerome Manis and Bernard Meltzer. Boston: Allyn and Bacon, 1972.

139

Turner, Jonathan, and Beeghley, Leonard. "Current Folklore in the Criticisms of Parsonian Action Theory." Paper presented at Meetings of the American Sociological Association, August 1972.

Weber, Max. *The Theory of Social and Economic Organization.* New York: The Free Press, 1947.

————. "Social Action and Its Types" in *Theories of Society.* Edited by Talcott Parsons, *et al.* New York: The Free Press, 1961.

Znaniecki, Florian. *Method of Sociology.* New York: Farrar and Rinehart, 1934.

————. *Social Actions.* New York: Farrar and Rinehart, 1936.

4

*The
Social
Behavior
Paradigm*

EXEMPLAR

Behaviorism has a long and honorable history in the social sciences, in particular in psychology. However, its modern resurgence in all of the social sciences, and in particular in sociology, can be traced to the work of B. F. Skinner. In my opinion, it is his work that is the exemplar for the sociologists who have endeavored to translate the principles of behaviorism into sociological tenets. Skinner's work, while single-mindedly devoted to the principles of behaviorism, has covered a broad spectrum including scientific tracts (Skinner, 1938), a utopian novel (Skinner, 1948), and polemical and political essays (Skinner, 1971). He has also been in the forefront of those who have tried to develop practical applications of behaviorism—a good example of which is the famous crib he designed for his daughter using the principles of behaviorism. His scientific, utopian, political, and practical work have all played a role in the development of a sociological variant of behaviorism. In recent years Skinner has become more of a public figure and less of a scientist. This has prompted criticism from some sociologists who were heavily influenced by his scientific work (*see* Homans, 1969:23). Despite these later shifts, the body of Skinner's work remains the exemplar for those who work within the social behaviorist paradigm.

We need not go into detail at this point on Skinner's behavioristic principles. They will be covered later in the discussion of the two sociological theories that are heavily behavioristic—behavioral sociology and exchange theory. It would be useful at this point to distinguish Skinner's views from the other two paradigms discussed in this book—social factism and social definitionism.

I think it is fair to say that Skinner regards both social factism and social definitionism as mystical perspectives. That is, they are both seen as constructing mystical entities that serve to distract the sociologist from the only concrete entities of study—behavior and contingencies of reinforcement. Skinner (1971) directly attacks the social definitionist in *Beyond Freedom and Dignity* and has only indirect criticisms of the social facts paradigm in that book. However, he does level some criticisms that can be seen as attacks on the social factist. Take, for example, Skinner's (1971:121) criticism of the concept of a culture defined by a typical social factist as "traditional (i.e. historically derived and selected) ideas and especially their attached values." He argues that this definition has created unnecessary mystical elements such as "ideas" and "values." One does not see ideas and values when he looks at society, instead he sees "how people live, how they raise their children, how they gather or cultivate food, what kinds of dwellings they live in, what they wear, what games they play, how they treat each other, how they govern themselves, and so on." (Skinner, 1971:121)   Thus, the culture of a community *is composed of behaviors.* In order to understand behaviors we do not need concepts like ideas and values; we need instead to understand contingencies of reinforcement.

Although Skinner is disturbed by the social factist paradigm, he levels his most acid criticisms at the social definitionists. One of Skinner's major goals in *Beyond Freedom and Dignity* is the elimination of an idea which he labels "autonomous man" from the social sciences (indeed, from the world). The idea of an autonomous man is an integral part of the social definition paradigm (for example, Parsons' idea of voluntarism is close to Skinner's hated autonomous man) and an attack on it is also an attack on the social definitionists. Thus, Skinner, speaking for social behaviorism, is in no mood to reconcile his differences with the social definitionists. It fact, he is interested in eliminating the social definition paradigm.

What is this notion of an autonomous man? To Skinner, we imply that man is autonomous when we attribute to him such things as feeling, minding, freedom, and dignity. Man, in this view, has some sort of inner core from which his actions emanate. He is able to initiate, originate, and create, because of this inner core. This active, creative, voluntaristic view of man is clearly in line with the social definitionist position. Thus, Skinner's effort to destroy the

143

idea that man is autonomous is, indirectly, an effort to destroy social definitionism.

To Skinner, the idea that man has an inner, autonomous core is a mystical, metaphysical position of the kind that must be eliminated from the social sciences: "Autonomous man serves to explain only the things we are not yet able to explain in other ways. His existence depends on our ignorance, and he naturally loses status as we come to know more about behavior." (Skinner, 1971:12)   It is *behavior* as well as the conditions (primarily other behaviors) that produce behavior, that is the focal subject matter to Skinner. We need not be concerned with mediating concepts such as "feelings"; all we need examine (and control) is behavior and the contingencies that affect it.

IMAGE OF THE SUBJECT MATTER

Social behaviorists are interested in the relationship between the individual and his environment. The environment is composed of a variety of social and nonsocial objects. The social behaviorist argues, however, that the principles governing the relationship between an individual and a social object *are the same* as those that govern the relationship between an individual and a nonsocial object. Bushell and Burgess (1969:27) define the nature of the subject matter of the behaviorist as "the behavior of individuals that operates on the environment in such a way as to produce some consequence or change in it which, in turn, modifies subsequent performances of that behavior." Thus, the focus is on the "functional relationship" between behavior and changes in the environment of the actor. This means that a child tossing a stone into a river is an object of study to the behaviorist in exactly the same way as a mother scolding a child, a teacher instructing his class, or a business executive meeting a board of directors.

Social behaviorists claim they are focusing on an interaction process, but it is conceptualized very differently from social definitionists. The actor, to the social definitionist, is a dynamic, creative force in the interaction process. He is not simply responding to stimuli, but interpreting these inputs and acting on the basis of the way he defines these inputs. The social behaviorist, on the other hand, allows the individual far less freedom. The individual's response is determined by the nature of the external stimuli. The image is of a much more mechanical man than that conceived by the social definitionists.

The image held by the social factist is almost as mechanistic as the perspective of the social behaviorist. The social factist sees the individual as determined by external norms, values, structures and the like. The difference between social factism and social behaviorism lies in the source of control over the individual. To the social factist, it is macroscopic structures and institutions that control the individual. The question is far more microscopic for the social behaviorist as he is concerned with the relationship between individuals and contingencies of reinforcement.

THEORIES

Behavioral Sociology

Behavioral sociology constitutes a theoretical effort to apply the principles of psychological behaviorism to sociological questions. The behavioral sociologist is concerned with the relationship between the consequences of behavior in the actor's environment and the behavior of the actor. In variable terms, the consequences are the independent variable while the occurrence of behavior is the dependent variable. This means that the behavioral sociologist seeks to explain behavior by the environmental consequences that follow it. It is obviously almost metaphysical to try to explain the present in terms of the future. What the behavioral sociologist is interested in is the relationship between the *history* of environmental consequences for behavior and the nature of present behavior. The behavioral sociologist is saying that the past consequences of a given behavior govern its present state. By knowing what elicited a certain behavior in the past, we can predict whether an actor will enact the same behavior in the present situation. This is admittedly a little confusing. We need to introduce some of the concepts of behavioral sociology in order to clarify the nature of this theory.

A key concept to the behavioral sociologist is *reinforcement,* which may be defined as a reward. There is nothing inherent in an object that makes it a reward. Reinforcers cannot be defined on *a priori* grounds apart from their effects on behavior. A reinforcer is defined in terms of its effect on the actor. Thus, a "reward" that does not affect the actor is *not* a reinforcer. Food might be considered a general reward in our society, but if a given individual is not hungry, it will not serve as a reinforcer. What, then, determines whether a given reward will, in fact, serve as a reinforcer? One crucial determinant is the actor's level of deprivation. If the actor has been deprived of food, he will be hungry and food will act as a reinforcer. If, on the other hand, he has just eaten, his level of deprivation will be minimal and food will not be an effective reinforcer.

The example used here is physiological deprivation. If we deny man food, sex, water, or air, they will serve as potent reinforcers. If, on the other hand, these physiological needs are well met, they will not be useful reinforcers. But reinforcers are not just physiological; they can also be learned. That is, we learn to need certain things. Once we learn to need these things, they serve as reinforcers when we are deprived of them.

Reinforcers may be either positive or negative. Positive reinforcement is defined as follows: ". . . where environment changes take the form of presenting or adding stimulus events which thereby increase the probability of behavior occurring in the future." (Bushell and Burgess, 1969:28–29) This is the situation in which the actor is rewarded, such as the salesman who knocks on a door and makes a sale. Negative reinforcement also acts to increase the likelihood of a behavior occurring in the future. This may take the form of something being removed or subtracted from the environment. The turning off of a noisy radio, for example, may improve one's ability to write or read. Thus, in the future, one's ability to write or read may be improved when the radio is turned off.

Obviously, if we are considering reinforcers, we must also take punishment into account. Bushell and Burgess (1969:29) define punishment as follows: "A consequence which decreases the frequency of the response that precedes it is a *punisher*." The whip, or even the mere threat of a whip, may serve to prevent someone from repeating a given act. Now it is clear that what is a punishment to one person may be a reward to another. A masochist may find the whip rewarding and would be more likely to repeat the act in question. We must know about the individual's physiological properties as well as his personal history in order to determine in many cases whether something will be a reward or a punishment.

Punishments, like reinforcers, can be either positive or negative, but remember, punishers are aimed at reducing the frequency of a response. Whipping a child every time he cries is an example of a positive form of punishment. Punishment can also take a negative form when we remove or threaten to remove a reward. This is labelled *response cost* or loss of reinforcers. If we remove or threaten to remove privileges enjoyed by a child because he is crying, we are employing a negative form of punishment. It is interesting to note that Bushell and Burgess (1969:30) argue that this form of punishment, response cost, "is the mainstay of control procedures in social organizations." Rather than reward or positively punish, most social organizations prefer to remove, or threaten to remove, rewards already being enjoyed.

As was pointed out in the beginning of this chapter, the behavioral sociologist is primarily concerned with the relationship between the actor and his environment. Contingencies are built into this relationship and the behaviorist focuses much of his attention upon these. The reinforcement-punishment relationship between the actor and his environment occurs in patterns, some of which are determined by nature and some of which are socially determined. The simplest pattern is when reinforcement follows each and every act. This pattern is most likely to be found in childhood where, for example, a child's cry is immediately followed by attention from parents. This is less likely to occur in adulthood. In fact, adult reinforcement is much more likely to be intermittent, with reinforcement occurring at a very uneven pace. The traveling salesman does not expect every knock on the door to produce a sale. The knocks on the door do lead to infrequent sales and this keeps the salesman on the job. If he was never rewarded, his sales behavior would be *extinguished* and he would cease functioning as a salesman. Interestingly, continuously reinforced behavior is more easily extinguished than intermittently rewarded behavior. The salesman becomes accustomed to intermittent reward and it takes him a great deal of time to realize that he is not going to be rewarded again. It would take him a long time to give up (for his behavior to be extinguished). If he had been rewarded continuously, and the rewards suddenly stopped, he might continue for a short time. He would cease his activities far more quickly than had he been rewarded intermittently.

Reinforcement is far more complex than simply doing something and receiving the desired (or undesired) reaction. There are many conditions in the environment that determine the probability for reinforcement of a given act. Some conditions serve to make response more likely while others make it less likely. These are things that have in the past been associated with a reinforcement or a punishment. If, for example, the person doing the reinforcing has always worn some sort of uniform, that uniform may elicit a given response even when it is worn by someone else. Similarly, if the classroom has always been associated with punishment, a suitable response to punishment will be elicited even if the student is transferred to a rewarding classroom situation. This is the process by which originally neutral stimuli became secondary or conditioned reinforcers. Once transformed, a neutral stimulus can become a positive reinforcer with the capability of increasing behaviors that precede it. Since reinforcement rarely occurs in a vacuum, a number of secondary reinforcers inevitably become associated with the original one. By this process the number of reinforcers inevitably mushrooms.

Although many reinforcers are specific to a given situation, there are some that are *generalized reinforcers*. Generalized reinforcers are defined by Bushell and Burgess (1969:38) as reinforcers that

. . . have great power and importance in social analysis because they retain their effectiveness in the absence of any specific deprivation. The term 'generalized' refers to the fact that these stimuli stand for, represent, or provide access to, a wide range of other reinforcers, both unconditioned and conditioned, which may differ from time to time and from person to person.

148

Money and status are two good examples of generalized reinforcers. They are reinforcers that can be used to acquire many other desirable things.

Since generalized reinforcers are discriminative for a number of other things, they became more and more reinforcing in themselves. The individual is also seen by the behavioral sociologist as difficult to satiate in terms of generalized reinforcers. Large amounts of money or status are not likely to dull the desire for more.

When a given response is reinforced, a whole series of other responses similar to the one being rewarded are almost inevitably rewarded at the same time. It is this fact that allows the behavioral sociologist to talk of *shaping behavior* or *behavior modification*. Let me illustrate this with a diagram adapted from one used by Bushell and Burgess: (1969:40) :

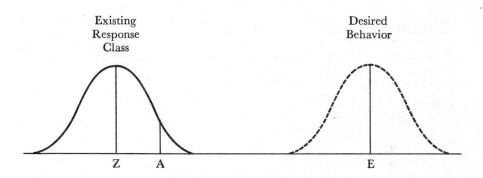

Because we possess a given reward, we are able to elicit behavior Z from an individual. Now in eliciting this behavior we are also eliciting a number of similar behaviors including A. Suppose the behavior we really want to elicit is E. How do we get our subject to elicit behavior E? We begin by rewarding A, which is already in our range of elicited responses. By repeatedly eliciting A, we move the center of the curve over A and bring behaviors closer to E, the desired behavior, within our range. By doing this over and over, we ultimately will elicit behavior E. This process is illustrated in the diagram on the following page:

149

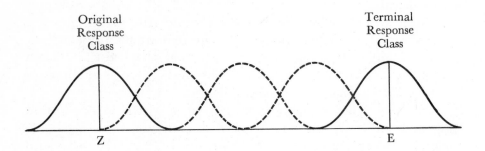

The process of shaping behavior outlined above has been adapted to therapeutic situations and labelled *behavior modification.* Behavior modification is seen as a six-step process:

1. The therapists must identify the specific final behaviors that they are interested in eliciting.
2. They must determine the nature of the existing response class of the subject, i.e. what range of behaviors are currently being elicited and how close are they to the desired behavior.
3. Construct a favorable training site. "This means eliminating distracting stimuli, the possibility of conflicting or incompatible behavior, and providing stimuli which are discriminate for the desired response." (Bushell and Burgess, 1969:43)
4. Establish motivation in the subject by acquiring an effective reinforcer. Although they can be specific reinforcers, general reinforcers such as money, social attention, and social status are most often used.
5. Begin the shaping process by "differential reinforcement of responses that are successively closer to the terminal state." (Bushell and Burgess, 1969:43–44)
6. Finally, when the modification has "taken," the therapist should allow the reinforcers to become more intermittent and slowly transform the reinforcement from an artificial device to the natural world.

Interestingly, it is the applied aspect of behavioral sociology that is one of the things that sets it apart from other sociological theories, including exchange theory. Very little applied sociology has emerged from other sociological theories. There are exceptions, of course, such as the human relations school, which sought to manipulate group processes in order to increase the productivity of workers. All in all, behavioral sociology has far more of an applied character than any other sociological theory.   Behavior modification has been used on retarded children (Birnbauer, *et al.,* 1965), autistic children (Brawley, *et al.,* 1969), preschool children (Bushell, *et al.,* 1969), and even college students (Miller, 1970).   Although applied activity distinguishes behavioral sociology from other sociological theories, I am more interested in exploring theoretical than practical differences.

All of these principles of behavioral sociology are virtually indistinguishable from psychological behaviorism.   Thus, behavioral sociologists have made a self-conscious effort to apply their ideas to phenomena that are the domain of sociology.

Take the sociological concept of socialization.   Burgess and Bushell (1969:275) define socialization as "an interactional process whereby an individual's behavior is modified to conform to the rules or standards of the groups to which he belongs."   This is a fascinating definition of socialization given our preceding discussion of social definitionism and social factism.   Behavioral sociologists do, if one can judge from this definition, recognize the importance of the interactional process and they admit the existence of something called a group.   This will be of some consolation to those who support the other two paradigms, but the thrust of their definition of socialization will not.   Socialization is seen by the behaviorist as simply a process of behavior modification.   This is clearly at variance with the views on the socialization process held by the adherents of the other paradigms. In both paradigms one finds the idea that there is a "mind" that intervenes between the socialization process and behavior.   It is true, however, that the mind is a very different entity to the supporters of the two paradigms.   To the social factist, the mind is often little more than a receptacle for that which is communicated during the socialization process. To the social definitionist, the mind is a much more active and creative force.   Nevertheless, in both paradigms, the mind intervenes between the socialization process and behavior.

Let us examine one more example of a definition of a traditional sociological concept by the behavioral sociologists.   "The 'self' may be parsimoniously defined as the overt and covert verbal statements an individual uses to describe his own physical characteristics and behavior patterns."   (Burgess and Bushell, 1969:284)   Again, the self is a very different thing to those who accept the other paradigms. Social factists devote relatively little attention to the self because it is the kind of active, creative aspect of the mind that they see controlled by external social forces.   Furthermore, it is far too microscopic an issue for most social factists to be concerned with.   On the other hand, the self is a central concept of social definitionists, in particular George Herbert Mead.   Mead's "self" is highly unpredictable and is a much more important component of social life than simply one's verbal descriptions of himself.   The self is an important source of voluntarism in Median theory and, more generally, in symbolic inter-actionism.

The position enunciated by Bushell and Burgess is not without its political opponents.   The social definitionist seems to be the most hostile to the social behaviorist because of his omission of the human-minding process.   This viewpoint is well-expressed by Kurt Back (1970:1100) in his review essay of Burgess and Bushell's *Behavioral Sociology*:*

> The other evasion technique . . . is the general flight from human-ity.   Many scientists exhibit a tremendous talent, even a joy, in find-ing some human behavior which can be explained in a non-human way by reference either to an animal model or to a completely me-chanical model . . . When the history of current social science is written, it will be largely a story of treating social science as if it were something else, or trying to get away from the human properties of human beings, and of the strange faith of scientists who can measure exactly stimulus and response to reinforcement.

The discussion of the way behavioral sociologists treat two socio-logical concepts, socialization and self, illustrates how they seek to redefine these concepts to be congruent with the basic tenets of behaviorism.   Such efforts offer little hope of reconciling social behaviorism with other sociological paradigms.

Exchange Theory

Although exchange theory can be traced back to the work of Cha-vannes (Knox, 1963) and Mauss (1954), it has enjoyed a contempo-

---

* George Homans, "Sociological Relevance of Behaviorism," in *Behavioral Sociology* by Robert Burgess and Don Bushell, Jr. (New York: Columbia University Press, 1969) .

rary boom in the work of George Homans. Much of Homans' exchange theory can be viewed as a reaction to the social facts paradigm. It will be useful to begin by outlining his criticisms of the social facts paradigm. Homans (1969) confronts the social factists by directly attacking the work of Emile Durkheim* on three points: the issue of emergence, his view of psychology, and his method of explanation. Let us examine each criticism.

Homans recognizes that during interaction new phenomena emerge. He feels that such a view is acceptable to social behaviorists. The question, however, is how do we explain that which emerges out of interaction? Do we need any new propositions to explain the emergent properties of interaction beyond those that apply to simple behaviors? Homans' rhetorical reply is, as you might have expected, negative. "All the usual examples of emergent social phenomena can readily be shown to follow from psychological propositions." (Homans, 1969:14)

Homans rightly points out that since Durkheim was writing in the late nineteenth century, he had an extremely primitive conception of psychology. After all, the psychology that Durkheim was attacking at that time was far less sophisticated than the present version. Psychology in his day focused primarily on instinctive forms of behavior and assumed that human nature was the same universally. Thus, Durkheim was right in disentangling sociology from the psychology of the day: "Sociology is surely not a corollary of the kind of psychology Durkheim had in mind." (Homans, 1969:18) Contemporary psychology is a far cry from the psychology of Durkheim's day and just because Durkheim was able to separate the two at that time, does not mean that the same feat can also be accomplished today.

Finally, Homans attacks Durkheim on his method of explanation. Homans argues that Durkheim considered something explained if we were able to find its cause or causes. More specifically, a social fact is explained when we can find the social facts that cause it. Homans admits that social facts are often the cause of other social facts, but such a finding does not in his view constitute an explanation. To Homans, what needs to be explained is the *relationship*

---

* We have already seen how Durkheim's work does not fit neatly into the social facts paradigm. He is a "paradigm bridger."

between cause and effect and that relationship is always explained by
psychological propositions.   We need to explain why one social fact
causes another social fact.   To Homans (1969:19), that explanation
is inevitably psychological.*   He cites the following as an example of
what he means:

> The price rise of the sixteenth century, which I take to be a social
> fact, was certainly a determining cause of the enclosure movement
> among English landlords.   But were we to construct an explanation
> why this particular cause has this particular effect, we should have
> to say that the price rise presented English landlords both with great
> opportunities for monetary gain and great risks of monetary loss,
> that enclosure tended to increase the gain and avoid the loss, that
> the landlords found monetary gain rewarding (which is a state of
> individual consciousness, if you like), and, finally, that men are
> likely to take actions whose results they find rewarding—which, as I
> cannot repeat too often, is a general psychological proposition.

Thus, psychological variables always intervene between social
facts; they are the effective cause of the dependent social fact.   Homans is arguing that social facts lead to psychological changes that
lead to new social facts, but that the essential factor is psychological,
not the social fact.

Homans also attacks the social facts paradigm more directly.   He
chooses to focus, on the explanation of *institutions*, which he defines
as "relatively persistent patterns of social behavior to whose maintenance the actions of many men contribute."   (Homans, 1969:6)
He argues that four methods have been used to analyze institutions
and the two he rejects are associated with the social facts paradigm.
The first is the *structural* explanation, which argues that a "particular institution exists because of its relation to other institutions in a
social system."   (Homans, 1969:6)   To Homans, to assert that
certain institutions are correlated with others does not explain them,
nor do *functional* explanations do the job.   Functional explanations
contend that "the institution exists because the society could not
survive or remain in equilibrium without it."   (Homans, 1969:6)
This, of course, is a vulgar form of functional explanation that ig-

---

* It should be noted that when Homans uses the term *psychological* he means *behavioral*, "the behavior of men as men," as he puts it.

nores the modern work on the subject, such as that of Robert Merton (1968). Having set up a straw man, Homans (1969:9) proceeds to the attack:

> The trouble with functional explanations in sociology is not a matter of principle but of practice. From the characteristic general proposition of functionalism we can draw the conclusion in logic that a society failing to survive did *not* possess institutions of type x —whatever x may be. Now there are societies—a very few—that have not survived in any sense of the word. For some of these societies we have accounts of the social organization before their disappearance, and it turns out that they did not possess institutions of type x. If these societies failed to survive, it was not for lack of social institutions, unless resistance to measles and alcohol may be a social institution. That is, there is inadequate evidence so far for the truth of the general propositions of functionalism—and after all truth does make a difference. It is conceivable that the difficulties will be overcome, that better statements of the conditions for the survival or equilibrium of any society may be devised, from which nothing but true conclusions will be drawn. But in spite of endless efforts nothing of the sort is in sight. Whatever its status in principle, functional explanation in sociology is in practice a failure.

We should not be surprised that Homans has succeeded in slaying functionalism. After all, he has depicted functionalism in such a way that he could not fail. He would have received more accolades had he chosen to attack structural-functionalism together since that is the way they are most often used by contemporary sociologists. If he had taken on Merton's functional paradigm, rather than a vulgar form of functionalism that no contemporary functionalist would support, we could take Homans more seriously. Taking only easy targets, Homans can cavalierly conclude that structural explanation is no explanation at all and functional explanation is unsatisfactory since it leads to false, as well as true, conclusions.

Homans uses the label *historical* for the third form of institutional explanation. Interestingly, he sees historical explanation as basically *psychological explanation*—the fourth type of institutional explanation according to Homans. He sees institutional change as ubiquitous and its study as central to sociology, but when we do an historical analysis correctly we must come to the conclusion that the explanation of this change lies at the psychological level:

155

All human institutions are products of processes of historical change. In fact, most institutions are continually changing. When we have enough factual information, which we often do not, even to begin explaining historical change, and when we try to supply the major premises of our unstated deductive systems, we find that there are certain premises we absolutely cannot avoid using, and that these premises are not propositions about the interrelations of institutions, as in structural explanation, or propositions about the conditions for the survival of societies, as in functional explanation, but propositions about the behavior of men as men, ... That is, they are psychological propositions; in their major premises history and psychology are one.   (Homans, 1969:11)

In sum, Homans is arguing that change must be explained by sociologists and any explanation of change will be psychological at its base.   Let us examine the example he uses to make this point.

Homans chooses to exemplify his position with the example of the introduction of power-driven machinery into the English textile industry in the eighteenth century.   He argues that this event is of great sociological importance since it was one of the first steps in the Industrial Revolution that led to many of our present-day institutions.   He takes as his starting point the growth in the English export of cotton in the eighteenth century which "led to an increased demand on the part of the industrial entrepreneurs for supplies of cotton thread, a demand that was not fully met by the existing labor force, spinning thread by hand on spinning wheels, so that the wages of spinners began to rise, threatening to raise the price of cloth and thus check the expansion of trade."   (Homans, 1969:10)   To prevent this, people associated with the textile industry, cognizant of power-driven machines in other sectors, discovered that water power or steam machines could spin several threads at a time and prevent a rise in wages that would, in turn, reduce trade.   Driven by the thought of higher profits, many tried to develop such machines, and some succeeded.

Homans argues that this process can be reduced to a deductive system that would explain why entrepreneurs took the actions they did.   This deductive system, based upon psychological principles, takes the following form:

1. Men are likely to take actions that they perceive are, in the circumstances, likely to achieve rewarding results.
2. The entrepreneurs were men.

3. As entrepreneurs, they were likely to find results in the form of increasing profits rewarding.　(Homans, 1969:11)

Starting with the basic assumption about the psychological nature of man, Homans argues that he has explained the coming of power-driven machines to eighteenth century English textile industry.　Using this example, Homans concludes that historical change can be explained only by psychological principles.　Homans has drummed the social facts paradigm out of sociology and argued that the only true sociology is based on psychological principles.　Homans, however, is more than simply polemical; he has tried to develop a theory based on psychological principles and I would like to turn to it now.

Homans' theory consists of five basic propositions.　Although some deal with at least two interacting individuals, he is careful to point out that they are psychological principles.　According to Homans, they are psychological for two reasons.　First, "they are usually stated and empirically tested by persons who call themselves psychologists."　(Homans, 1967:39–40)　More importantly, they are psychological because of the level with which they deal with the individual in society: "they are propositions about the behavior of individual human beings, rather than propositions about groups or societies as such; and *the behavior of men, as men,* is generally considered the province of psychology." (italics mine)　(Homans, 1967: 40)　This last reason is, of course, the more important explanation and is what causes me to include Homans' views in this chapter on the social behavior paradigm.

Although Homans makes the case for psychological principles, he does not think of individuals as isolated.　He recognizes the obvious fact that man is social and spends a considerable portion of his time interacting with other men.　Thus, he is interested in explaining man's social behavior, but with psychological principles: "What the position [Homans'] does assume is that the general propositions of psychology, which are propositions about the effects on human behavior of the results thereof, do not change when the results come from other men rather than from the physical environment."　(Homans, 1967:59)　Homans does *not* deny the Durkheimian position that something new emerges from the interaction of men.　Homans argues that those emergent properties can be explained by psycho-

logical principles. There is no need for new sociological propositions to explain social facts; psychological principles will suffice. He
uses the basic sociological concept of a norm to illustrate what he
means:

> The great example of a social fact is a social norm, and the norms of
> the groups to which they belong certainly constrain towards con-
> formity the behavior of many individuals. The question is not that
> of the existence of constraint, but of its explanation . . . . The
> norm does not constrain automatically: individuals conform, when
> they do so, because they perceive it is to their net advantage to con-
> form, and it is psychology that deals with the effect on behavior of
> perceived advantage.   (Homans, 1967:60)

Thus, Homans does not deny the existence of social facts, he simply
argues that their effect on individuals is explained through the use of
psychological principles.

In numerous publications Homans has detailed a program to, in
his words, "bring men back in" to sociology. In addition to polem-
ics, Homans has tried to develop a theory that focuses on psychology,
man, and/or the "elementary forms of social life." That theory has
come to be called *exchange theory*. Exchange theory, according to
Homans, "envisages social *behavior* as an exchange of activity, tangible or intangible, and more or less rewarding or costly, between at
least two persons." (italics mine)

In the example discussed above, Homans sought to explain the
rise of motor-driven machinery, and thereby the industrial revolution, through the psychological principle that men are likely to act
in such a way as to increase their rewards. In his version of exchange
theory, he seeks to explain elementary social behavior in terms of
rewards and costs. He is motivated in part by the work of the social
factists, in particular the structural functional theories of his acknowledged "colleague and friend," Talcott Parsons. He argues that such
theories "possess every virtue except that of explaining anything."
(Homans, 1961:10)   The social factists, as epitomized by Parsons, have done little more than create conceptual categories and
schemes. Homans admits that a scientific sociology needs such categories, but sociology "also needs a set of general propositions about
the relations between the categories, for without such propositions

explanation is impossible.   No explanation without propositions!"
(Homans, 1961:10)   Homans, therefore, sets for himself the task
of developing these propositions that focus on the psychological level
and form the groundwork of exchange theory.

In *Social Behavior: Its Elementary Forms* (1961), Homans acknowledges that his exchange theory is derived from both behavioral
psychology and elementary economics, although in his later work its
economic component is played down.   The basic ideas of exchange
theory are traceable to economic theory.   The models there are the
exchange of goods in a barter economy and the exchange of money in
a capitalistic economy.

Homans begins his development of exchange theory with a discussion of the exemplar of the behaviorist paradigm, B. F. Skinner's
work, in particular his study of *pigeons*.

> Suppose, then, that a fresh or naive pigeon is in its case in the labo-
> ratory.   One of the items in its inborn repertory of behavior which
> it uses to explore its environment is the peck.   As the pigeon wan-
> ders around the cage pecking away, it happens to hit a round red
> target, at which point the waiting psychologist or, it may be an auto-
> matic machine, feeds it grain.   The evidence is that the probability
> of the pigeon's emitting the behavior again—the probability, that is,
> of its not just pecking but pecking the target—has increased.   In
> Skinner's language, the pigeon's behavior in pecking the target is an
> *operant;* the operant has been *reinforced;* grain is the *reinforcer;* and
> the pigeon has undergone *operant conditioning*.   Should we prefer
> our language to be ordinary English, we may say that the pigeon has
> learned to peck the target by being rewarded for doing so.   (Ho-
> mans, 1961:18)

It is on the humble backs of Skinner's pigeons and the principles
derived from their study, that George Homans sought to develop
his brand of social behaviorism.   The difference in this instance is
that Skinner is interested in pigeons while Homans is interested in
humans.

According to Homans, Skinner's pigeons are not engaged in a
true exchange relationship with their mentor.   The pigeon is engaged in a one-sided exchange relationship while human exchanges
are always two-sided.   The pigeon is being reinforced by the grain,
but the psychologist is not truly being reinforced by the pecks of the

pigeon. The pigeon is carrying on the same sort of relationship with the psychologist as he would with the physical environment. Since there is no reciprocity, Homans defines this as individual behavior. Homans seems to relegate the study of this sort of behavior to the psychologist, while the sociologist is urged to study social behavior "where the activity of each of at least two animals reinforces (or punishes) the activity of the other, and where accordingly each influences the other." (Homans, 1961:30)   However, and this is important, *no new propositions* are needed to explain social behavior as opposed to individual behavior. The laws of individual behavior as sketched by Skinner in his study of pigeons fits social behavior as long as "the complications of mutual reinforcement are taken into account." Homans admits that he may ultimately have to go beyond the principles derived by Skinner, but only reluctantly.

Before turning to the actual propositions developed by Homans, we need one more piece of information—the kind of behavior he is focusing on. Homans in his theoretical rather than polemical work restricts himself to everyday, ordinary, elementary social interaction. It is clear that Homans believes that a sociology built on his principles will ultimately be able to explain all social behavior. This expansion aside, let me give you the case Homans (1961:31) uses to exemplify the kind of exchange relationship he is interested in:

> Suppose that two men are doing paper-work jobs in an office. According to the office rules, each should do his job by himself, or, if he needs help, he should consult the supervisor. One of the men, whom we shall call Person, is not skillful at the work and would get it done better and faster if he got help from time to time. In spite of the rules he is reluctant to go to the supervisor, for to confess his incompetence might hurt his chances for promotion. Instead he seeks out the other man, whom we shall call Other for short, and asks him for help. Other is more experienced at the work than Person; he can do his work well and quickly and left with time to spare, and he has reason to suppose that the supervisor will not go out of his way to look for a breach of rules. Other gives Person help and in return Person gives Other thanks and expressions of approval. The two men have exchanged help and approval.

Although Homans will ultimately deal with more complex social behavior, this is basically the level at which his exchange theory is aimed, at least initially.   Focusing on this sort of situation, and based on Skinner's findings on pigeons, Homans develops five propositions that lie at the base of his exchange theory of social behavior.

Homan's first proposition focuses on the relationship between past and present behavior.   "If in the past the occurrence of a particular stimulus-situation has been the occasion on which a man's activity has been rewarded, then the more similar the present stimulus-situation is to the past one, the more likely he is to emit the activity, or some similar activity, now."   (Homans, 1961:53)

To illustrate this proposition, as well as the others, Homans uses the example of Person and Other in the office situation described above.   A substantial proportion of the activity each emits in that situation is both a reward *and* a stimulus for further activity.   When Person is helped by Other he is being rewarded by Other, while at the same time Other is stimulating Person to reward him by expressing his thanks.   Some activities may, in themselves, have little reward-value.   Homans uses the example of Person's original request of help from Other.   This may, in itself, carry no reward for Other. It still can be an effective stimulus if in the past such a request has been followed by action on the part of Other for which he did receive a reward, such as an expression of appreciation.   Other is more likely to help in the present if in the past such action has proven rewarding to him.   This, of course, is a conditional statement.   If Other has not been rewarded in the past, he will not help now.   If the present situation is similar to past situations, and Other has been rewarded in the past, Other will be likely to help Person.   The more similar the present situation is to past situations, the more likely Other is to help.

Even at this early stage in the development of his position Homans is forced to admit the inadequacies of his analysis.   He admits that men are far more complicated than pigeons and it is, therefore, not an easy matter to determine what makes a man discriminate between stimuli.   According to Homans, (1961:58) language makes the analysis more problematic for man than pigeon: "With a man the discriminations may be the result not only of his everyday experience but also of his formal education, his reading, and the verbal arguments he may have listened to."   It is this type of complexity that causes Homans (1961:53) to throw up his hands: "Obviously the problem of the relations between stimuli, past activities, and

161

present ones is of the first importance, yet we shall state no further general propositions about it, and accordingly this book falls *far short* of being a complete psychology." (italics mine)   In effect, Homans is ignoring the concerns of the social definitionists and he recognizes that this severely limits the generality of his position.

Having dealt with the relationship between past and present behavior, Homans turns to the issue of the frequency of reward and activity, and offers a second proposition, "The more often within a given period of time a man's activity rewards the activity of another, the more often the other will emit the activity."   (Homans, 1961: 54)

This proposition places the burden of maintaining a relationship on *both* Person and Other.   If either party reduces the frequency with which he rewards the other, the frequency of response by the other party will correspondingly fall off.   If Person reduces the number of times he thanks Other for his help, there will be a decline in the number of times Other will help Person.   Ultimately, the relationship could theoretically be terminated if Person ceases thanking (rewarding) Other altogether.   Conversely, the more Person thanks Other, the more Other will help Person.

Frequency is only one of the variables Homans considers in analyzing interaction.   Value of the activity is also important and the addition of this factor leads Homans (1961:55) to his third proposition: "The more valuable to a man a unit of the activity another gives him, the more often he will emit activity rewarded by the activity of the other."

We must consider the value of an activity in addition to its frequency.   If either party ceases to consider the activity of the other as valuable (isn't this a social definition?), their relationship will be terminated.   Conversely, if Person decides, for whatever reason, that an activity of Other has grown in importance to him, he will respond by offering more rewards than he has in the past.   Frequency of interaction between Person and Other is contingent on both the frequency with which one rewards the other and value each places upon those activities.

Here Homans introduces a new concept that he labels *rate of exchange*.   The rate of exchange between two activities is defined by the "number of units of activity Person emits within any limited period of time in return for a specific number of units emitted by Other." (Homans, 1961:55)   Homans makes it clear here that his exchange theory is really a nonmonetary form of economics and that the idea of rate of exchange is analogous to price. In economics, the price of a commodity specifies the number of its units needed to be exchanged for another commodity. Interaction, in Homans' view, operates much the same way as the economic system. In terms of his third proposition, Homans (1961:55) says: ". . . the rate of exchange between approval and help should tend to equal the ratio between the value Person puts on help and the value Other puts on approval; for if Person values help relatively more than Other values approval, then he is likely to give relatively more approval than Other gives him." The economic character of Homans' social behaviorism is clearest at this point.

In his fourth proposition, Homans gets into the issue of satiation. He begins to take into account the fact that if you have been rewarded in the recent past, additional units of reward are going to become increasingly less valuable to you. In terms of the example of Person and Other, the more help Person has recently received, the less likely he is to ask for help or to reward Other by thanking him. This kind of thinking leads Homans to his fourth proposition: "The more often a man has in the recent past received a rewarding activity from another, the less valuable any further unit of that activity becomes to him." (Homans, 1961:55)

Homans' orientation becomes even more like economics at this point, as he introduces the concepts of costs and profits to his notion of rewards. He defines the cost of a unit of an activity as the value of the reward that could have been attained through an alternative activity which was foregone because the given activity was emitted. For example, the cost to Other of helping Person is the rewards he could have received doing his own work, but which he surrendered in order to help Person. Profit is defined as reward minus cost and Homans argues that no exchange relationship continues unless both parties are making a profit. Thus, Other will keep giving advice to Person until such time as that activity is no longer profitable to him.

Homans introduces one final proposition that deals with why people get angry in exchange relationships. To explain this, Homans introduces the notion of distributive justice: are the rewards and costs distributed fairly among the individuals involved? The relationship between distributive justice and anger leads Homans (1961:75) to his last proposition "The more to a man's disadvantage the rule of distributive justice fails of realization, the more likely he is to display the emotional behavior we call anger."

As you might have guessed, Homans' exchange theory unleashed a torrent of criticism in sociology and that debate lingers to this day. To illustrate the controversy, I will analyze some of Abrahamsson's (1970) criticisms of exchange theory. Abrahamsson is most upset by the fact that the concept of "reward" is not clearly defined by Homans. The way it now stands, contradictory sorts of events can be fitted under the heading of rewards; doing something good and doing something evil can both qualify as rewards. Obviously, we must be able to specify whether something will be rewarding by examining the nature of the person and the situation. Some types of people may find doing good deeds rewarding, while others may find malevolence similarly rewarding. What is rewarding in one situation may not be rewarding in a different situation.

Abrahamsson also argues that in order to make exchange theory useful, we must be able to quantify the "merchandise" exchanged. It is not enough to say that "some" advice is given and "some" social approval is returned. The need to quantify clearly opens a whole can of worms. How, for example, can we quantify social approval? Such things as social approval are created at the moment of exchange and therefore cannot be quantified because they do not exist prior to the occurrence of the act of exchange.

Finally, in Abrahamsson's view, Homans tends to focus an overt behaviors and ignores the inner experiences of the actors: "Knowing the *experiences* of individuals and their perceptions of rewards of certain acts is often of great importance for understanding and predicting their behavior." (Abrahamsson, 1970:283)   This constitutes an effort to push exchange theory into the social definitionist camp. Such an effort has also been made by Singelmann (1972) and we shall deal with it later in this chapter. Abrahamsson concludes his analysis of exchange theory by calling it a tautology and "no theory at all." He asserts that it is "highly convenient for extensive *ex post facto* interpretations." That is, exchange theory is useful in terms of explaining something after it occurs, but far less useful in predicting future occurrences.

I could obviously expand at this point summarizing and cataloging the numerous criticisms of Homans' position. However, I prefer to discuss it in relation to the other two paradigms discussed in this book. I want to focus on the attacks of the social factists and social definitionists on the behaviorist paradigm as it is expressed in the theories of George Homans. In order to accomplish this, I will include the following in the remainder of this section. First, I will examine Talcott Parsons' criticisms of Homans from the social facts position. Then I will turn to the work of Peter Blau and his effort to respond to the criticisms of the social factists by extending exchange theory beyond elementary social behavior. Finally, I will examine Singelmann's effort to reconcile exchange theory and social definitionism. His work is important because it simultaneously represents a criticism of social behaviorism from the social definitionist perspective and an effort to reconcile the two.

Taking the social facts position, Parsons (1964) criticizes Homans' use of, and orientation toward, *elementary* social behavior. Parsons' (1964:207) basic quarrel with Homans concerns "just how far Homans wishes to press his claims of generality." Homans defines elementary social behavior as uninstitutionalized action and interaction taking place on a face-to-face basis in small groups.

> Yet Homans' discussion of the relevance of psychological principles to social behavior is, although worked out and illustrated entirely at this elementary level, apparently generalized to cover all social systems at whatever level. . . . The sense, however, in which for example, the relation of the frequency of psychological reward to the emission of given types of behavior governs the relations between the United States and the Soviet Union, is not immediately clear. The point is that Homans has never attempted to show how the "reduction" of sociology to psychological principles is useful at the macroscopic levels. Yet he generalizes his doctrine to sociology as a whole. (Parsons, 1964:207)

In other words, Parsons charges that Homans has only *said* his elementary principles govern social facts, but he has never demonstrated that to be true.

Parsons pinpoints two basic differences between himself and Homans. First, he contends that Homans tends to "slur" over the difference between the behavior of men as men and animals as animals. Parsons, on the other hand, sees a very clear line dividing the behavior of men from the behavior of other animals. Thus, to Parsons, principles that can be used to explain human behavior are qualitatively different from those used to explain animal behavior. Parsons objects to Homans' derivation of human exchange principles from Skinner's study of pigeons.

Parsons' (1964:216) second objection is even more crucial: "I would insist that the most general formulations applicable to men as men (which *I* would call principles of *action,* rather than psychological) do *not* suffice to explain the phenomena of organization of the complex subsystems of action."*   In other words, psychological principles do not, indeed cannot, explain social facts. Homans has been unable to show how psychological principles apply at more macroscopic levels. As Parsons (1964:216) says, "At the very least Homans is under obligation to show how his principles can account for the principal structural features of large scale social systems and the generalized media of exchange within them. . . ." He concludes that even if Homans were to try, he would inevitably fail because social facts are independent variables capable of explaining, and being explained, beyond Homans' psychological principles:

> The alternative to this (Homans') emphasis is to see acting units as part of organized systems, which have properties other than those attributable to isolated units and the most general conditions of interaction between "men as men." They have languages, cultural values, legal systems, various kinds of institutional norms and generalized media. Concrete behavior is not a function simply of elementary properties, but of the kinds of systems, their various structures and the processes taking place within them. From this point of view it is quite legitimate to be concerned with the organization of complex systems when the features of these organizations must be described, classified, and otherwise ordered long before their properties can be derived from elementary principles. . . .   (Parsons, 1964:219)

In reply to Parsons, Homans (1971) maintains that the key issue concerns explanations of the structures and institutions of complex societies: "Here is the nub of the matter. Parsons thinks psychological propositions do not suffice to explain them; I think they do."

---

* It is interesting to note that Parsons is also admitting a discontinuity between his earlier interest in action and his later interest in structure.

(Homans, 1971:375)   This quotation has a childish quality about it with each party steadfastly asserting his rightness and the other's wrongness. Nevertheless, it is the nub of the issue. Homans recognizes that social facts emerge out of interaction, but he thinks they can be explained by psychological principles. Conversely, Parsons thinks that only social facts explain social facts.

Homans (1971:376) replies to Parsons' (and others) attack on his position with a counterattack aimed at social factists:

> Let them therefore specify what properties of social behavior they consider to be emergent and show, by constructing the appropriate deductive systems, how they propose to explain them without making use of psychological propositions. I guarantee to show either that the explanations fail to explain or that they in fact use psychological propositions, in however disguised a form.

We are, thus reduced to a series of charges and countercharges with both parties claiming that the other's theory has little explanatory power. Replying to Parsons' statement that he is under an obligation to show how his principles can explain the structural features of large-scale societies, Homans (1971:376) says: "I am under no more obligation than Parsons is under himself, who has not shown how his principles can explain the existence of these principal structural features. Indeed, it is not at all clear what his principles *are*." And here is where we are left. Parsons says Homans has not explained structure and Homans says Parsons has not explained structure. This kind of polemical dialogue between exchange theory and social factism clearly is futile. However, it does succeed in clarifying once again the battle lines between the social facts and behaviorist paradigms.

While Homans and Parsons do not move beyond a simple declaration of the boundaries that separate them, Peter Blau (1964) does in his effort to develop an exchange theory that combines social behaviorism and social factism. Blau's (1964:2) goal is "an understanding of social structure [based upon] an analysis of the social processes that govern the relations between individuals and groups. The basic question . . . is how social life becomes organized into increasingly complex structures of associations among men." Blau is clearly, in his first paragraph, charting a course carrying him beyond Homans' concern with elementary forms of social life into complex structures. In working in this middle ground, Blau focuses on the process of exchange which, while not guiding all of human behavior, does direct much of it. To Blau, exchange underlies relationships among individuals, as well as among groups. In effect, Blau sees a four-stage sequence leading from interpersonal exchange to social structure to social change:

- Step one: Personal exchange transactions between people, gives rise to
- Step two: Differentiation of status and power, which leads to
- Step three: Legitimation and organization, that sows the seeds of
- Step four: Opposition and change.

Let us briefly follow Blau through each of these steps in order to better understand how he seeks to bridge the gap between social behaviorism and social factism.

On the microscopic level Blau and Homans are interested in similar processes. However, Blau's concept of social exchange is limited to actions that are contingent, rewarding reactions from others, which cease when expected reactions are not forthcoming. People are attracted to each other for a variety of reasons; it is this force that induces people to establish social associations. Once initial ties are forged, the rewards they provide each other serve to maintain and enhance the bonds. The opposite situation is also possible with insufficient rewards causing an association to weaken or break. Rewards that are exchanged can be either intrinsic (e.g. love, affection, respect) or extrinsic (e.g. money, physical labor). Both parties cannot always reward each other equally, and out of this fact stems a differentiation of power within an association.

When one party needs something from the other, but has nothing comparable to offer in return, he has four alternatives open to him. First, he can force the other person to help him. Second, he can find another source to obtain what he needs. Third, he can attempt to get along without what he needs from the other. Finally, and most important, he can subordinate himself to the other, thereby giving the other person generalized credit in their relationship which the other person can draw on when he wants him to do something.

All of this sounds very close to Homans' position, but there is an importance difference—Blau extends his theory to the level of social facts.   He notes, for example, that we cannot analyze these processes of social association apart from the social structure that surrounds them.   While it is true that social structure emerges from social associations, once social structures emerge they have a separate existence that affects the processes of association.

Social associations exist first within social groups.   A person is attracted to a group of people when he feels that the association will offer more rewards than alternatives open to him.   Because he is attracted to them, he wants to be accepted by them.   In order to be accepted in the group he must offer others rewards, thereby demonstrating that he has something to offer to them.   In order to do this, he seeks to impress the group members by showing that associating with him will be rewarding.   His relationship with the group members will be solidified when they are impressed by him and he, in turn, receives the rewards he expects.   Yet, while trying to be impressive leads to cohesion, it can also lead to competition and ultimately social differentiation when a number of individuals are actively seeking to impress others with their abilities to reward.   The paradox here is that although an impressive person can be an attractive associate, his distinguishing characteristics arouse fears of dependence in other group members and cause them to acknowledge their attraction to him only reluctantly.   In the early stages of group formation, competition for social recognition among group members is actually a screening test for potential leaders of the group.   Those best able to reward are most likely to end up in leadership positions. Other group members with less ability to reward will want to continue to receive the rewards offered by the potential leaders and this will usually more than compensate for their fears of becoming dependent on them.   Ultimately, those individuals with the greater ability to reward emerge as leaders and the group is differentiated.

The inevitable differentiation of the group into leaders and followers creates a renewed need for integration.   Once they have acknowledged the leader's status, followers have an even greater need for integration.   In the past, followers flaunted their impressive qualities.   Now, in order to achieve integration among the followers, they flaunt their weaknesses.   This flaunting of weaknesses is, in effect, a public declaration of the fact that they no longer want to be leaders. This self-deprecation leads to sympathy and social acceptance from the other also-rans.   The leader (or leaders) also engages in some self-deprecation at this point, in order to improve group integration. By admitting that subordinates are superior to him in some areas, the leader reduces the pain associated with subordination and demonstrates that he does not seek control over every area of group life. These types of forces serve to reintegrate the group despite its new, differentiated status.

All of this is reminiscent of George Homans' exchange theory, but about midway through his book Blau extends Homans' reductionism to social factism.   Blau differentiates between two types of social organization.   The first type, in which Blau recognizes the emergent properties of social groups, emerges from the processes of exchange and competition discussed above.   Exchange theorists and behavioral sociologists also recognize this differentiation, but there is, as we will see, a basic difference between Blau and "purer" social behaviorists on this issue.

The second type of social organization is not emergent but is explicitly established for the purpose of achieving specified objectives—whether manufacturing goods that can be sold for a profit, participating in bowling tournaments, collective bargaining, or winning political victory.   (Blau, 1964:199)

When Blau begins discussing these complex social organizations, he moves beyond the "elementary forms of social behavior" that are typically of interest to the social behaviorist.   Given these two types of organizations we find that differentiation either emerges out of the process of interaction or is given in the construction of an organization.   Out of this inevitable differentiation are sown the seeds of opposition and conflict.

When Blau moves beyond Homans' elementary forms of behavior and into complex social structures, he must adapt exchange theory to the social facts paradigm.   Blau (1964:253) recognizes the essential difference between small groups and large collectivities while Homans minimizes this difference in his effort to explain all social behavior in terms of basic psychological principles:

> The complex social structures that characterize large collectives differ fundamentally from the simpler structures of small groups.   A structure of social relations develops in a small group in the course

of social interaction among its members. Since there is no direct social interaction among most members of a large community or entire society, some other mechanism must mediate the structure of social relations among them.

This statement is interesting and requires careful scrutiny. Blau is, on the one hand, clearly ruling out social behaviorism as an adequate paradigm for dealing with complex social structures. Interestingly, he is also ruling out the social definitionist paradigm since he argues that social interaction and the social definitions that accompany it do not occur directly in a large-scale organization. Thus, starting from the social behavior paradigm, Blau is clearly aligning himself with the social facts paradigm when it comes to dealing with more complex social structures. Let us explore how Blau seeks to transform exchange theory into social factism.

For Blau, the mechanisms that mediate between the complex social structures are the norms and values (the value consensus) that exists within society:

> Commonly agreed upon values and norms serve as media of social life and as mediating links for social transactions. They make indirect social exchange possible, and they govern the processes of social integration and differentiation in complex social structures as well as the development of social organization and reorganization in them. (Blau, 1964:255)

There are other mediating mechanisms between social structures, but Blau focuses upon value consensus. Looking first at social norms, Blau argues that they serve to substitute indirect exchange for direct exchange. One member conforms to the group norm and receives approval for that conformity and, implicitly, for the fact that conformity contributes to the group's maintenance and stability. In other words, the group or collectivity (either is a social fact) is now engaged in an exchange relationship with the individual. This is in contrast to Homans' simpler notion that only allowed for interpersonal exchange. Blau gives a number of examples of collectivity-individual exchanges replacing individual-individual exchanges:

> Staff officials do not assist line officials in their work in exchange for rewards received from them, but furnishing this assistance is the offi-

cial obligation of staff members, and in return for discharging these obligations they receive financial rewards from the company.

Organized philanthropy provides another example of indirect social exchange. In contrast to the old-fashioned lady bountiful who brought her baskets to the poor and received their gratitude and appreciation, there is no direct contact and no exchange between individual donors and recipients in contemporary organized charity. Wealthy businessmen and members of the upper class make philanthropic contributions to conform with the normative expectations that prevail in their social class and to earn the social approval of their peers, not in order to earn the gratitude of the individuals who benefit from their charity. (Blau, 1964:260)

The norm in Blau's formulation moves us to the level of exchange between an individual and collectivity, but it is the concept of values that moves Blau to the most macroscopic level and the analysis of the relationship between collectivities. The central role played by values in Blau's more macroscopic conception of exchange theory is clear in the following quotation:

Common values of various types can be conceived of as media of social transactions that expand the compass of social interaction and the structure of social relations through social space and time. Consensus on social values serves as the basis for extending the range of social transactions beyond the limits of direct social contacts and for perpetuating social structures beyond the life span of human beings. Value standards can be considered media of social life in two senses of the term; the value context is the medium that molds the form of social relationships; and common values are the mediating links for social associations and transactions on a broad scale. (Blau, 1964: 264)

In Blau's view there are four basic types of values, each of which performs different functions. *Particularistic* values are the media of integration and solidarity. These values serve to unite the members of a group "and extend the scope of integrative bonds far beyond the limits of personal feelings of attraction." (Blau, 1964:267) These are seen as being similar at the collective level to sentiments of personal attraction that serve to unify individuals on a face-to-face basis. Particularistic values also serve to differentiate the in-group from the out-group, thereby enhancing their unifying function.

172

The second type of values are *universalistic* values. These are standards by which the relative worth of the various things that can be exchanged are assessed. It is the existence of these standards that allows for the possibility of indirect exchange. An individual may make a contribution to a sub-segment of a community and the existence of universalistic values allows the community to assess the value of the contribution, rewarding the individual in an appropriate manner (e.g. give him higher social status) .

The social values that legitimate *authority* are the third type. The value system that accords some people more power than others extends the scope of organized social control. This is particularly related to the final type of value system—values of *opposition*. The existence of opposition or revolutionary values allows for the spread of a change—orientation beyond that possible as a result of personal contact between revolutionaries. These values serve to legitimize opposition to those whose power is legitimated by authority values.

This discussion of Blau's four types of values has carried us far from Homans' version of exchange theory. The individual and his behavior, which is paramount for Homans, has almost disappeared as one works his way through Blau's conception. In place of the individual we find a wide variety of *social facts!* We are treated to discussions of groups, organizations, collectivities, societies, norms, and values. By the time we come to the end of Blau's analysis we are concerned with what holds macroscopic social units together and rends them apart, clearly traditional concerns of the social factist.

Although Blau argues that he is simply extending exchange theory to the macroscopic level, in so doing he is twisting it beyond recognition. He is even forced to admit that processes at the macroscopic level are fundamentally different from those that occur at the microscopic level. Clearly antithetical to Homans' position, it is nearly congruent with the social facts paradigm. Thus, in his effort to extend exchange theory, Blau has managed to transform it into another theory closely congruent with the social facts paradigm.

Blau (1968:457) seemed to recognize his failure to extend exchange theory to the level of social facts when he later said: "Exchange theory is most directly concerned with face-to-face relations, and thus it must be complimented by other theoretical principles that focus on complex structures with institutionalized values."

173

Peter Singelmann (1972) has performed a similar function for those who subscribe to the social definition paradigm. In his effort to reconcile exchange theory and symbolic interactionism, he has managed to transform exchange theory to fit the social definitionists' perspective.

Singelmann begins with Mead's triple categories of mind, self, and society, in establishing convergences between exchange theory and symbolic interactionist theory.

Mind

According to Singelmann (1972:416), the concept of mind to the social definitionist "reflects the human capacity to *conceive* what the organism *perceives,* define situations, evaluate phenomena, convert gestures into symbols, and exhibit pragmatic and goal-directed behavior." The actor is an active agent to the social definitionist and, according to Singelmann, to the exchange theorist as well. He argues that the social definitionist conception of the mind has been "explicitly recognized" by exchange theorists. As evidence that such a conception of mind exists among exchange theorists, Singelmann cites discussions by exchange theorists of such things as the following: the awareness by individuals of alternatives open to them, the fact that they have aspirations and expectations, and Homans' concept of distributive justice. The idea of distributive justice implies that one subjectively evaluates different rewards in order to determine whether the law of distributive justice has been violated. On the basis of this kind of analysis Singelmann (1972:417) concludes: "Current exchange theory has thus gone beyond the purely 'behavioristic' approach of many reinforcement theories by recognizing, more or less explicitly, that the human mind mediates the relationships between stimuli and behavioral responses." Thus, a reward is not a reward in itself, but must be defined as a reward in order to operate as a reinforcer. This process of definition brings exchange theory in Singelmann's view in line with the social definitionist position.

Most behaviorists would concur only partially with Singelmann. They would agree that there is nothing inherent in an object that makes it a reward. A reward may be defined as a reinforcer, if it in fact affects behavior. The behaviorist, Singelmann aside, is aware of the process of social definition, but he is *not* concerned with it. He is only concerned with the behavioral manifestations of the definition process, not that process itself.

It is important to note here that, in general, I feel comfortable with Singelmann's efforts at reconciliation. In fact, I also appreciate Blau's similar effort to extend exchange theory to the level of social facts. All of these levels *can be integrated*. But the exchange theorist is likely to reject both Singelmann's and Blau's efforts. Singelmann, in fact, transforms exchange theory into a social definitionist perspective. This can be done, but the end product is no longer exchange theory, nor does it fall within the behaviorist paradigm. Similarly, Blau's macroscopic extension of exchange theory is also possible, and even worthwhile, but it too, as we have seen, is no longer subsumable under the behaviorist paradigm.

Self

Singelmann points out that social definitionists are concerned with the idea of self both in the sense used by Mead as "a process in which actors reflect on themselves as objects," and in the sense of the "self-concept" held by actors. Singelmann suggests that exchange theorists understand that an individual has a self and a self-concept, and that these ideas are perfectly amenable to exchange theory. For exchange relationships to develop and persist, for example, each party must be able to take the role of the other, as well as the generalized other, in order to determine what rewards they should offer and what rewards they are likely to receive. In my opinion this is a useful insight, but the exchange theorist is likely to throw his hands up in disgust. I think he would say that while it is true that people take roles, have a self, etc., it is really not relevant to his concerns. He is not concerned with the process by which an individual decides what rewards he will offer, but only in the exchange relationship itself. He would want to know about behavior and not about such "soft" concepts as self, generalized other, and taking the role of the other. These are for a philosopher to dabble in, not something of concern to the "scientist" who identifies with the behaviorist paradigm. Burgess and Bushell's (1969:284) definition of self, which is totally foreign to the conception of the social definitionist, demonstrates this distance. "The 'self' may be parsimoniously defined as the overt and covert verbal statements an individual uses to describe his own physical characteristics and behavior patterns." A similarly antithetical definition of self is offered by Skinner (1971:189): "A self is a repertoire of behavior appropriate to a given set of contingencies."

Society

Singelmann argues that both social definitionists and exchange theorists focus on the microsocial level in analyzing social structure. He sees two further points of convergence. First, he argues that symbolic interactionists focus on how people fit their interaction patterns together, while Homans is concerned with stabilizing relationships on the basis of the most profitable exchanges. Both imply a constant construction and reconstruction of interaction patterns. Secondly, and more bluntly, Singelmann argues that "exchange may be conceptualized as symbolic interaction." Here he means that exchange entails a communication of symbols. This is a clue to Singelmann's whole argument, which is basically that exchange theory can be subsumed under symbolic interactionism. Exchange theory is transformed beyond recognition by Singlemann, but symbolic interactionism remains unscathed.

    Singelmann (1972:422) sees several other points of convergence, but of greatest import is his theoretical synthesis, which consists of four basic points:

1. In exchange, actors construct normative and existential definitions of themselves, others, actions, goals, and assessments of "fairness."
2. These definitions are not only subjectively constructed but to a large extent socially shared and thus constitute a constraint external to individual actors.
3. In exchange, hedonistic strivings of actors are limited and qualified by the nature of the subjective and socially shared definitions of the objective world, which includes the self and others.

4. In exchange, actors will change their behaviors or definitions when the following apply:
    a. Changes in the objective world render existing behaviors and definitions problematic.
    b. Changes in some of their subjective definitions render other definitions or existing objective conditions and behaviors problematic.

The word that appears over and over in Singelmann's four propositions is "definition." He has transformed exchange theory beyond recognition and placed it squarely in the camp of the social definitionist.* In so doing, he has actually done the same thing that Blau did in trying to move exchange theory into the social facts camp. Nevertheless, we must applaud both Blau and Singelmann for the efforts to reconcile the disparate paradigms. It is problematic, however, whether transforming another paradigm into your own favorite is really a contribution to reconciliation of paradigms.

METHODS

All of the methods discussed in this book *could* be used by the social behaviorist. The behaviorist *could* use observation techniques to study behavior. He could venture into the field and observe the behavior of the taxi driver, prostitute, or physician. He could then write up his observations and write an essay describing their behaviors. This is, in fact, what the social definitionist does, but he uses his description of behaviors to infer things about intrasubjective and intersubjective states of mind. However, the social behaviorist is likely to shy away from the "soft" methodology of the observation technique because of his origins in psychology and its commitment to rigorous methods, statistical analyses, and elaborate equipment. Although the social behaviorist could apply the observation technique, he rarely does.

---

* After this section was written, the social behaviorists published a bitter reply to Singelmann in the *American Sociological Review*. In effect, they accused Singelmann of distorting behaviorism by integrating it with social definitionism. They were resisting Singelmann's effort to distort "pure" behaviorism with this political attack on him. *See* Abbott, Brown, and Crosbie, 1973.

The behaviorist *could* also utilize the interview/questionnaire technique. He could, for example, ask people to describe their behaviors in a questionnaire or in an interview. Although the interview/questionnaire is more acceptable to the social behaviorist because it is a more rigorous method than observation, employs statistical techniques, and requires some elaborate equipment, it is not frequently used by the behaviorist. The behaviorist finds an individual's description of his behavior to be far less valid than actual observations of his behavior in a controlled setting. In addition, despite its greater methodological rigor, the interview/questionnaire is simply not viewed as being as rigorous as the experimental technique.

Although he could utilize the observation or interview/questionnaire techniques, the behaviorist almost invariably uses the experimental method. The issue should be raised at this point of how well the experimental method fits the study of behavior. We have already seen that the interview/questionnaire is not well suited to the study of social facts. Similarly, the observation technique has limitations in terms of the study of social definitions. In both cases, the information that is gathered is far removed from the subject of study. The researcher is forced to make inferences about his subject from the data he is able to collect.

The experimental method is clearly better suited to the study of behavior than the relationship between the other methods and their objects of study. Nevertheless, the social behaviorist, like all other sociologists, must make inferences from what he can observe. Although he can observe and measure some aspects of some behaviors, he is forced to make inferences about the rest of the behavior patterns from these bits and pieces.

There are two basic types of experimental methods open to the social behaviorist—field experiments and laboratory experiments. In either case, the behaviorist argues that the experiment has assets for the study of behavior unmatched by any other method: "The experimental analysis seeks to gain sufficient control of its subject matter to be capable of drawing direct comparisons between phenomena which are different by virtue of the experimenter's actions. When successful, this is indeed a powerful form of analysis, for the clearest way to account for a phenomena lies in the ability to control its appearance." (Bushell and Burgess, 1969:144–145) Both field and laboratory

experiments have these strengths, but they are obviously more difficult in a field than a laboratory setting. Although social behaviorism has been dominated by laboratory experiments, in recent years
there has been a growing propensity to conduct laboratory research
in a field setting. Three reasons seem to motivate behaviorists to
leave the confines of the laboratory and venture into the field. First,
he may want to use the field setting to test principles developed in
the laboratory in more real-life situations. Second, he may want to
use the natural setting to discover new relationships and/or extend
already discovered relationships. Finally, the experimenter may wish
to apply principles developed in the laboratory to practical problems. (Bushell and Burgess, 1969) Whatever the motivation,
the social behaviorist must retain the ability to alter a portion of the
environment so that he can observe resulting changes in behavior.

The great asset of the experiment is the ability of the researcher
to contol many of the relevant conditions. In contrast, the observer
has almost no control over what goes on in his research setting. Users
of questionnaires and interviews have some control, but not nearly as
much as the experimenter.

Let us examine some of the ways in which the sociological experimenter can control his research. Keep in mind that although
the experimenter can have a great deal of control, such control is
never absolute. In any experiment there are going to be factors (e.g.
what happened to respondents before they entered the experimental
setting) that will affect the results. A fight with one's girlfriend or
an upset stomach can affect the way someone behaves in a research
setting. There is little the experimenter can do about these factors.
Such factors will always intrude in the research setting, but the experimenter has far more control over the *immediate environment* of
the research setting than the other researchers discussed to this point.

The basic concern in an experiment is to determine whether
some change takes place in a group of subjects as a result of something the experimenter does to it or because of environmental
changes. To ascertain whether changes occur, the experimenter generally needs two groups. The first, the *experimental group,* is the
group to which the outside force is applied. No effort is made to
induce changes in the second, the *control group.* The researcher's
ability to apply stimuli to one group and not to another is an important source of his control. He can ascertain whether the change

that occurs in the experimental group is a reaction to the stimulus by comparing what happens in the experimental group to what happens in the control group. If only the experimental group changes in the predicted way, he can infer that it was induced by the force he applied and not some other factors that might have been controlled.

The researcher must also be sure that the control group and the experimental group are matched. That is, they are as identical as possible in terms of such factors as age, sex, occupation, and education, if he deems them to be factors that can affect the results. This ability to make the groups as similar as possible is another way in which the experimenter has control over what occurs.

He also controls the environment so that he can be sure that the only thing that happens to the groups during the experiment is what he wants. The experimenter can match groups, apply the stimuli he wants, and prevent other stimuli from intervening. By being able to control these things he can be fairly sure the differences between what happens to the experimental group and the control group are caused by the stimuli he applies.

Another step is the presentation to both groups of a pretest before the experiment begins measuring attitudes relevant to the study. After the experiment, the researcher gives both groups the same test. He then calculates the changes that have occurred in both groups. The differences between the changes in the control group and the changes in the experimental group demonstrate the effect of the stimuli applied by the experimenter.

The classical before-after experiment with one control group can be schematically outlined as follows: (Phillips, 1971:114) *

Steps	Experimental Group	Control Group
1. Matched selection of subjects	Yes	Yes
2. Matched experimental conditions	Yes	Yes
3. Pretest—the before measure	Yes	Yes
4. Application of experimental stimuli	Yes	No
5. Posttest—the after measure	Yes	Yes

* Bernard Phillips, *Social Research*, 2d ed. (New York: Macmillan Publishing Co., Inc., 1971).

Everything is the same for both groups except the application of the experimental stimuli. By controlling everything else, the experimenter can ascertain whether the stimuli he applies has any effect on the group.

There are many variations on this basic experimental design. In some cases a before-after experiment is performed using only an experimental group and *no* control group. At other times, an after-only experiment is performed which omits the pretest phase. There are much more complex designs which use multiple experimental and control groups. Each variation in design is aimed at solving a basic problem or problems with other designs, but in the process of solving them new problems are inevitably created.

Despite its obvious rigor compared to other sociological methods, the experiment is not without its critics. Naturally, the major criticisms come from those who support the other paradigms and their attendant methods. Although it is the "purist" of sociological methods, it is also criticized by experimentalists from other, more "scientific" fields. The physicist or chemist who uses experimental techniques might denigrate the behaviorist's experiments. After all, the behaviorist has far less control over his subjects than the physicist or chemist has over his. The human subject might have an argument prior to his participation in an experiment that affects his performance. This, in turn, would affect the validity of the experimental findings. Obviously, no such possibility exists when one studies a chemical.

The criticisms that interest us most, however, are those levelled by supporters of other paradigms and methods. The social factist is most critical of the level of analysis of the experimentalist. By the very nature of the experiment, one is able to study only microscopic questions with it. This is an asset in studying behavior, but one would obviously have great difficulty studying the way a society changes or adapts to external threats in a laboratory setting. As an extension of this, the social factist feels that the experimental method substitutes methodological rigor for the study of truly important sociological questions. He feels that the experimentalist suffers from a "displacement of goals." Instead of studying important problems, the goal of the experimentalist may well become methodological rigor with little regard for the issues being examined.

The social definitionist criticizes the experimental method on other grounds. For example, he is particularly upset by the fact that the experiment often distorts the behavior of the participants. An individual may not behave normally because of the fact that he is being studied, because he is in an artificial situation, or because he thinks the experimenter expects him to behave in a certain way, etc. For all these and other reasons experimental behavior may be atypical.

The social definitionists often point to the famous studies at the Hawthorne plant of the Western Electric Company to buttress their case. In this field experiment, the researchers were interested in examining the changes in a variety of conditions (e.g. amount of lighting) on the productivity of the worker. In the lighting experiment, they found that productivity increased in the groups studied irrespective of whether the room was well, or poorly, lit. In fact, they found that the productivity of the experimental group went up even when the lighting was reduced almost to the level of moonlight. Critics of this experiment have argued that the increases in productivity had nothing to do with the changes in lighting, but occurred because the subjects knew they were being studied and they worked that much harder because they were part of a select group picked for scientific research. This phenomenon has come to be known as the "Hawthorne effect," which was coined as a result of this research.

Social definitionists also criticize the experimental method for distorting normal behavior in other ways. Take the example of a pretest questionnaire. In experiments, such a questionnaire is often used as a baseline to determine what changes, if any, have taken place during the experiment. The difference between the post-experiment test and the pretest are presumed to be caused by the experimental stimulus. But the social definitionist argues that the pretest serves to "wise up" the subject to what the experiment is about and what is going to be expected of him in the experiment. As a result, he may alter his behavior during the experiment as a result of the preconceptions he developed as a result of the pretest.

One other criticism by the social definitionist will suffice at this point to give you a feel for the kinds of objections raised against the experimental method. This objection relates to the kinds of subjects used in experimental studies. Most frequently the subjects are college students who can be coerced (often as a part of their course work) into participating in their professor's research project. Critics note that college students are not representative of the population as a whole and findings on this select group cannot be generalized to the total population.

Like the supporters of all methods and paradigms, the experimenter does not sit idly by in the face of criticisms from his adversaries. He generally finds other methods rather "soft" and primitive and underscores the "hardness" of the experimental technique.

The strength of the experiment vis-à-vis the other methods discussed in this book is the relatively great control of the experimenter and his ability to code what takes place. In fact, the ability to code what occurs is a good index into the "hardness" or objectivity of the method. Obviously, the field notes of a sociological observer are relatively difficult to code into specific categories that can be analyzed objectively. The same is true of open-ended interviews. What can we do with reams of notes describing the way a gang operates or long descriptions of an interviewee's sex habits? In most cases, all the researcher can do is examine them carefully and get some "feel" for uniformities in the group he has studied. These kinds of data cannot be reduced to specific categories that can be assigned numbers and analyzed with the aid of the computer. In contrast, answers to closed-ended questionnnaires and data derived from experiments can be categorized, assigned number codes, and computer analyzed. The difference between the closed-ended questionnaire and the experiment lies in the control of the researcher. When he mails a questionnaire, the researcher has no control over the conditions that affect how the respondent will answer the questions. He may answer at work, on the train going home from work, at home, or may even delegate the answering of the questionnaire to a subordinate. Where he answers, who answers, and the particular events that occur prior to answering the questionnaire will obviously affect the results. In contrast, the experimenter has much more control over these things, but it must be remembered that even his control is far from absolute.

Conclusion

In this chapter I have summarized the basic components of the social behavior paradigm. The exemplar for the social behaviorist is the work of the psychologist, B. F. Skinner.*   The social behaviorist believes the subject matter of sociology to be the study of behavior and the attendant contingencies of reinforcement.   Theoretically, behavioral sociology and exchange theory are encompassed by this paradigm.   Stemming as it does from psychology we should not be surprised to find that the preferred method of the social behaviorist is the experiment.   This concludes the in-depth discussion of each of the sociological paradigms.   In the next chapter I summarize the basic thesis of this book as well as raise a number of issues suggested by the preceding analysis.

BIBLIOGRAPHY

Abbott, Carroll, Brown, Charles R., and Crosbie, Paul V.   "Exchange as Symbolic Interaction: For What?" *American Sociological Review* 38 (1973) :504–6.

Abrahamsson, Bengt.   "Homans on Exchange."   *American Journal of Sociology* 76 (1970) : 273–85.

Back, Kurt.   "Review of Robert Burgess and Don Bushell, Behavioral Sociology." *American Sociological Review* 35 (1970):1098–1100.

Birnbauer, J. S., *et al.*   "Classroom Behavior of Retarded Pupils with Token Reinforcement."   *Journal of Experimental Child Psychology* 2 (1965) : 219–35.

Blau, Peter.   *Exchange and Power in Social Life.*   New York: John Wiley, 1964.

Brawley, Eleanor, *et al.*   "Behavior Modification of an Autistic Child." *Behavioral Science* 14: (1969) :87–96.

Burgess, Robert, and Bushell, Don.   "A Behavioral View of Some Sociological Concepts."   *Behavioral Sociology.*   New York: Columbia University Press, 1969.

Bushell, Don, and Burgess, Robert.   "Some Basic Principles of Behavior." *Behavioral Sociology.*   New York: Columbia University Press, 1969.

————.   "Characteristics of the Experimental Analysis."   *Behavioral Sociology.*   New York: Columbia University Press, 1969.

* Skinner's role has recently been underscored by an article in *The American Sociologist* by Donald Tarter entitled, "Heeding Skinner's Call."   It is a blatantly political tract written on behalf of social behaviorism.   Also see Robert Friedrichs, "The Potential Impact of B. F. Skinner upon American Sociology."

————. "Applying 'Group' Contingencies to the Classroom Study of Behavior of Preschool Children." *Behavioral Sociology.* New York: Columbia University Press, 1969.

Friedrichs, Robert. "The Potential Impact of B. F. Skinner upon American Sociology." *The American Sociologist* 9 (1974) :3–8.

Homans, George. *Social Behavior: Its Elementary Forms.* New York: Harcourt, Brace and World, 1961.

————. "Contemporary Theory in Sociology" in Robert E. L. Faris *Handbook of Modern Sociology.* Edited by Robert E. L. Faris. Chicago: Rand McNally, 1964a.

————. "Bringing Men Back In." *American Sociological Review* 29 (1964b) :809–18.

————. *The Nature of Social Science.* New York: Harcourt, Brace and World, 1967.

————. "The Sociological Relevance of Behaviorism" in *Behavioral Sociology.* By Robert Burgess and Don Bushell. New York, Columbia University Press, 1969.

————. "Commentary" in *Institutions and Social Exchange.* Edited by Herman Turk and Richard Simpson. Indianapolis, Indiana: Bobbs-Merrill, 1971.

Knox, John. "The Concept of Exchange in Sociological Theory: 1884 and 1961." *Social Forces* 41 (1963) :341–46.

Mauss, Marcel. *The Gift.* Translated by Ian Cunnison. London: Cohen and West, 1954.

Merton, Robert. "Manifest and Latent Functions" in *On Theoretical Sociology.* New York: The Free Press, 1968.

Miller, L. Keith. "A Token Economy for the University Classroom." Paper read at Meetings of the American Psychological Association, Miami, Florida, 1970.

Parsons, Talcott. "Levels of Organization and the Mediation of Social Interaction." *Sociological Inquiry* 34 (1964a) :207–20.

Phillips, Bernard. *Social Research: Strategy and Tactics.* New York: Macmillan, 1971.

Singelmann, Peter. "Exchange as Symbolic Interaction." *American Sociological Review* 38 (1972) :414–24.

Skinner, B. F. *The Behavior of Organisms: An Experimental Analysis.* New York: Appleton-Century-Crofts, 1938.

————. *Walden Two.* New York: Macmillan, 1948.

————. *Beyond Freedom and Dignity.* New York: Knopf, 1971.

Tarter, Donald. "Heeding Skinner's Call: Toward the Development of a Social Technology." *The American Sociologist* 8 (1973) :153–58.

5

Paradigmatic Differences in Sociology: An Assessment

Three tasks remain for this final chapter. First, I will briefly summarize major themes of the preceding four chapters. Second, I will assess the current status of paradigmatic differences in sociology. Finally, I will venture some predictions on changes that can be anticipated in the paradigmatic status of sociology in the future.

Summary

The starting point for this book was Thomas Kuhn's (1962, 1970) provocative analysis of revolutionary changes in science. Kuhn contradicted the lay conception of science developing in a cumulative manner. In his view, this is a myth promulgated by authors of beginning science textbooks which often have a vested interest in presenting a coherent image of their field. While some scientific development has been cumulative, most important changes in science have come about as a result of scientific revolutions. Focusing on these revolutions, Kuhn presented the following model of the development of science:

PARADIGM I → NORMAL SCIENCE → ANOMALIES →
CRISIS → REVOLUTION → PARADIGM II

Briefly, a paradigm gains preeminence in a science and is refined and extended during the period of normal science. Researchers are inevitably confronted by anomalies that cannot be adequately explained by Paradigm I. As anomalies increase, a crisis is reached when the paradigm itself comes to be questioned. If the crisis is sufficiently serious, a revolution occurs and a new paradigm, viewed as

188

capable of coping with the issues handled by Paradigm I as well as the anomalies it failed to explain, emerges.

Although revolution is the theme of Kuhn's work, the key term in his scheme, and in this book, is *paradigm*. Kuhn never defines the term precisely; in fact he uses it in no less than twenty-one different ways. Utilizing Masterman's (1970) effort to differentiate various types of paradigms, I offer the following definition of that concept:

> A paradigm is a fundamental image of the subject matter within a science. It serves to define what should be studied, what questions should be asked, and what rules should be followed in interpreting the answers obtained. The paradigm is the broadest unit of consensus within a science and serves to differentiate one scientific community (*or sub-community*) from another. It subsumes, defines, and interrelates the exemplars, theories, and methods and tools that exist within it.

It is this term, paradigm, that anchors this book, in which my primary objective has been to assess the paradigmatic status of sociology.

The first question is whether one *can* identify the paradigmatic status of sociology. Using Masterman's four types of science (paradigmatic, nonparadigmatic, dual paradigmatic, and multiple paradigmatic), I conclude that sociology is presently a multiple paradigm science. Sociology's multiple paradigms are in conflict within the discipline as a whole as well as in all of the sub-areas within the field. Thus, "normal science" is almost impossible in sociology because disciples of each paradigm are constantly having their basic assumptions questioned by those who accept other paradigms.

Kuhn did not develop the concept of a paradigm to be applied to social sciences such as sociology. It is necessary to demonstrate its applicability to sociology. If the paradigm concept can be fruitfully applied to a field that stands somewhere between sociology and the natural sciences, namely linguistics, we are on firmer ground in trying to apply it to sociology. The paradigm concept proves to be of great utility in explaining the sources of controversy within contemporary linguistics. Of greater importance is the fact that the applicability of Kuhn's ideas to linguistics demonstrates the political character of the conflicts between supporters of different paradigms. There is not one science which is a totally rational enterprise. Irrational factors constantly intrude. The struggle between adherents of different paradigms is often a political battle in which a paradigm's scientific or intellectual merit is subordinated to the issues of relative power among competing paradigm adherents or claimants.

Having analyzed the sources of paradigm conflict in linguistics, it is safe to consider the question of paradigms and sociology. As a starting point, the work of other sociologists who have attempted to apply the paradigm concept to sociology must be reviewed. The most important of these efforts is Robert Friedrichs' (1970) *A Sociology of Sociology*. Friedrichs' effort is marred by the fact that he is forced to work with Kuhn's definition, or rather Kuhn's twenty-one different definitions of a paradigm. Working with such a muddled definition, it is little wonder that Friedrichs comes to such a muddled conception of the paradigmatic status of sociology.

When he applies the paradigm concept to sociology, Friedrichs arrives at a wide array of perspectives that qualify, in his eyes, for the status of a paradigm. Among these are system theory, conflict, Marxism, dialectics, action theory, and exchange theory. These are theories, not paradigms. They are components of larger paradigms, but they are not themselves paradigms. Friedrichs is obviously uncomfortable with such a large number of paradigms, so he decides that Kuhn's model does not adequately fit sociology. He finds it necessary to differentiate between first-order and second-order paradigms. The first-order (most controlling) paradigms in sociology are seen as those that relate to the sociologist's image (either priestly or prophetic) of himself as a scientist. Through the device of developing two orders of paradigms, Friedrichs achieves a parsimonious perspective of the paradigmatic status of sociology. But this step is unnecessary. Had Friedrichs started with a more precise definition of a paradigm, he would have come to a very different conclusion about the fundamental differences in sociology. He would have seen that the truly important differences in sociology relate to the image of the subject matter and not to the sociologist's self-image. I think we can use Kuhn's orientation and still come up with a parsimonious view of the paradigmatic status of sociology.

Given these criticisms of Friedrichs' perspective, it is incumbent to outline my own view of the paradigmatic status of sociology.

There are, in my opinion, three paradigms in contemporary sociology*; *social facts, social definition,* and *social behavior* paradigms, each of which is discussed in Chapters 2 through 4. I shall briefly summarize their essential elements.

The exemplar for the social facts paradigm is the work of Emile Durkheim, in particular his books *Suicide* (1951, originally published in 1897) and *The Rules of Sociological Method* (1964, originally published in 1895). Durkheim develops the concept of a social fact and then applies it to the study of suicide. Durkheim develops this concept to distinguish the emergent discipline of sociology from the competing fields of psychology and philosophy. In Durkheim's view, a social fact must be treated as a thing external to the individual and coercive on him. However, Durkheim is not prepared to give all social facts the ontological status of a real, material entity. Most of them are only to be treated as things; they are not necessarily real, material entities with an existence separate from the minds of men. Some social facts have a material existence (e.g. laws), but the most important are more evanescent "currents" that exist within, and between, consciousness; they are intrasubjective and intersubjective realities.

Contemporary social factists tend to ignore these equivocations in Durkheim's work and believe that social facts are not merely to be treated as things, they *are* things. This view is best expressed by Charles Warriner, who argues that groups *are* real, and, by implication, that other social facts are just as real. There are two basic types of social facts—structures and institutions. Both are dealt with by the modern social factist who is primarily interested in the relationship between structures and institutions, and their coercive power over individuals.

Several theories can be subsumed under the social facts paradigm—including structural-functionalism, conflict theory, systems theory, and macrosociology. However, structural-functionalism and conflict theory are by far the most important. They differ in their conceptualization of the relationship between social facts. To the structural-functionalist the various structures and institutions within society tend to mesh rather neatly. Society is viewed as being in a state

---

* Although I emphasize differences in this book, there is a common core of agreement in sociology that serves to set it apart from other social sciences.

of gradually moving equilibrium. On the other hand, conflict theorists have a far less sanguine perspective. They see social facts in
varying degrees of conflict with one another. If society is in equilibrium, it is a consequence of the coercive power of those who control
society.

In examining these two theoretical perspectives, I chose recent
and representative statements that underscored the similarities,
rather than the differences, between them. Thus, Robert Merton's
(1968) structural-functionalism overcomes many of the conservative
biases of earlier versions. By focusing on such things as dysfunctions,
net balance, and functional alternatives, Merton is perfectly capable
of dealing with conflict and change. This is exemplified by Herbert
Gans' (1972) application of Merton's model to the study of poverty.
Gans demonstrates that structural-functionalism can be used to
achieve radical conclusions on this question, as well as many others.
Concerning conflict theory, Ralf Dahrendorf's (1959) ideas are
analyzed because they closely resemble the tenets of structural-functionalism. Dahrendorf argues that the two theories should be used
alternatively. Conflict theory can be used to analyze conflict and
structural-functionalism can be used to analyze order. This, to me,
is an ultimately unsatisfying position. Genuine efforts toward a
reconciliation of these two perspectives are needed, and the work of
people like van den Berghe (1963), Coser (1956), and Coleman
(1971) represent at least beginning efforts toward reconciliation.

Methodologically, the social factist tends to use interviews and/
or questionnaires when he engages in social research. Because he is
oriented toward scientific sociology, he finds the rigor of these methods to his liking. Alternative methods, on the other hand, are not
well suited to the study of social facts. One would find it difficult to
study social structures and institutions in an experimental setting.
Similarly, the observation technique is not designed for the study of
social facts. Thus, the social factist is left with the interview/ques-
tionnaire. Many methodologists have been concerned with this in-
congruity, and several techniques have been developed to aid in the
studying of social facts. This is not to say that this technique is well
suited to the study of social facts—it is not. I suggest that the best way
of studying social facts is through the historical and comparative
methods. A good example of this is Weber's comparative study of

religion and capitalism.   However, historical and comparative studies are not favored by contemporary social factists because they are
costly, time-consuming, and considered "unscientific."

The second major paradigm in sociology is social definitionism.
The exemplar for the social definitionist is Max Weber's (1961)
work on social action.   Weber is interested in the subjective meaning individuals attach to their actions.   He is concerned with the
intrasubjective and intersubjective states of mind that characterize
social behavior.   Weber is not, in this interpretation, interested in
studying macroscopic social facts such as structures and institutions.
His focus is far more microscopic.   The social definition process and
the resulting action and interaction constitute the subject matter of
sociology for Weber.   In order to study such phenomena, Weber urges
use of interpretative understanding or *verstehen.*

Although a portion of Weber's work serves as an exemplar for
the social definition paradigm, the bulk of his work falls squarely
within the social facts paradigm.   Thus Weber, like Durkheim, does
not fit well within the paradigm for which his work is the exemplar.
As we will discuss later in this chapter, both Weber and Durkheim
were "paradigm bridgers."

To the social definitionist, man is in certain respects an active
creator of his own social reality.   Conversely, social facts are not seen
as static or coercive.   Such a stance leads to concern with man's social
definitions or his social construction of reality.   In addition, the social definitionist is interested in the social processes that flow from the
social definitions of the individuals.   In fact, he must observe social
processes in order to make inferences about the largely invisible intrasubjective and intersubjective states of the participants.

Three major theoretical perspectives are subsumed by the social
definition paradigm: action theory, symbolic interactionism, and phenomenological sociology.   Other more minor theories such as drama-
turgy (Goffman, 1959) and existential sociology (Manning, 1973)
also may be subsumed under social definitionism.

Action theory is directly derived from Max Weber's work.   Although many sociologists have worked with action theory, it was Talcott Parsons (1937) who first brought it (and Max Weber) before
a large American audience.   Parsons' action theory is similar to
Weber's and he, like Weber, moved from microscopic to more macro-

scopic concerns. Action theory itself has not made a crucial contribution to American sociology, but its significance lies in the role it played in the development of the more important theory of symbolic interactionism.

Many early symbolic interactionists (e.g. Cooley, Mead, Park, Faris, and Thomas) were associated with the tenets of action theory, and symbolic interactionism was intimately related to the Chicago school of sociology. It is distinguished by its single-minded objections to the other two major paradigms. Symbolic interactionists respond negatively to the behaviorists' contention that man simply reacts to external stimuli. Symbolic interactionists argue that there is a "minding" process that intervenes between stimulus and response. It is this mental process, and not simply the stimulus, that determines how a man will react. On the other hand, the symbolic interactionist opposes the social factist's emphasis on macroscopic structures and institutions and the coercive power they are purported to have over individuals. To the symbolic interactionist, structures and institutions are simply the shell within which the truly important processes of social definition and interaction take place.

The final theoretical perspective discussed within the social definitionist paradigm is phenomenological sociology. Although emerging from a tradition different from action theory or symbolic interactionism, phenomenology also is indebted to Max Weber. The relationship between the social construction of reality and action is the object of study for the phenomenologist, as with the action theorist and symbolic interactionist. Phenomenologists are distinguished from the other theorists by their greater focus on the "taken for granted world" of everyday life. Some of them may also be distinguished by their use of methods designed to disrupt social situations so that the "taken for granted world" can be studied.

Methodologically, the social definitionist generally employs the observation technique. One cannot observe the minding process and can, at best, only catch glimpses of interaction. Thus, the social definitionist must infer the existence of intrasubjective and intersubjective forces from that which he can observe. The observation technique, like the interview/questionnaire, is not particularly well-suited to the paradigm in which it is most frequently used. The overwhelming goal of the social definitionist is to study life *in vivo*.

The alternate methods, interview/questionnaire and experiment, clearly do not permit this. The interview/questionnaire yields only self-reports, while the experiment is ordinarily quite artificial.

Finally, we have the social behavior paradigm. The exemplar of this paradigm is the work of B. F. Skinner (1971), who has been in the forefront of psychological behaviorism for many years, and has enunciated its principles in scientific tracts, novels, and polemical essays.

The subject matter of sociology to the social behaviorist is behavior and contingencies of reinforcement. As Bushell and Burgess (1969) put it, the social behaviorist focuses on "the behavior of individuals that operate on the environment in such a way as to produce some consequence or change in it which, in turn, modifies subsequent performances of that behavior." Such a focus is very different from the image of subject matter in the other two paradigms. Social behaviorists vehemently reject the social definitionist's idea that there is a voluntaristic mind that intervenes between reinforcement and behavior. They regard such entities as metaphysical constructs. They tend to take a similarly negative view of the social factist and his focus on structures and institutions. It is behavior that is important, and such concepts as mind, social structure, or social institution serve to distract us from a concern with it.

There are two basic theories subsumed under the heading of the social behavior paradigm. First is behavioral sociology. It represents an effort to directly translate psychological principles of behaviorism to sociological questions. We have examined some of these translations and it is clear that they are unlikely to be acceptable to sociologists who accept other paradigms. One of the distinguishing characteristics of behavioral sociology is its applied aspect. Unlike any other theoretical perspective in sociology, behavioral sociology has been successfully applied to a number of practical problems.

The other major theoretical perspective in the social behavior paradigm is exchange theory. This approach is closely identified with the work of George Homans (1961) who is heavily and directly affected by B. F. Skinner's operant conditioning of pigeons. While Homans integrates behavioral and sociological principles at the microscopic level, Peter Blau (1964) seeks to extend exchange theory to the macroscopic level. He tries to integrate social behaviorism and social factism, and in the process he produces an orientation that is not likely to be acceptable to the disciples of either paradigm.

Stemming as it does from psychology, social behaviorism's preferred method is the experiment. Behaviorists have traditionally preferred laboratory experiments, although in recent years they have been more prone to venture into field experiments. The experiment allows the researcher great control over his subjects and the surrounding conditions. This allows the experimenter to make highly precise judgments about the effect of changes he has induced on the behavior of the subjects involved. Although the experiment is a fairly direct way of studying behavior, the experimenter must still make inferences from short glimpses of behavior he is actually able to observe.

Given this overview, we come to a key question: How can one determine that sociology is, in fact, divided into these three, and *only* these three, paradigms? How can you be sure that I have not missed a paradigm? On the other hand, how can you be sure that sociology is not better characterized as a dual paradigm or even a single paradigm science? How can the reader be sure that the analysis presented in this book is more accurate than Friedrichs', Effrat's, or any other work that has dealt with this issue? The answer, of course, to all of these questions is that there is no way that the reader can be *sure* that sociology is divided into the three paradigms discussed in this book. However, for a variety of reasons, I believe in the orientation taken here. Let me enumerate some of my reasons.

The split between structural-functionalism and conflict theory has frequently been perceived as sociology's most basic division. In fact, using the paradigm concept, Friedrichs tended to affirm this view. This perspective has always bothered me. In my experience a structural-functionalist never had any difficulty communicating with a conflict theorist. They often found that they shared many assumptions and perspectives. If the basic split in sociology is between structural-functionalism and conflict theory, functionalists should have had difficulty with conflict theorists. The fact that they did not, led me to look for other differences within sociology.

As I examined my own contacts with sociologists, I found that functionalists did have trouble communicating with those who accept what I now term the social definition and social behavior paradigms. They simply had very different images of the subject matter of sociology. They operated from totally different perspectives. Given my own experience, I came to believe that there were more basic splits in sociology than the differences between conflict and structural-functional theory. A tangential point that emerges from this book, therefore, is that it is time for sociologists to disabuse themselves of the notion that the split between structural-functionalism and conflict theory is their most basic difference.

I find the tripartite division of sociological paradigms to be esthetically pleasing. It fits my own experience in the field. It pinpoints our major and basic differences without raising every one of our different perspectives to the level of a paradigm. The various components of each of the paradigms seem to fit together rather neatly. The exemplars for each are acknowledged by almost everyone within the paradigm as basic to their entire approach. All of the theoretical approaches within each of the paradigms have well-recognized basic similarities, although they differ in terms of their theoretical orientations. The favored method of each paradigm has a clear linkage to each of the paradigms. In my opinion, therefore, the paradigms cohere and exhaust most of our present basic differences. There are perspectives that I have been unable to categorize. One is the critical theory which has emerged from the Frankfurt school and seems to defy classification. It may well represent the basis for an emerging fourth paradigm. The other is the increasing significance of biologism in sociology.

Up to this point, all you have are my assertions that my schema is valid. However, assertions are not evidence. Is there any evidence to support my case? I have already discussed in Chapter 1 some empirical support offered by Brown and Gilmartin (1969). In their research, they identified three variables that were most frequently analyzed in research studies published in the *American Journal of Sociology*. The three variables closely parallel my three paradigms:

Variable	Paradigm
Individual	Social Behavior
Individual-Group	Social Definition
Group	Social Facts

The correspondence here is only suggestive. I would certainly not argue, for example, that all of those who focus on the individual accept the social behavior paradigm. Nevertheless, Brown and Gilmartin's findings on these three basic variables is supportive of the tripartite paradigmatic schema presented here. Approximately a third of all the studies done during two periods (1940–1941 and 1965–1966) used each of the three variables supporting my contention that there are three powerful paradigms extant in sociology. The fact that they marshall data from the early 1940s and late 1960s also supports my belief that we have never had a dominant sociological paradigm.

Theoretical support for the position advanced here is found in Theodore Abel's (1970) *The Foundation of Sociological Theory*. Abel is not dealing with issues as broad as those covered in this book. He is *only* dealing with the *theoretical* component of the broader paradigm, and he is focusing only on a *single* specific issue—the question of the nature of social collectivities. Although he is only dealing with theoretical views on a specific issue, the similarities between Abel's analysis and the one advanced in this book are striking. Abel argues that there are three theoretical conceptions of collectivities. These parallel *precisely* the three paradigms discussed in this book. Abel's three theoretical perspectives, and the three paradigms that they parallel, are as follows:

Abel's Theoretical Perspectives	Ritzer's Paradigms
Social Nominalism	Social Behavior
Social Realism	Social Facts
Social Humanism	Social Definition

Let us examine each of Abel's theoretical perspectives on the nature of collectivities.

According to Abel, *social nominalism* takes both an extreme and a moderate form. He uses the views of Floyd Allport to represent extreme social nominalism. In Abel's view, Allport considers it fallacious to see "the group as an object that can be studied, that obtrudes itself upon experience and is capable of being manipulated and measured." More strikingly, Allport regards it as a fallacy "to assume that we can say something about the group that cannot be said equally well about the individuals who compose it." (Abel, 1970:30)

The reader will note that this view is remarkably close to the position of social behaviorist George Homans. The group is nothing more than repeated individual behaviors to the social nominalist. It is my contention that those who support the social behavior paradigm also enunciate this perspective.

There is a more moderate position encompassed by Abel's social nominalism. This stance is exemplified by May Brodbeck, who accepts the position of methodological individualism. She recognizes, however, that there are times when one would be required to treat social phenomena *as if* they are holistic. Thus, such things as "the Reformation, the church, capitalism, the cold war, and army morale" (Abel, 1970:32) should be treated as if they are real, whole entities. Nevertheless, Brodbeck accepts the social behaviorist view that there are no observable group properties that cannot be defined in terms of either individual behavior or interaction. Brodbeck's views, as well as what Abel calls social nominalism, are similar to what I have called social behaviorism.

A second theoretical perspective, according to Abel, is *social realism*. The social realist maintains that social facts are real, material entities. Like social nominalism, social realism can be subdivided into extreme and moderate positions. The extreme form is organic theory, which states that collectivity is analogous to an organism. In sociology, this view can be traced to the work of Herbert Spencer. In later years the organic analogy was carried to ridiculous extremes with "individual persons viewed as 'cells,' military and penal bodies as 'skin and protective system,' trading and manufacturing organizations as 'metabolism,' vocational groups as 'tissues,' administrators, judges, politicians, and priests as 'receptors,' and so on." (Abel, 1970:34) In its more moderate form, social realism resembles the position taken by Charles Warriner (1956) in *Groups Are Real*. Sorokin is Abel's exemplar of this position:

> an organized group is truly real; it is real as an ontological entity, as a definite, even material structure, as a causal-functional unity, as a

meaningful system. . . . As such this reality is fundamentally different from the total sum of these components taken in the state of mutual isolation.

Sorokin's position, as well as the entire social realism position, is clearly congruent with what I have termed the social facts paradigm.

Finally, Abel discusses the perspective of *social humanism,* which parallels the social definition paradigm. The social humanist focuses on the social construction of a group by those involved. It is "the group as it is imagined by its participants" that is the basic focus of this perspective. Such a subjective orientation fits well into the broader idea of the social definition paradigm.

The correspondence between my three paradigms and Abel's three theoretical orientations, as well as Brown and Gilmartin's empirical data, obviously does *not* prove that the position taken in this book is correct. Nevertheless, this empirical and theoretical work can be taken as strong support for my thesis.

I obviously cannot prove the viability of my three-fold classification of paradigms. The reader will have to make his own judgment based on the arguments I have presented. Beyond the available evidence, the reader is encouraged to use the schema presented in this book to examine sociology. I believe that such an examination will enable the reader to find some order in sociology where he previously found only chaos.

A caveat is needed at this point. Although an understanding of the paradigms in sociology is important, the reader should be careful not to reify paradigms. That is, paradigms are not real things but simply handy constructs for understanding the nature of sociology or any other field. They are simply descriptions of the way sociologists currently practice their craft. The ultimate goal, however, is not to understand sociological paradigms but to understand social reality. Thus, an understanding of the nature of paradigms is not an end itself, but a means for gaining greater insight into social reality. I think many sociologists forget this ultimate goal and spend their academic lives defending the legitimacy of their chosen paradigm. They would be better advised to spend less time in political machinations and more time examining social reality from the perspective of their chosen paradigm.

**The Current Status of
Paradigmatic Differences
in Sociology**

As we have seen, contemporary sociology is radically divided among three competing paradigms, each of which is striving to achieve dominance within the discipline. At the same time, they are competing for preeminence within nearly every sub-area within sociology. No supporter of a paradigm is immune from criticism from those who accept the others. This has been previously emphasized and each of the paradigms has been described in detail. However, we have yet to address ourselves to the implications of this multiple paradigm state for contemporary sociology.

I have chosen to approach the paradigmatic status of contemporary sociology by considering some of the positive and negative consequences of these paradigmatic differences. As Merton has pointed out, it is important to specify the unit examined when conducting such an analysis. Consequently, I will look at the positive and negative consequences of paradigmatic differences for the discipline *as a whole*. I will begin with a discussion of negative consequences.

**Negative Consequences of
Paradigmatic Differences**

Perhaps the major negative consequence of paradigmatic differences for sociology is that they stand in the way of "normal science." Remember that during the period of normal science the scientist is able to work on highly specific questions that serve to articulate and expand the dominant paradigm. This is the period of cumulation of knowledge in a science but it is generally lacking in sociology. Because there is no dominant paradigm in sociology, sociologists find it difficult to do the highly specialized work needed for the cumulation of knowledge. Instead of concentrating on their specialty, they must spend a good portion of their time defending their basic assumptions in the face of criticisms from those who accept other paradigms.* This serves to distract them from practicing normal science, making it difficult to accumulate knowledge. Although the cumulation of knowledge is important, this book is based on the theme that the truly important advances in science come about as a result of revolution, not cumulation. However, the inability to practice normal science also acts as an impediment to revolutionary advances. Let us examine why this is the case.

The difficulty in pursuing normal science in sociology makes it difficult to uncover anomalies within a paradigm. Anomalies are usually uncovered by those engaged in the highly-detailed work of normal science. If anomalies are not uncovered, it becomes difficult to mount a serious critique of any of the paradigms. Those who accept a given paradigm are unlikely to question it since serious questions cannot be raised about a paradigm because of the failure to uncover anomalies. Without anomalies, the crisis phase of Kuhn's model will never be entered and this, in turn, means that paradigmatic revolutions are highly unlikely to occur. Both cumulation and revolution are less likely to occur in sociology than the natural sciences because the sociologist finds it difficult to engage in normal science. Both small increments and great leaps in knowledge are less likely to be found in sociology as a result of the inability to practice normal science.

Another major negative consequence of paradigmatic splits in sociology is traceable to the political character of debates between paradigms. We have seen that all paradigmatic debates in all sciences are highly political phenomena. However, in the social sciences, and in sociology in particular, political factors are preeminent. Intellectual factors play a much smaller role in paradigmatic debates in sociology that the natural sciences. These debates in sociology often take the form of efforts to discredit the positions taken by the adherents of other paradigms. Comparatively little time is spent in assessing the intellectual merits of paradigms, their weaknesses, or what they have to offer to those who accept other paradigms. Sociology is dominated by the highly-unprofitable process of trying to annihilate opposing paradigms with verbal assaults. Politics is an

---

* Although I have emphasized inter-paradigmatic conflict in this book, it is also true that there is much intra-paradigmatic conflict in sociology. A good example is the battle between structural-functionalism and conflict theory.

important part of paradigmatc conflict in all sciences but it takes exaggerated proportions in sociology.   The examples of such political attacks in sociology are legion.   We have noted B. F. Skinner's acid attack on the social definition paradigm and its notion of autonomous man.   George Homans' criticisms of social factism have been discussed, as have George Herbert Mead's attacks on the principles of behaviorism.   Preoccupation with this kind of global political attack has far more negative than positive consequences for sociology.   Sociologists would be better advised to engage in efforts to articulate their paradigm and assess the intellectual merits of opposing paradigms than to engage in verbal assaults on other sociological paradigms.

Another aspect of this political process, with equally negative consequences, is the attempt by supporters of a given paradigm to exaggerate its explanatory powers.   Of this genre, we have discussed George Homans attempt to argue that principles of behaviorism can be used to explain such macroscopic phenomena as the Industrial Revolution.   Although others are less overt, many sociologists appear seemingly incapable of resisting the temptation to exaggerate their paradigm's significance.   Such blatant political maneuvering is designed to win converts.   While it may be successful on that score, it is certainly not designed to advance the state of sociological knowledge.   Given the entire thrust of this book, I would be the last to deny the importance of political machinations in any science, but I think that sociologists often completely forget the question of knowledge advancement in their efforts to politically advance the cause of their paradigm.

A further negative consequence of the blatantly political character of paradigmatic debates in sociology is the propensity to set up one's opponents as "straw men" by exaggerating their position in order to dismiss it more easily.   While this may be a useful device to the critic in "winning" his case, it is certainly not useful to the cause of advancing knowledge within the discipline as a whole.   Too much time is spent in replies arguing that the critic has misrepresented the original author's position.   All that is left, after all the smoke has cleared, are two statements of one position sandwiched between an irrelevant critique.   However, even when a critic has attacked a straw man, there can still be some positive effects.   For example, in replying to exaggerated criticism an author may succeed in clarifying aspects of his ideas that previously were ambiguous.   Let us examine an example of the straw man controversy.

No sociologist has had his work distorted more frequently than Talcott Parsons, in particular his structural-functional theory.   A favorite theme of Parsons' critics is that he has ignored social change and focused instead on social order.   Critics say he has neglected the forces that tear society apart in order to focus on what holds it together.   The critics then impute a conservative bias to Parsons, implying that he favors maintaining the status quo rather than changing the existing society.

The classic example of this is C. Wright Mills' famous attack on Parsons in his very influential book *The Sociological Imagination* (1959).   Mills (1959:42) accuses Parsons of being incapable of dealing with social change: "The magical elimination of conflict, and the wondrous achievement of harmony, remove from this [Parsons'] 'systematic' and 'general' theory the possibilities of dealing with social change, with history."   From this supposed emphasis on order and inability to deal with change flows the accusation that Parsons favors maintenance of the status quo and that his theory "functions as a general legitimizing ideology of the dominant interest group."   (Szymanski, 1972:23)

Two issues are embedded in this critique: Is Parsons, in fact, incapable of dealing with change? Did Parsons downplay social change because of his conservative ideology?

First, Parsons does not ignore social change.   He deals with it in his earliest works and, in fact, two of his most recent books are exclusively concerned with the process of social change.   Thus, Mills misrepresents Parsons' work when he accuses it of being incapable of dealing with social change.   It is true that Parsons pays far more attention to order than to change.   Does Parsons downgrade social change because of his ideological views?   I think not, but his critics are anxious to set up a conservative (even reactionary) straw man to demolish.   Parsons' reasons for focusing on social structure rather than social change are theoretical rather than ideological, as the following quotation from *The Social System* illustrates:

> It is processes of social change in social systems as a whole, that is, of societies, which are problematical.   The above treatment has been

designed to illustrate two things. First, it brings home the fact that, as was stated at the beginning of the chapter, we do *not* in the present state of knowledge possess a *general* theory of the processes of change in societies as a whole. Therefore what we have been able to outline is not an "explanation" of such processes in a complete sense, but only a partial explanation in terms of certain elements. But, secondly, we hope we have been able to show that the theory of social systems in its present state is by no means devoid of relevance to the analysis of such processes of change, processes which pose precisely the most difficult empirical problems we have in our field. We very definitely have *something* to say about these problems. We can distinguish elements in them which we know to be of strategic importance, and we are by no means completely in the dark about many quite specific propositions about many of these elements. For example, whether or not it is possible completely to abolish coercive power from a society, or to do without any inequality in social stratification in an industrial society, is *not* simply a matter of opinion, in which the social scientist who takes the position stated here is merely "stating one view." The question of what elements in an ideology are utopian is, with a certain margin of error, a scientifically answerable question, and with it the question of the probable consequences of attempting to institutionalize such values literally in a large-scale society.

Above all, the treatment of the society deliberately and systematically *as a social system,* taking care to consider every problem indicated by the conceptual scheme as being germane to the functioning of a complete social system, constitutes an extremely powerful instrument of analysis in this connection as in so many others. It permits us to mobilize and apply, in the proper place and order, the empirical and theoretical knowledge we possess. But just as important, it forces us to recognize the gaps in our knowledge, to locate the unsolved problems, and to attempt to state accurately just what these problems are, and what we need to know in order to solve them. Thus, while we repeat we do not have a complete theory of the processes of change in social systems, we do have a canon of approach to the problems of constructing such a theory. When such a theory is available the millennium for social change will have arrived. This will not come in our time and most probably never. But progress toward it is much more likely to be assured and rapid if we know what we want and need. We submit that, without conceiving the problems in terms of the social system as a conceptual scheme, it is not possible to know what you want and thus even to measure progress toward the goal of attaining such a theory.

Perhaps one final word may be permitted. It has persistently been alleged that the "structural-functional" approach to the problems of theory in the sociological field suffers from a "static" bias. It has been held that the problems of change were outside its purview and since, the argument runs, these are obviously the really important problems, such a theory only succeeds in cutting itself off from genuine empirical relevance. Perhaps the first major example of large-scale processes of change introduced above, that of the processes of change arising from the institutionalization of science and technology, will serve to convince the reader that the author is aware of the fact that we live in what is sometimes called a "dynamic" society. Perhaps, even, it is not too much to hope that this chapter as a whole will convince him that there is a certain falsity in the dilemma between "static" and "dynamic" emphases. If theory is *good theory,* whichever type of problem it tackles most directly, there is no reason whatever to believe that it will not be *equally* applicable to the problems of change and to those of process within a stabilized system.   (Parsons, 1951:533–535) *

Parsons is not ideologically opposed to social change; he simply does not feel that sociological theory can deal with it until it has successfully coped with social structure. Those inclined to criticize Parsons should focus on the validity of the theoretical issue of dealing with social structure prior to social change. This is a difficult theoretical issue. Instead of dealing with this issue, many critics attack Parsons (and I think incorrectly) ideologically rather than theoretically because it is easier to set up an ideological straw man than a theoretical straw man. Further, if his opponents can paint him as a conservative or a reactionary, they will win over most sociologists (who consider themselves liberals or radicals). Setting Parsons up as a straw man may help his opponents score debating points, but it does not contribute to the development of a theory of social change. We need to critique his theoretical position, not his supposed conservatism, to move toward a theory of change. Do we need a theory of social structure before we can determine a theory of change? That is the question to which Parsons' critics should address themselves.

Another negative consequence of political debates between paradigms is the propensity to engage in name calling. In the heat of the political battle between adherents of different paradigms, combatants are sometimes reduced to calling their opponents names.* It is diffi-

* Reprinted by permission of Macmillan Publishing Co., Inc. from *The Social System* (Free Press, 1951) by Talcott Parsons. Copyright 1951 by Talcott Parsons.
* Name-calling is not restricted to inter-paradigmatic conflict. Much intra-paradigmatic conflict is also characterized by an abundance of vituperation.

cult, to say the least, to think of any positive functions performed by name-calling. Of the literally thousands of vituperations from which I could have chosen, I have selected the following criticisms of ethno-methodologist-social definitionist Harold Garfinkel's (1967) work *Studies in Ethnomethodology* by the social factist, James Coleman (1968:126–130) :

> . . . it would be fortunate if the reader could leave the book (or, rather, non-book: it is actually a disconnected collection of papers. . . .) after having read only Chapter 2 . . .
> Garfinkel simply fails to generate any insights at all from the approach. His other chapters constitute unrelated excursions into research, in some cases with disastrous results. Perhaps the program would be more fertile in the hands of someone more carefully observant, but it is strangely sterile here. . . .
> In sum, this chapter appears to be not only an ethnomethodological disaster in itself but also evidence of the more general inadequacies of ethnomethodology.
> In short, this chapter is another major disaster, combining the rigidities of the most mathematically enraptured technicians with the technical confusions and errors of the soft clinician, and without the insights or the technical competence of the creative and trained sociologist.
> Once again, Garfinkel elaborates very greatly points which are so commonplace that they would appear banal if stated in straightforward English. As it is, there is an extraordinarily high ratio of reading time to information transfer, so that the banality is not directly apparent upon a casual reading.

Another negative consequence of these political battles is the propensity to criticize someone for not doing what you would have done. Thus, the supporter of one paradigm frequently criticizes the work done by someone associated with another paradigm for its omissions. The fact is, however, that these omissions are usually foreign to the paradigm within which the author is working.

Useful criticism in any academic field focuses on what an author did rather than what he should have done. A critic should examine the validity of the author's assumptions, concepts, methods, theories, interpretations, or conclusions. It is his responsibility to point out weaknesses in these and other facets of the sociologist's work. The true critic addresses himself to the question: Did the author adequately carry out the task he carved out for himself? The following excerpt from a review of a book on the interviewing method is a classic example of a useless criticism that could lead to a highly dysfunctional controversy. The details of what the critic has to say are not important; what is important is his propensity to criticize the author for what he did not do.

> The effort to present the whole approach in terms of a theory of communication is laudable; but having gone that far, why not go farther? Gordon does not consider the seminal work on the audience and social transactions by Raymond Bauer and Arthur F. Bentley. There is also a great deal of illumination to be gained from literary work, a source which Gordon entirely ignores (e.g. the great James Boswell himself was a serious, professional interviewer). He overlooks, too, that anthropological literature which raises some of the really tough problems of empathy, insight, and policy (e.g., Dollard's *Caste and Class in a Southern Community,* Chs. II and III). Less serious but worth noting; he has also ignored the by now considerable literature of oral history.   (Dexter, 1970:186).*

What have we learned from this critique? We have not learned anything about the utility of what the author actually did. Instead we have learned about some issues that interest the critic and which should be (and perhaps are) the subject of a book of his own.

Positive Consequences of
Paradigmatic Differences

Despite many seriously negative consequences of paradigmatic differences within sociology, they are not without positive consequences. This should not be surprising since paradigmatic splits exist within almost all sciences and, in fact, go to the heart of the scientific enterprise. Let me suggest some positive consequences for sociology.

Debates between adherents of different paradigms can serve to test new ideas. The existence of multiple and conflicting paradigms in sociology makes it likely that those ideas that survive the attacks for any length of time are very useful ones. For example, Max

---

* Lewis Anthony Dexter, Review of Raymond L. Gordon's "Interviewing: Strategy, Techniques and Tactics," *American Sociological Review* 35 (1970) :186.

Weber's ideas on the relationship between Protestantism and Capitalism have been severely criticized. Yet they have survived, as have Durkheim's work on social facts, Mead's thoughts on the relationship between mind, self and society, and behaviorism's basic tenets. These have endured, despite the best efforts of adherents of competing paradigms.

Relevant criticisms from those accepting other paradigms may help an author clarify his ideas or even correct errors in his initial formulation. This assumes, of course, that the criticisms are relevant. We have previously discussed the irrelevancy of many critiques. Yet the perspective of a different paradigm can offer an author useful clarifications and corrections.

Debates between adherents of different paradigms can clarify issues or areas of inquiry that might have been obscured. In the process of arguing over one issue, combatants may well unearth other issues that could be dealt with fruitfully.

Finally, and most importantly, criticisms by adherents of other paradigms can serve to show an author that the premises of other paradigms have something to contribute to his own thinking. While this is potentially the most important contribution of paradigmatic debates, in practice it rarely occurs. The reason is a sociologist is usually committed to a given paradigm and unalterably opposed to others. He has often effectively closed himself off from these potential contributions. Nevertheless, on the rare occasions when it does occur, there is the possibility of great sociological insight.

There are certainly other positive and negative consequences of paradigmatic differences in sociology, but I believe I have enumerated the major ones. It is now necessary to turn to the question of "net balance." That is, do the positive consequences outweigh the negative consequences? This is not an easy question to answer since the concept of net balance is one of the weakest in Merton's model. It requires the sociologist to eventually make a value judgment regarding whether positive or negative consequences predominate. We cannot simply sum them and arrive at a precise quantity for each. I must at least venture an opinion on the status of paradigmatic differences in sociology.

It should be clear from the relative amount of space devoted to positive and negative consequences in the preceding discussion that, in my opinion, the negative consequences outweigh the positive consequences. Paradigmatic differences have more negative conse- quences for sociology because of the highly politicized conflict existing between adherents of the three paradigms. Much time is wasted in efforts to score political points at the expense of those who subscribe to other paradigms.

I do not want to imply that because of the greater number of negative consequences that sociology would be better off with para- digmatic unity. All sciences have paradigmatic differences and soci- ology is no exception. But these differences in sociology lead to an undue number of useless political squabbles. Again, some political conflicts are endemic to the scientific enterprise, but they go far be- yond the range of utility in sociology. Thus, paradigmatic differ- ences have more negative than positive consequences in sociology because of the large number of relatively useless political conflicts. I think we will continue to have paradigmatic differences in soci- ology, but they would be far more useful if the sociologists involved would tone down the rhetoric and concentrate on furthering socio- logical knowledge.

The Future of
  ## Paradigmatic Debates

We come now to the final portion of this book in which I will venture some predictions about the future of paradigmatic differences in soci- ology. Let me first point out the role I hope this book plays in that future. It is my belief that *most sociologists are unaware of the na- ture of the basic differences in the field.* Most sociologists in the past have believed that the debate between conflict theory and structural- functionalism comprised the basic difference in the field, a conception this book has sought to dispel. More importantly, I hope it will show sociologists the sources of their basic differences. I have discussed at several points how sociologists become committed to a particu- lar paradigm and seek to elevate it, while at the same time down- grading its opposition. However, a paradigm commitment is most often unconscious since the nature of the basic paradigms and their differences have been largely hidden. With the attainment of a better knowledge of the multiple paradigms in sociology, I hope that the sociologist is in a better position to assess the validity of his paradigm as well as those he has heretofore found objectionable. Perhaps we will see fewer blind defenses of, and attacks on, paradigms.

The most popular conclusion I could come to is that in the near future we will see paradigmatic reconciliation in sociology. However, there are several reasons why I do *not* think that in a short period of time we will see a single dominant paradigm in sociology. First, it is rare to find any science at any time dominated by a single paradigm. Second, although adherents of each paradigm claim all of sociology, their approach *seems* best suited to a particular facet of social reality. The social behaviorists *appear* to be best able to deal with behavior and contingencies of reinforcement. The social definitionists *apparently* cope best with the social construction of reality and the ensuing action. Finally, the social factists *seem* to work best with social structures and social institutions. I have emphasized the words *appear, apparently* and *seem* in the preceding sentences because it is my view that none of the paradigms is able to cope well with its facet of reality. *In fact, no aspect of social reality can be adequately explained without drawing on insights from all of the paradigms.* I will return to this point in a moment. The third, and most important, reason why we will not see paradigmatic reconciliation in the near future is the political allegiances and goals of the supporters of each of the paradigms. We will not witness significant steps toward the development of a single paradigm because many sociologists are more committed to their paradigm than the development of sociological thinking. Their major commitment is to the "victory" of their paradigm.

Given the current political situation in sociology, the best we can hope for in the near future is an expansion of our common core of agreement. In addition, it is possible that adherents of each of the paradigms will relax their political allegiances enough to allow for the infusion of insights from the other paradigms. It is in these two rather restricted ways that I see the possibility of some paradigmatic reconciliation.

Although paradigmatic reconciliation will not occur because of the reasons discussed above, there is no rational reason for the continuation of many of our paradigmatic differences. The simple fact is that each of the paradigms is, in itself, incomplete and incapable of adequately explaining any social phenomenon.*   In any sociological study we need to simultaneously understand structures, institutions, definitions of the situation, action, contingencies of reinforcement and behavior.

In order to fully understand each of the three sociological paradigms we must understand their structure, the norms and values encompassed by each, the definitions of the situation and resulting action of the sociologists who accept each of the paradigms, and the behavior of sociologists as well as the contingencies of reinforcement involved in that behavior. A sociological paradigm encompasses structures, insitutions, definitions of the situation, action, contingencies of reinforcement and behavior. Given this fact, we need all of the paradigms in order to understand the paradigmatic status of sociology. The same is true of *every* other social phenomenon. An adequate explanation requires the use of all of the sociological paradigms.

Despite my own views on the subject, I recognize that the political realities of the situation militate against the development of a single paradigm. The best I can hope for is some paradigm bridging and isolated efforts at paradigmatic reconciliation, As an aid in this, I would like to turn to several past, current sociological works that offer us leads on how at least this limited reconciliation might take place. There have been sociologists, "the paradigm bridgers," who have been able to integrate and/or draw from multiple paradigms. In addition, we have witnessed, in the last few years, a number of specific sociological works that have sought to integrate paradigms. I will now discuss paradigm bridgers and efforts at paradigmatic reconciliation.

PARADIGM BRIDGERS

It is my thesis that virtually all of the great sociological theorists were able to bridge paradigms. They were capable of moving, more or less

* I would like to thank Gary Long for making this point clear to me.

comfortably, between the two, or more, of the paradigms discussed in this book. This was not an entirely conscious process, although I think that most theorists felt a need to deal with social reality in diverse ways. Some tried to deal with multiple paradigms simultaneously, while others have shifted from paradigm to paradigm over time. Still others have shifted their theoretical perspectives or methodological techniques but remained within the same paradigms.

I would include among the paradigm bridgers in sociology Emile Durkheim, Max Weber, Karl Marx, and Talcott Parsons, each of whose efforts to bridge paradigms will be explored. I will deal with the first three briefly and Talcott Parsons in greater detail. This relative emphasis does not reflect their capabilities as theorists, but rather the fact that only Parsons has dealt with all three of the paradigms discussed in this book. However, it is sometimes difficult to speak of Parsons as a paradigm bridger since he tended to move from one paradigm to another during the course of his career rather than systematically dealing with all paradigms simultaneously. In fact, much of the discussion of Parsons focuses on his propensity to "leap" from one paradigm to another.*

In my view, Durkheim (as well as Weber and Marx) attempted to bridge the social facts and social definition paradigms. In Chapter 2, I discussed at length the fact that Durkheim, despite the fact that he coined the term "social fact," could not be fitted into that paradigm. He certainly recognized that material social facts exist and are external to, and coercive on, the individual. He accorded such phenomena as law and architecture the status of material social facts. On the other hand, he recognized that the most important social facts were nonmaterial "social currents" that could only exist as intrasubjective and intersubjective social phenomena. It was his ability to discuss both material and nonmaterial social facts that enabled Durkheim to bridge the social facts and social definition paradigms. As I pointed out in Chapter 2, it is more accurate to think of Durkheim as a social definitionist than a social factist. This would certainly come as a shock to those social factists who believe that they are following in Durkheim's footsteps. In any case, the relevant point is not the category in which Durkheim is placed but the fact

---

* I would like to thank Gary Long for this observation.

that he was capable of bridging paradigms. One of his major, if not often noted, contributions was his ability to integrate social factism and social definitionism.

Starting from a polar position, Max Weber accomplished the same feat—bridging social factism and social definitionism. Weber's work, chosen here as the exemplar for the social definition paradigm, clearly played a major role in the development of the three theories subsumed by that paradigm; action theory, symbolic interaction, and phenomenological sociology. Although Weber defined social action as the subject matter of sociology, he spent a substantial portion of his life studying social facts. The best known example was his cross-cultural studies of the relationship between religion and capitalism. The comparative method he employed in those studies provides a model of social facts analysis. In addition, much of his work was devoted to the study of other social facts such as bureaucracy, the city, class, status, and party.

There are times in Weber's work when you have the feeling that he has forgotten his dual orientation. In particular, when he dealt with various social facts, he frequently remained at that level without relating social facts to social definitions. For example, his classic discussion of bureaucracy focused primarily on the structural level, discussing such things as the structural characteristics of bureaucracy or the relationship between bureaucracy and a money economy. Although he briefly mentioned the relationship between bureaucracy and personality, he certainly does not concentrate on it as one might expect. This task was fulfilled by later authors such as Merton (1968) and Cohen (1970).

In his cross-cultural studies of religion, Weber was clearly dealing with both social factism and social definitionism. He was interested in the macroscopic question of the relationship between a variety of structural factors and the rise of the capitalistic system. He was also concerned with the relationship between various structural occurrences and the rise of a certain economic "mentality." Along these lines he discusses such things as "the spirit of capitalism," and the "spirit" of the Indian caste system. At some points these seem to be the kind of nonmaterial social currents discussed by Durkheim, while at others they appear to be subjective states of the actors in the system. In either case, they are clearly either intrasubjective or intersubjective states of consciousness.   Although Weber bridges social definitionism and social factism, he is not always careful to deal with both levels or to interrelate them.

Karl Marx is the third early figure in sociology whom I would classify as a paradigm bridger.   Like Durkheim and Weber, Marx was able to work with both the social facts and social definition paradigms.   Marx, of course, was also a polemicist, but this is not terribly distinctive, since Weber and Durkheim were also.   The causes that Marx championed (and his positions) served to give him far more notoriety as a polemicist than both Weber and Durkheim.   It was this notoriety—basically a political judgment—that made Marx unacceptable to sociologists and, until fairly recently, obscured the import of his sociological theories.   In addition, we cannot ignore the fact that most sociologists found Marx's ideology repugnant, while the ideology of Max Weber was more acceptable.

Careful examination of Marx's work reveals remarkable correspondence with Weber's work.   Indeed, Weber was often called the "bourgeois Marx."   Marx dealt with many of the same issues as Weber, e.g. religion, capitalism, and bureaucracy, though the two theorists often came to different conclusions about the same phenomenon.

Marx focused upon a wide range of structural phenomena.   In fact, at certain points he seemed to give external reality priority over the acting individual.   He criticized Hegel for taking an extreme phenomenological position: "Hegel makes man *the man of self-consciousness* instead of making self-consciousness the *self-consciousness of man,* or real man, man living in a real objective world and determined by that world."   (Bender, 1970:141)   At another point, Marx expresses his social factist position in more positive terms: "The mode of production in material life determines the general character of the social, political and spiritual processes of life.   It is not consciousness of men that determines their existence, but, on the contrary, their social existence determines their consciousness." (Bender, 1970:161–162)

Thus, Marx accords coercive reality to various social facts, but he does not neglect social definitionism.   In fact, the two perspectives are interwoven because of the dialectical character of Marx's thinking.   The following description of the position of the dialectician expresses well Marx's ability to integrate social factism and social definitionism:

> In a more interesting case, that of the growth of a child, the dialectician would reject as one-sided both the approach that the child is simply "unfolding his nature" as well as that which understands the child solely in terms of the all-pervasive influence of his environment. Rather, for the dialectician, the child is a purposeful being (i.e. his growth is a process) and the psychologist must understand the way in which the environment has *significance* for the child (i.e. he neither unfolds his "potentialities" as in a vacuum nor does he merely passively accept stimuli; rather he plays an active role in reacting to and integrating meaningful experiences). (Bender, 1970:4)

Marx, therefore, fully recognizes the creative, active aspect of man: "what distinguishes the worst architect from the best of bees is this, that the architect raises his structure in imagination before he erects it in reality." (Bender, 1970:360)

Of the three theorists (Marx, Weber, and Durkheim), I believe Marx best integrated social factism and social definitionism. I think this is traceable to his dialectical image of the relationship between man and society. In any case, each was fully aware of these two modes of analysis and the need to integrate them.

I have reserved Parsons for last because he alone has dealt with all three of the paradigms discussed in this book. I am not arguing that Parsons' theory is superior to the theories of Weber, Durkheim, or Marx; but Parsons, more than any other theorist, has been very conscious of building a general theory integrating insights from a wide variety of sources and perspectives. Parsons has not even been content to intergrate social factism, social definitionism, and social behaviorism. He has also integrated insights from anthropology and even Freudian psychology.

Parsons' stance in *The Structure of Social Action* (1937) is clearly of an action theorist squarely in the social definitionist camp. His concepts of the unit act, voluntarism, and Verstehen reflect this orientation even though there were hints of his later defection to social factism in this early period. There is a lively debate over whether Parsons ever actually deserted social action theory. Schwanenberg (1971) argues that Parsons has consistently employed the action approach, while Scott (1963) outlines the opposing position of inconsistency. To resolve this issue, let us examine the fate of the three social definition concepts basic to his initial work-unit act, voluntarism, and Verstehen.

The unit act lies at the very core of the theoretical contribution of *The Structure of Social Action,* but it progressively disappears from view as Parsons' theories develop. In *The Social System* (1951) the unit act has already begun to fade from the scene. In fact, it is cited only three times in a book of nearly six-hundred pages. When it is cited, one receives the impression that Parsons is simply using it to legitimize his earlier work and that it is irrelevant to the project at hand. In *The Social System,* Parsons prefunctorily remarks that the unit act is still the basic unit, but

> for most purposes of the more macroscopic analysis of social systems, however, it is convenient to make use of a higher order unit than the act, namely the status-role . . . it is the *structure* of the relations between the actors as involved in the interactive process which is essentially the structure of the social system . . . it is the *participation* of an actor in a patterned interactive relationship which is for many purposes the most significant unit of the social system. (Parsons, 1951:25)

I can see no real relationship between the unit act and the status-role. Similarly, Parsons developed the concept of need-disposition as the most significant unit of the personality level and value orientations occupy the same position in the cultural system. Now the issue is whether these three new units have "emerged" from the unit act or whether they are entirely new concepts. Of these three, only the value orientation is traceable directly to the unit act and Parsons' thinking in 1937. The other two, status-role and need-disposition, are entirely new concepts emerging from thought after publication of *The Structure of Social Action.* In his preface to its second edition, written in 1949, Parsons admitted that he did not include two critical inputs (those of Freud on the psychological side and anthropologists such as Boas) in his original formulation. It is from these sources, ignored in 1937, that Parsons' concepts of need-disposition and status-role arose. Therefore, the concept of unit act is unnecessary to understand at least two of the later units. Furthermore, Par-

217

sons himself does not need (nor use) the unit act to analyze the social, cultural, and personality systems; the unit act increasingly became a piece of excess baggage. In a recent book, *Societies* (1966), the unit act was not even mentioned.

The second basic concept developed in *The Structure of Social Action* is voluntarism. It is often cited in *The Structure of Social Action,* but is not indexed in *The Social System.* It is interesting to note that in *Toward a General Theory of Action* (Parsons and Shils, 1951) the concept of voluntarism is indexed, but it is cross-referenced to the category "choice." Scott calls this one of Parsons' crucial equivocations. Talking of Parsons' 1951 work, Scott says: "Parsons now does not say definitely, as he did before the war, that free choice is a *fact* of human life which the action scheme cannot afford to ignore." (Scott 1963:726) Just as Parsons found it impossible to work with the unit act, he also found it untenable to assume that man possessed free will or, as he called it, voluntarism.

Finally, there is the concept of *verstehen* or the need to analyze action from the subjective perspective. Says Parsons: "Contrary to the point of view held by the author in *The Structure of Social Action,* it now appears that [the subjective point of view] is not essential to the frame of reference of the theory of action in its most elementary form." (Parsons, 1951:54) Thus, *verstehen* follows the unit act and voluntarism into Parsonian oblivion. In fact, the subjective perspective had to go when Parsons deserted the unit act and voluntarism. It was because he was looking at a voluntaristic unit act that Parsons needed a subjective methodology. According to Scott, the influence of Tolman's behaviorism moved Parsons away from the need for *verstehen.*

Parsons had all but deserted the social definition paradigm for social factism by the 1950s. Nevertheless, he retained ties to his original action orientation even though he often only paid lip-service to it. Parsons' work would have been far stronger had he truly integrated social factism and social definitionism instead of leaping from one to the other. It was as a social factist, that Parsons gained his greatest fame. The status-role became his basic unit of analysis and this was clearly a structural phenomenon. He spent most of his time dealing with social systems and, more recently, with the ways in which they change.

Social behaviorism is least developed in Parsons' work, but he came under the influence of the psychologist Edward Tolman in the 1940s and sought to integrate his thinking on behaviorism into his schema. Note the following statement in which Parsons (1951:64) attempted to reconcile his earlier social definitionism with his then recent interest in social behaviorism:

> We do *not* postulate a substantive entity, a mind which is somehow dissociated from the organism and the object world. The organization of observational data in terms of the theory of action is quite possible and fruitful in modified behavioristic terms, and such formulation avoids many of the difficult questions of introspection or empathy.

Although Parsons did not succeed in truly integrating the three paradigms, he at least made the attempt.

I have discussed Weber, Durkheim, Marx, and Parsons because they have demonstrated that it is possible to deal with two or more paradigms. I do not think that any of them have done it very well, but that does not mean that the task cannot be done, and done well. The work of these men represents a resource from which those who wish to reconcile paradigmatic differences can draw. Much can be learned from their work, both in terms of their successes and their failures. With their work as background, it might prove possible to reconcile paradigms.

Efforts at Paradigm Reconciliation

Although it is rare to find theorists who have been able to bridge paradigms, there have been increasing attempts to show points of convergence between divergent perspectives. I believe that the future will bring even greater efforts to reconcile these differences. Again, let me remind the reader that I do not think a complete reconciliation of the three paradigms is likely, given the political climate in sociology, but there are aspects of each that can be unified. I would like to briefly examine several of the efforts at paradigm reconciliation in the next few pages. I do not intend to deal with the works in great depth. I simply want to demonstrate the emerging effort to reconcile at least some of the outstanding differences between paradigms.

We can begin with an effort to reconcile social factism and social definitionism by Peter Berger and Thomas Luckmann (1966). Their book, *The Social Construction of Reality,* has been one of the most influential of the recent works in sociological theory. One gets the impression from the title that the authors are squarely within the social definitionist paradigm. Although the book is heavily slanted in that direction, the authors do make an effort to integrate the social facts and social definition paradigms. They tend to overplay social definitionism, but, as we will see, most efforts aimed at paradigmatic reconciliation tend to overemphasize one paradigm at the expense of the other. The following quotation from Berger and Luckmann (1966:18) makes clear their desire to reconcile paradigms (as well as their recognition that Weber and Durkheim were paradigm bridgers) :

> One was given by Durkheim in *The Rules of Sociological Method,* the other by Weber in *Wirtschaft und Gesellschaft.* Durkheim tells us: "The first and most fundamental rule is: *Consider social facts as things.*" And Weber observes: "Both for sociology in the present sense, and for history, the object of cognition is the subjective meaning-complex of action." These two statements are not contradictory. Society does indeed possess objective facticity. And society is indeed built up by activity that expresses subjective meaning. And, incidentally, Durkheim knew the latter, just as Weber knew the former. It is precisely the dual character of society in terms of objective facticity *and* subjective meaning that makes its "reality *sui generis,*" to use another key term of Durkheim's. The central question for sociological theory can then be put as follows: How is it possible that subjective meanings *become* objective facticities? Or, in terms appropriate to the afore-mentioned theoretical positions: How is it possible that human activity (*Handeln*) should produce a world of things (*choses*)? In other words, an adequate understanding of the "reality *sui generis*" of society requires an inquiry into the manner in which this reality is constructed.

In their effort at reconciliation, Berger and Luckmann are operating primarily as phenomenologists. Charles K. Warriner (1970) has recently tried to reconcile the same two paradigms (social factism and social definitionism) although he emphasizes symbolic interaction and action theory rather than phenomenology.* The following passage demonstrates Warriner's (1970:128–129) effort to reconcile paradigms:

> In short, I believe that the approach developed in this book shows how the paradox can be eliminated without destroying Durkheim's central insights. When we start with the basic orientations provided by Mead we can show that on the evidence available it is possible for men to be the agents of social action and of social facts without at the same time having those facts reflected in their essential natures. Conversely, what they are as total beings is not reflected in the social facts which are characteristic of any particular society in which they participate.
>
> This proposition—men can be the agents of action which is defined, articulated with other acts, and programmed by factors external to their personalities—is the key-stone on which society as *sui generis* is defended.

Warriner, therefore, recognizes the importance of both symbolic action and interaction, as well as social facts. Despite his previous work on the group as a social fact, Warriner chooses to emphasize action and interaction rather than society.* He summarizes his position: "I recognized the importance of two ideas: (1) the philosophy of emergence which suggested that new forms and structures could be created out of the interactive relationships between simpler or more primitive forms; and (2) the principle of the focus upon action as the only direct, observable phenomenon of society, person and culture." (Warriner, 1970:157)

Turning to the reconciliation of social factism and social behaviorism, I have previously discussed Peter Blau's efforts to extend exchange theory to the level of social facts analysis. Although clearly a laudatory effort, I have pointed out that Blau's macroscopic exchange theory is unlikely to be acceptable to the social behaviorist.

---

* As an aside, this is the same Warriner whose work on groups as real entities was one of the exemplars for the social facts paradigm. Fourteen years later Warriner engaged in an effort to reconcile that position with social definitionism.

* Warriner believes that this does not represent a change in his orientation. *The Emergence of Society* is the first of three projected books; Warriner intends to deal with "social facts" in the two later works.

At the microscopic level, he remains close to Homan's version of behaviorism, but when he moves to the level of social facts, he stretches exchange theory beyond recognition by trying to discuss exchanges between social facts. This is obviously unacceptable to someone like Homans, who believes that all sociological questions are reducible to principles of psychological behaviorism.

Finally, we confront the issue of the reconciliation between the social definition and social behavior paradigms. Peter Singlemann's (1972) effort in this regard was also discussed earlier in this book. Instead of reiterating his argument at this point I would like to discuss a critical reaction to Singelmann's paper.

Singelmann's effort to reconcile exchange theory and symbolic interactionism generated a political response. In this case, the exchange theorists felt most threatened since Singelmann emphasized symbolic interactionism rather than exchange theory. Their reaction came in the form of a paper entitled "Exchange as Symbolic Interaction: For What?" by Carroll W. Abbott, Charles R. Brown, and Paul V. Crosbie (1973). They make their position quite clear in the opening paragraph: "The theoretical integration which Singelmann proposes would destroy both perspectives; and incorporating of concepts seems of little benefit, at least to the exchange theorist." The political battle lines are clearly drawn.

They do not agree with Singelmann's charge that exchange theory ignores the issue of subjective meaning, although they confess that the way subjectivity is currently handled by exchange theorists is "incomplete." Nevertheless, they reject Singelmann's effort: "We doubt, however, that integrating symbolic interactionist assumptions as Singelmann proposes would do the job. Indeed, such an integration would be useless and apt to diminish predictive efficiency." (Abbott, et al., 1973:504)   They feel that the basic premises of exchange theory and symbolic interaction are different and therefore, any effort to integrate the two would be futile.

Although they make a strong case for basic differences between the perspectives, they do not prove to my satisfaction that such an effort is not worthwhile. In my opinion, their reaction is motivated out of fear that a movement toward integration of the perspectives would weaken the distinctive character of exchange theory. While this is undoubtedly true, the goal of sociological theory is not purity but the explanation of man in society. It seems to me that Abbott, et al. have lost sight of this fact in their effort to defend the sanctity of exchange theory. This however, is likely to be the fate of all efforts aimed at paradigmatic integration. That is, they are likely to be faced with opposition from vested interests in each paradigm whose position would be threatened by any change in their paradigm's orientation.

Singelmann's (1973:508) reaction to the Abbott, et al. critique is interesting for two reasons. First, he argues against the sanctity of paradigms and for the integration of perspectives. Secondly, Singelmann incorporates some aspects of the argument presented in this book into his response:

> Exchange theory and symbolic interactionism are not monolithic constructs, and I reject any claim by a particular school to either. Ritzer suggests that what is called exchange theory originated within the behavioral paradigm and that my article transformed it into the definitional paradigm. Apparently Abbott, Brown and Crosbie see my paper in a similar manner and deny the utility of transforming exchange theory from one paradigm into another. However, I am not very interested in paradigms beyond their utility in making sense out of the world . . . If we are interested in the world as it is, let us select our constructs according to whether they help us elucidate that world.*

Singelmann's emphasis is crucial. Sociologists tend to forget the real world and focus instead on the perspective within which they work. The point is, however, to understand the world and not defend our vested interests in our own "pet" paradigm.

I have dealt with several efforts at reconciling theoretical differences between paradigms, but there have also been efforts at reconciling methodological differences that I would like to touch upon at this point.

On a general level, Webb (1966) has argued for *triangulation*, which means that researchers should use multiple methods on the same research problem. Thus, a researcher might simultaneously study the same issue using interviews, mail questionnaires, observation, and experiments. Should he come to the same conclusions

---

* Peter Singelmann, *American Sociological Review* 38 (1972) :414–24.

using these multiple methods, we would feel far more confident in his findings. This is not always possible since some research questions are not amenable to all techniques, but it is often possible to use more than one method. This underscores the point that there is no necessary incompatibility between methods and, more generally, paradigms. Although specific methods fit best into given paradigms, we can draw on methods external to the paradigm in which we are working when the situation demands it.

Sam Sieber's (1973) effort to integrate fieldwork (observation) and survey methods is more recent. He acknowledges the fact that both methods have a series of strengths and weaknesses and that they could be used to complement each other quite nicely. Details of the integration need not concern us here. Suffice it to say that the two methods can be used together to make up for weaknesses inherent in each and to make for a stronger overall study.

A point that does deserve underscoring is Sieber's recognition that debate between the adherents of these two methods is political in nature:

> In fact, two methodological subcultures seemed to be in the making —one professing the superiority of "deep, rich" observational data and the other the virtues of "hard, generalizable" survey data. That the fieldworkers were more vocal about the informational weaknesses of surveys than were the survey researchers with respect to fieldwork suggests the felt security of the latter and the defensive stance of the former.   (Sieber, 1973:35)

A political struggle exists and it is one in which the survey researcher seems to be in a stronger position than the fieldworker. This strength is, of course, traceable to the growing scientism within sociology.

Conclusions

This book has underscored the political character of paradigmatic differences in sociology. Although these political factors militate against the degree of reconciliation that is clearly needed and desirable, I think proliferation of the kind of work discussed in the preceding section will pave the way for at least limited reconciliation.

There is a continuity within sociology that has been blurred by our political allegiances. This view is also held by Theodore Abel (1970:94) who has developed a three-fold schema similar to the one used in this book:

> In general, the classification of sociologists into different schools (each one, presumably, competing for exclusive control of the entire domain of sociology) created a distorted view of the sociological enterprise and is neither fruitful nor illuminating. Its chief shortcoming is that it blurs the recognition of continuity in sociological thought by presenting different ideas as conflicting viewpoints rather than as a number of ideas relevant to the growth of a science in process that frequently supplement each other.

Although the major sociological paradigms are clearly supplementary, the political allegiances of sociologists blind them to this reality.

Although there are some ongoing efforts at limited paradigm reconciliation, there are also other trends that point to a further splintering of sociology. In fact, there are two sociological perspectives that may well emerge in the near future as sociological paradigms. One of these paradigms is likely to develop from what is now labelled "critical theory." Critical theory has emerged out of the so-called Frankfurt school and the ideas of such men as T. W. Adorno, Herbert Marcuse, and Max Horkheimer. (Jay, 1973)

Owing a clear debt to Marx, this orientation is markedly different from any of the three paradigms currently existent in sociology. According to Schroyer (1970), such a critical science has three basic principles. First, it sees man as both active and historically limited, which is clearly in line with Marx's dialectical view of the relationship between social facts and social definitions. Second, critical science is "concerned with the assessment of the socially unnecessary modes of authority, exploitation, alienation, repression." (Schroyer, 1970:225) Finally, it is "a speculative science in that it tries to reflect about the 'necessity' for the conditions of lawlike patterns in society and history." (Schroyer, 1970:225)

In my opinion, critical theory is a combination of social factism and social definitionism, with a heavy emphasis upon social criticism.

Does this peculiar combination of elements qualify it for the status of a new paradigm? Only time will tell, but my feeling is that it will resonate well with many new and aspiring sociologists. It is its political attractiveness that may well allow it to acquire status as sociology's next paradigm.

An intriguing possibility for paradigmatic status in sociology is the burgeoning interest in biological factors and their role in social phenomena.* (Mazur and Robertson, 1972) Were it to be demonstrated that biology plays a greater role in social phenomena than has heretofore been recognized, many of the ideas associated with all of the current sociological paradigms would be called into question. The political conflict discussed in the preceding pages would be minor in terms of the battle that would occur were a biological paradigm to begin to gain a significant foothold in sociology.

Let me conclude this chapter, as well as the book, with a restatement of some of the numerous implications of this analysis:

1. Behaviorism is, despite the preferences of many sociologists, a major perspective in contemporary sociology. Most analyses of the sociological state of sociology neglect or underestimate the significance of behaviorism.
2. The common conception that the basic split in sociology is between structural-functionalism and conflict theory is misleading. These two theories share many more commonalities than differences since both are encompassed by the same paradigm. The fundamental differences in sociology are among the three paradigms discussed in this book.
3. Another implication is the linkage between theory and method, which are often thought of as being practiced in virtual isolation from each other. There is a general, but far from perfect, congruence between theory and method.
4. There is considerable irrationality involved in sociology. Many of those involved in theoretical and methodological work do not understand the linkages between them. Theorists who think they stand in stark opposition to one another (e.g. conflict theory and structural-functionalism) are, in reality, interrelated. We have seen that researchers often use methods ill-suited to achieve their ends. This is particularly true of the use by social factists of the interview/questionnaire method and the social definitionist's utilization of the observation technique. All of these underscore Kuhn's emphasis, at least in the first edition of his book, on irrationality in science.

* I am indebted to Norman Yetman for this insight.

5. Finally, and most importantly, this book has underscored the highly political nature of paradigmatic conflict in sociology. Each paradigm competes with the others in every area of sociology. Much effort is expended in rhetoric designed merely to overwhelm one's paradigmatic rivals with a verbal barrage. Much of this political conflict is of little utility in the development of sociology. We need to spend less time attacking adversaries and more time examining their positions. We might then begin to understand how we can use insights from other paradigms and in the process develop a more unified perspective.

BIBLIOGRAPHY

Abbott, Carroll, Brown, Charles R., and Crosbie, Paul V. "Exchange as Symbolic Interaction: For What?" *American Sociological Review* 38 (1973) :504–6.

Abel, Theodore. *The Foundation of Sociological Theory.* New York: Random House, 1970.

Bender, Frederick, ed. *Karl Marx: The Essential Writings.* New York: Harper, 1970.

Berger, Peter, and Luckmann, Thomas. *The Social Construction of Reality.* Garden City, New York: Doubleday Anchor, 1966.

Blau, Peter. *Exchange and Power in Social Life.* New York: John Wiley, 1964.

Brown, Julia, and Gilmartin, Brian G. "Sociology Today: Lacunae, Emphases and Surfeits." *American Sociologist* 4 (1969):283–90.

Bushell, Don, and Burgess, Robert. "Some Basic Principles of Behavior" in *Behavioral Sociology.* Edited by Robert Burgess and Don Bushell. New York: Columbia, 1969.

Cohen, Harry. "Bureaucratic Flexibility. Some Comments on Robert Merton's 'Bureaucratic Structure and Personality.' " *British Journal of Sociology* 21 (1970) :390–99.

Coleman, James. "Community Disorganization and Conflict" in *Contemporary Social Problems.* 3rd ed. Edited by Robert Merton and Robert Nisbet. New York: Harcourt, Brace and Jovanovich, 1971.

———. "Review of Harold Garfinkel, *Studies in Ethnomethodology.*" *American Sociological Review* 33 (1958) :126–30.

Coser, Lewis. *The Functions of Social Conflict.* New York: The Free Press, 1956.

Dahrendorf, Ralf. *Class and Class Conflict in Industrial Society*. Stanford: Stanford University Press, 1959.

Dexter, Lewis Anthony. Review of *Interviewing: Strategy, Techniques, and Tactics*. By Raymond L. Gordon. *American Sociological Review* 35 (1970) :186.

Durkheim, Emile. *Suicide*. New York: The Free Press, 1951.

———. *The Rules of Sociological Method*. New York: The Free Press, 1964.

Effrat, Andrew. "Power to the Paradigms: An Editorial Introduction." *Sociological Inquiry* 42 (1973) :3–33.

Friedrichs, Robert. *A Sociology of Sociology*. New York: The Free Press, 1970.

———. "The Potential Impact of B. F. Skinner upon American Sociology." *The American Sociologist* 9 (1974) :3–8.

Gans, Herbert. "The Positive Functions of Poverty." *American Journal of Sociology* 78 (1972):275–89.

Garfinkel, Harold. *Studies in Ethnomethodology*. Englewood Cliffs, New Jersey: Prentice-Hall, Inc., 1967.

Goffman, Erving. *The Presentation of Self in Everyday Life*. Garden City, New York: Doubleday Anchor, 1959.

Homans, George. *Social Behavior: Its Elementary Forms*. New York: Harcourt, Brace and World, 1961.

Jay, Martin. *The Dialectical Imagination*. Boston: Little, Brown and Co., 1973.

Kuhn, Thomas. *The Structure of Scientific Revolutions*. Chicago: University of Chicago Press, 1962.

———. *The Structure of Scientific Revolutions*. 2d ed. Chicago: University of Chicago Press, 1970.

Manning, Peter. "Existential Sociology." *Sociological Quarterly* 14 (1973) :201–25.

Masterman, Margaret. "The Nature of a Paradigm" in *Criticism and the Growth of Knowledge*. Edited by Imre Lakatos and Alan Musgrave. Cambridge: Cambridge University Press, 1970.

Mazur, Allan, and Robertson, Leon S. *Biology and Social Behavior*. New York: The Free Press, 1972.

Merton, Robert. "Manifest and Latent Functions" in *On Theoretical Sociology*. New York: The Free Press, 1968.

Mills, C. Wright. *The Sociological Imagination*. New York: Oxford University Press, 1959.

Parsons, Talcott. *The Structure of Social Action*. New York: The Free Press, 1937.

————. *The Social System.* New York: The Free Press, 1951.

————. *Societies.* Englewood Cliffs, New Jersey: Prentice-Hall, Inc., 1966.

Parsons, Talcott, and Shils, Edward, eds. *Toward a General Theory of Action.* New York: Harper Torchbooks, 1951b.

Schwanenberg, E. "The Two Problems of Order in Parsons' Theory: An Analysis." *Social Forces* 49 (1971) :569–81.

Schroyer, Trent. "Toward a Critical Theory for Advanced Industrial Society" in *Recent Sociology.* Edited by Peter Drietzel. New York: Macmillan, 1970.

Scott, John Finley. "The Changing Foundations of the Parsonian Action Scheme." *American Sociological Review* 28 (1963) :716–35.

Sieber, Sam. "The Integration of Fieldwork and Survey Methods." *American Journal of Sociology* 78 (1973) :1353–59.

Singelmann, Peter. "Exchange as Symbolic Interaction." *American Sociological Review* 38 (1972) :414–24.

————. "On the Reification of Paradigms: Reply to Abbott, Brown and Crosbie." *American Sociological Review* 38 (1973):506–9.

Skinner, B. F. *Beyond Freedom and Dignity.* New York: Macmillan, 1972.

Szymanski, Albert. "Toward a Radical Sociology" in *Issues, Debates and Controversies: An Introduction to Sociology.* Edited by George Ritzer. Boston: Allyn and Bacon, 1972.

van den Berghe, Pierre. "Dialectic and Functionalism: Toward a Reconciliation." *American Sociological Review* 28 (1963) :695–705.

Warriner, Charles K. *The Emergence of Society.* Homewood, Illinois: Dorsey Press, 1970.

————. "Groups Are Real: A Reaffirmation." *American Sociological Review* 21 (1956) :549–54.

Webb, Eugene. "Unconventionality, Triangulation and Inference." Proceedings of the Invitational Conference on Testing Problems. Princeton, New Jersey, Educational Testing Service, 1966.

Weber, Max. "Social Action and Its Types" in *Theories of Society.* Edited by Talcott Parsons, *et al.* New York: The Free Press, 1961.

Subject Index

Name Index

Glaser, Barney, 131, 138
Goffman, Erving, 124, 138, 193, 228
Gold, Raymond, 127, 131, 138
Gordon, Gerald, 2, 16–19, 34
Gordon, R. L., 208, 228
Gouldner, Alvin, 48, 82
Gumplowicz, Ludwig, 93
Gurvitch, George, 122

Heidegger, Martin, 115
Himes, Joseph, 63, 65–66, 82
Hinkle, Roscoe, 92–93, 138
Homans, George, 30, 33, 99, 142, 153–
    168, 170–171, 173, 174, 185, 195,
    199, 203, 222, 228
Horkheimer, Max, 225
Hughes, Everett, 130, 138
Husserl, Edmund, 28, 33, 109–114,
    116, 119, 138

James, William, 97
Jay, Martin, 225, 228

Knox, John, 152, 185
Kuhn, Manfred, 107–108
Kuhn, Thomas, 2–13, 15, 16, 19, 20,
    23, 34, 188–190, 228

Lakatos, Imre, 2, 34, 228
Lodahl, Janice, 2, 16–19, 34
Luckmann, Thomas, 122, 132, 220, 227
Lyman, Stanford, 123, 138

MacIver, Robert, 28, 34, 91–92, 138
Malinowski, Bronislaw, 42
Manis, Jerome, 138, 139
Manning, Peter, 193, 228
Marcuse, Herbert, 225
Marx, Karl, 34, 57, 61, 63, 88, 213,
    215–216, 219, 225
Masterman, Margaret, 4–6, 11, 12, 34,
    189, 228
Mauss, Marcel, 46, 82, 152, 185
Mazur, Allan, 226, 228
McCluggage, Marston, 29
Mead, George H., 28, 34, 93, 97, 98,
    102, 106, 114, 153, 175, 194, 203,
    209
Meltzer, Bernard, 103, 105, 108, 138,
    139
Merleau-Ponty, Maurice, 115
Merton, Robert, 49–52, 74, 82, 155,
    185, 192, 209, 227, 228
Miller, L. Keith, 151, 185
Mills, C. Wright, 22, 27, 33, 34, 204,
    228
Musgrave, Alan, 2, 34, 228

Natanson, Maurice, 121
Newton, Isaac, 11, 12
Nisbet, Robert, 82, 227

Pareto, Vilfredo, 93
Park, Robert, 93, 97, 194
Parsons, Talcott, 28, 34, 47, 48, 56,
    63, 82, 84, 88, 89, 92–97, 138, 140
    144, 158, 165–167, 185, 193, 204–
    206, 213, 216–219, 228, 229
Peterson, Richard, 49, 82

Petras, James, 108, 138
Phillips, Bernard, 180, 185
Phillips, Derek, 2, 10, 24, 34
Porter, John, 82
Psathas, George, 121, 138

Ratzenhofer, Gustav, 93
Ritzer, George, 73, 82, 131, 138, 223,
    229
Robertson, Leon, 226, 228
Rose, Arnold, 100–106, 138, 139
Ross, E. A., 92
Roy, Donald, 130, 139
Royce, James, 97

Scheler, Max, 122
Schroyer, Trent, 225, 229
Schutz, Alfred, 28, 32, 34, 112–116,
    119, 121, 139
Schwanenberg, E., 216, 229
Scott, John F., 95, 139, 217, 218, 229
Scott, Marvin, 123, 138
Searle, John, 13–15, 34
Selznick, Phillip, 41, 81
Sieber, Sam, 224, 229
Simmel, Georg, 64, 93, 97
Singelmann, Peter, 164, 174–177, 185,
    222–223, 229
Skinner, B. F., 29, 34, 90, 142–144,
    159, 166, 176, 184, 185, 195, 203,
    228, 229
Small, Albion, 92
Spencer, Herbert, 36–38, 93, 199
Spiegelberg, Herbert, 110, 139
Strauss, Anselm, 131, 138
Szymanski, Albert, 57, 82, 229

Tarde, Garbriel, 93
Tarter, Donald, 184, 185
Thomas, W. I., 27, 28, 34, 93, 97, 114,
    120, 194
Tiryakian, Edward, 95, 139
Tolman, E., 218–219
Trow, Martin, 134–137, 139
Troyer, William, 106, 139
Turner, Jonathan, 95, 140

van den Berghe, Pierre, 63, 82, 192,
    229
Vera-Godoy, Hernan, 46, 82
Vierkandt, Alfred, 122
Volkhart, E. H., 34

Ward, Lester F., 92
Warriner, Charles K., 25, 34, 41–45,
    47, 68, 81, 82, 191, 192, 220–221,
    229
Watson, J. B., 6, 34, 98, 106
Webb, Eugene, 223–224, 229
Weber, Max, 27, 28, 71, 74, 84–89, 91,
    93, 95, 96, 113, 121, 137, 140, 192–
    193, 208–209, 213, 214–215, 219,
    220, 229
Wilensky, Harold, 74, 82
Wirth, Louis, 42

Yetman, Norman, 226

Znaniecki, Florian, 91, 140